The Restaurants Book

The Restaurants Book

Ethnographies of Where We Eat

Edited by
David Beriss and David Sutton

Oxford • New York

English edition
First published in 2007 by
Berg
Editorial offices:
First Floor, Angel Court, 81 St Clements Street, Oxford OX4 1AW, UK
175 Fifth Avenue, New York, NY 10010, USA

Berg is the imprint of Oxford International Publishers Ltd.

Library of Congress Cataloging-in-Publication Data

The restaurants book : ethnographies of where to eat / edited by David Beriss and
David Sutton.
    p. cm.
Includes bibliographical references and index.
ISBN-13: 978-1-84520-754-0 (cloth)
ISBN-10: 1-84520-754-8 (cloth)
ISBN-13: 978-1-84520-755-7 (pbk.)
ISBN-10: 1-84520-755-6 (pbk.)
  1. Food habits—United States. 2. Restaurants—United States—Social
aspects. 3. United States—Social life and customs. I. Beriss, David. II. Sutton,
David E. (David Evan)

  GT2853.U5R47 2007
  394.1'2—dc22

                                                                    2007039584

British Library Cataloguing-in-Publication Data

A catalogue record for this book is available from the British Library.

ISBN   978 1 84520 754 0 (Cloth)
       978 1 84520 755 7 (Paper)

Typeset by JS Typesetting Ltd, Porthcawl, Mid Glamorgan
Printed in the United Kingdom by Biddles Ltd, King's Lynn

www.bergpublishers.com

Contents

Illustrations

Acknowledgments

This collection began as a conference session organized for the American Anthropological Association meetings in 2004. When we first put out a call for papers under the "big tent" title of "Restaurants," we were astounded by the response we received. Over thirty inquiries resulted in more than twenty abstracts, which, with great difficulty, we winnowed down to twelve. We did not try to have these papers "cover the territory." We received submissions on restaurants in Burkina Faso, Malaysia and Dubai, on 4-star restaurants, diners and Chinese takeaways, but, surprisingly nothing on McDonalds or other fast-food chains. We chose papers that were ethnographically grounded in the goings-on inside restaurants, or in restaurants' relationships to larger communities. The positive response suggested that our own fascination with restaurants was not idiosyncratic. It indicated that perhaps the time for a book on the anthropology of restaurants had indeed arrived

Unfortunately, the ill-fated 2004 meeting took its toll on the panel, with only three of the twelve papers being presented in Atlanta. However, we had a lively discussion with panelists and audience members and were encouraged to proceed. In the process, we lost a number of papers and added others. Sadly, a number of our papers on restaurants in non-Western locations did not make it to the final version. On the plus side, though, we were able to add papers that added disciplinary perspectives from sociology (Erickson) and anthropological history (Ray).

In the course of these revisions, we received encouragement from a number of scholars, and would particularly like to thank Sidney Mintz and Susan Tax-Freeman. Kathryn Earle, as always, provided warm encouragement, and Hannah Shakespeare was a most patient editor in the long process of submission and review, and they both deserve much thanks. A number of colleagues offered advice in the editing process. Thanks, in particular, go to Jeffrey Ehrenreich, Antonio Lauria, Linda Smith, Connie Sutton, Martha Ward and Peter Wogan. Thanks, also, to Connie (mother of one editor, teacher of the other) for bringing us together to think about these issues in the first place. Finally, thanks go to Mae Poblete, for her yeoman's work as research assistant, to Kaitlin Fertaly for her proofreading, and to Aimee Hosemann and Qiaoyun "Janet" Zhang for their indexing.

A few chapters have appeared earlier in a different form. A longer version of Chapter 2 appeared as Erickson 2004; parts of Chapter 3 appeared as Trubek 2004; and an earlier version of Chapter 6 appeared in *The China Review* 5:2 (2005), pp.

125–50. Each is reprinted with the permission of the respective journal. We would also like to thank New Orleans restaurant owner and chef Jacques Leonardi, whose restaurant art figures in the cover photo. May Crabby Jack's and Jacques-Imo's, his two New Orleans joints, long keep the spirit of that much-battered city alive!

Contributors

David Beriss is Associate Professor and Chair of Anthropology at the University of New Orleans and author of *Black Skins, French Voices: Caribbean Ethnicity and Activism in Urban France* (Westview, 2004).

Karla Erickson teaches Sociology at Grinnell College, where she is currently working on a book-length project entitled *Sweat and Salsa: Working for the Hungry Cowboy*. Erickson has also co-edited an anthology entitled *Feminist Waves, Feminist Generations: Life Stories from the Academy* (forthcoming). She received her Ph.D. in American Studies and Feminist Studies from the University of Minnesota in 2004.

Michael Hernandez Jr. is a Ph.D. student in the Department of Anthropology at Southern Illinois University. Michael's work focuses on the topics of food, the senses and museums studies. Michael is currently working on a food exhibit that will act as a research site for his dissertation.

Michael Herzfeld, Professor of Anthropology at Harvard University, is the author of nine books, including *The Body Impolitic: Artisans and Artifice in the Global Hierarchy of Value* and *Cultural Intimacy: Social Poetics in the Nation-State* (2nd edition, Routledge, 2005). He has served as Editor of *American Ethnologist* (1994–8). In 2005 he was elected to an honorary doctorate of the Université Libre de Bruxelles, Belgium, and in 1994 he won both the J. I. Staley Prize of the School of American Research and the Rivers Memorial Medal of the Royal Anthropological Institute.

Jennifer Hubbert teaches anthropology at Lewis & Clark College, Portland, Oregon. Her research areas include issues of historical representation, collective memory, visual anthropology and popular culture. She is currently researching nationalism and the built environment in the Beijing 2008 Olympics.

Eve Jochnowitz, Yiddish instructor at YIVO and Yugntruf, is a lecturer in Jewish Culinary History at The New School University. She worked for several years as a cook and baker in New York, and is currently working on a doctoral dissertation on the subject of Jewish culinary ethnography in the department of Performance Studies at New York University She has lectured both in the United States and abroad on food in Jewish tradition, religion, and ritual, as well as on food in Yiddish performance and popular culture, and has published a number of articles on Jewish food practices.

Winnie Lem is an anthropologist and Professor of International Development Studies and Women's Studies at Trent University, Canada. Her research has focused on the political economy of regional nationalism in rural France and international migration between Asia and Europe. Her books include *Cultivating Dissent: Work Identity and Praxis in Rural Languedoc; Culture, Economy, Power*; and *Memory, Mobility and Mobilization* (forthcoming).

Gerald Mars is Honorary Professor of Anthropology at University College, London and at London Metropolitan University. In 2003 he received The Royal Anthropological Institute's Lucy Mair Medal 'for consistent excellence in Applied Anthropology'.

Derek Pardue is an Assistant Professor of Anthropology and International and Area Studies at Washington University in St Louis. His work has concentrated on the power of popular culture to shape contemporary understandings of race, class, gender, and nation. This point of inquiry has led to the publication of various articles on Brazilian hip-hop and soccer as well as casual restaurants in the US. His ethnography *Hip-Hop as Cultural Design: A Retelling of Marginality in São Paulo, Brazil* is currently under review by Duke University Press.

Krishnendu Ray is an assistant professor in the Department of Nutrition, Food Studies and Public Health at New York University. Before that – from 1996 to 2005 – he taught at The Culinary Institute of America. He is the author of *The Migrant's Table: Meals and Memories in Bengali-American Households*.

David Sutton is Associate Professor of Anthropology at Southern Illinois University, Carbondale. For the past 15 years he has been conducting research on the Greek island of Kalymnos in the eastern Aegean Sea. He has published two books based on this research: *Memories Cast in Stone* and *Remembrance of Repasts,* and is conducting ongoing research on cooking as local knowledge in the context of the growth of fast food and cooking shows.

Amy B. Trubek teaches at the University of Vermont. She is the author of *Haute Cuisine: How the French Invented the Culinary Profession* and *The Taste of Place: Food Culture and the Pleasures of Terroir*, and has always done research on the interface between food, cooking and culture.

Christine Yano is Associate Professor of Anthropology at the University of Hawai`i. Her latest work is *Crowning the Nice Girl; Gender, Ethnicity, and Culture in Hawaii's Cherry Blossom Festival*. In 2007 she is a Verville Fellow at the Smithsonian's National Air and Space Museum, conducting research on Pan Am stewardesses.

Starter

Restaurants, Ideal Postmodern Institutions
David Beriss and David Sutton

Restaurants Matter

The idea for this book began with the observation that many of the most interesting aspects of social and cultural life in our contemporary world are featured in restaurants. Restaurants bring together nearly all the characteristics of economic life studied by cultural anthropologists – forms of exchange, modes of production, and the symbolism behind consumption – under one roof. Restaurants provide a context in which questions about class, ethnicity, gender and sexuality all play out. Many of the central concepts used to define cultural worlds – such as the distinction between domestic and private life, or the rules surrounding relations with kin or with strangers – are challenged in restaurants. Religious practices sometimes frame their organization, while political life often takes form in and through restaurants. Moreover, restaurants have become important symbols of postmodern life itself, with chefs transformed into media stars and restaurants increasingly carrying out symbolic work previously reserved for monuments and parades, representing the ethos of cities, regions, ethnic groups and nations. From the sensual and local, to the symbolic and global, restaurants, we believe, constitute ideal total social phenomena for our postmodern world.

As we prepared this collection, Hurricane Katrina devastated New Orleans, a city famous for its restaurants. Like most of the residents of New Orleans, restaurant owners and chefs were forced to evacuate the city for weeks after the storm. They were among the first to return, trying to assess the damage and to determine if and when they might reopen.[1] The challenges they faced were large. Some of the restaurant community's leading figures had perished in the floods or in exile. Many restaurants were so severely damaged that they seemed unlikely ever to reopen. Locals considered that the disaster threatened to destroy New Orleans' cultural distinctiveness permanently. The challenges faced by the restaurant industry seemed to illustrate that threat as well as anything.

In the months following the disaster, restaurants became an index of the city's recovery, as well as an essential social space in which New Orleanians, working to rebuild their communities, sought each other out. Those returning flocked to restaurants, seeking the camaraderie of other New Orleanians, and conversing with

Figure S.1 Shrimp Po-Boy, Crabby Jack's, New Orleans, LA. Photo credit David Beriss.

complete strangers at bars and at nearby tables about their experiences. Sharing emblematic local foods in reopened restaurants proved to be an essential part of reconnecting with the city, as one of the editors of this volume learned while eating a shrimp po-boy (see Figure S.1) at Crabby Jack's in mid-October 2005. If eating out was a major part of social life in New Orleans before Katrina, after the disaster, eating in restaurants turned into one of the central ways the city's social fabric was to be rewoven. Chefs became heroes of the recovery, in a way that parallels first responders such as medical personnel or the Coast Guard. Perhaps this is only logical in a city where the usual heroes – the police, the city's political leaders – were thought by many to have failed to rise to the crisis (Baum 2006).

In post-Katrina New Orleans, restaurants seemed to be governed by a logic that transcends business. Rumors that some famous chefs might not return set off panicky discussions on the internet about the city's future and about the proper relationship between chefs and local culture. The reopening of the totemic old-line Creole restaurants was celebrated as a sign of the city's resilience. At the same time, the devastation wrought on neighborhood restaurants was portrayed as a warning that the city's African-American cultural framework had been dangerously damaged. Opinions people held about the future of the city, about who can claim ownership of the local culture, about the ethnic makeup and political leadership of the recovering city were reflected in debates about which restaurants would recover and about which segments of the industry might never return.

These debates transcended the city and became part of the broader national discussion about the consequences of the disaster. In May 2006, as part of the James Beard Foundation annual award ceremony, the New Orleans restaurant community collectively received an award for "Humanitarian of the Year." The restaurants of New Orleans had, according to the foundation, gone beyond their supporting role in reproducing and sustaining the city's cultural distinctiveness. According to the foundation, "their generosity carried the first evidence for many outsiders and for the few remaining locals, that New Orleans is a city worth saving" (*Times-Picayune* 2006). This may be an extreme example of industry hyperbole, but it nevertheless raises the question of how and why restaurants have become so important, in New Orleans, and elsewhere. That is the subject of this book.

Restaurants as Total Social Phenomena

New Orleans is the site of a historic culinary culture, in which restaurants have long been central to structuring social life. Restaurants seem, however, to play an important role in social and cultural life in many places; a role that is perhaps revealing of deeper social trends. Although the organization of relations within restaurants is framed by the market, those relations also reflect non-market relations, including kinship, gender and politics, and, we would suggest, call into question the very categories public/private, market/nonmarket. Restaurants can be sites for the deployment of practices of social distinction, where chefs struggle for recognition as stars, and where artists and patrons insist on being seen to eat and to eat particular things. Restaurants can define urban landscapes, reflecting and shaping the character of neighborhoods or even the reputation of whole cities and regions. In many cases, restaurateurs and their clients collaborate self-consciously at a variety of levels in creating this thoroughly postmodern performance.

Whether they spread authoritarian French organizational models in *haute cuisine* restaurants or the putatively uniform menus and practices of American fast-food chains, restaurants have often been accused of contributing to the homogenization of culture on a global scale. At the same time, restaurants have played a central role in the reassertion of the local. Restaurants and the people involved in running them have become powerful cultural brokers and potent symbols for protests against a globalized and industrialized food system. Moreover, they form a bustling microcosm of social and symbolic processes focused on the formation and maintenance of identities in the context of highly sensory environments. Despite seeming to provide an ideal research setting for participant observation and thick description, and despite the efflorescence of food studies in recent years, there are only a handful of published anthropological studies on restaurants. This book seeks to remedy that by bringing together current research focused on restaurants as social and symbolic spaces, as well as on their relationship to larger historical and politico-economic processes.

Yet while restaurants have become a central institution in many societies, it does not follow that "eating out" carries the same meaning across a variety of cultures. What, really, is being produced, exchanged and consumed when people dine outside their homes in different societies? The studies collected here explore a variety of settings and themes, from the *Grand Guignol* performances at Russian-Jewish restaurants in New York to the soundscapes deployed in suburban American chain restaurants. We examine the ways that processes of identity and memory are "emplaced" in different sites, as restaurants come to stand for the larger places they inhabit and for social relations within cities or between nations. Through a focus on both the material practices and the symbolic elaboration of food service, these studies ground identity formation in practices of kinship, exchange and ritual, in debates over authenticity and in the sensory embodiment of history and memory.

The Ethnography of Restaurants

The rise of restaurants as a social practice and institution has been the subject of a great deal of recent historical analysis (see, for examples, Mennell 1996; Spang 2000; Trubek 2000; Ferguson 2004). However, as a topic for ethnographic investigation, restaurants have until recently suffered from serious neglect. The first, and in some ways the most thorough, ethnography of restaurants was the Chicago-school sociologist William Foote Whyte's *Human Relations in the Restaurant Industry* (1948), commissioned by the National Restaurant Association in 1943 and carried out in a number of Chicago restaurants during the Second World War. It is written, in the tradition of occupational sociology, as a kind of extended personnel manual for restaurant managers. Thus it is particularly concerned with issues of status among the different jobs in restaurants, as well as race and gender relations among staff and between staff and customers. Despite this managerial focus, Whyte provides a sensitive picture of the many interactions that make up the daily tasks of restaurant work, including extended passages of *mise-en-scène*, a view of the personalities of many restaurant workers, and extended analyses of different restaurant processes, such as that of moving food from kitchen to table, of cliques within the restaurant, and of the views of restaurant workers on unions. While discussing "human relations," Whyte is also attentive to the symbolic dimensions of restaurant work, including tipping, as well as those of food itself. He notes, for example, that the fish-preparation supervisor was accorded a lower status on the basis of the fact that most restaurant workers viewed fish as having an unsavory aroma (Whyte 1948: 41–6). Many of the questions he poses continue to inform more recent studies of restaurant work.

While Whyte's book makes for an auspicious start, restaurant work was neglected in the 1950s and 1960s, outside of the important contributions of Erving Goffman. Goffman's research focused on many different occupational contexts, one of which was the kitchen and dining- room of a hotel on one of the Shetland Islands north of Scotland. Goffman's signal contribution is in developing the "performance" metaphor to describe interpersonal interaction in the restaurant, as well as its metonymic extension to notions such as scripts, a cast of players, setting, dramatic action and frontstage and backstage: "All the world is not, of course, a stage, but the crucial ways in which it isn't are not easy to specify" (Goffman 1959: 72). Particularly useful has been the concept of front- and backstage, with the kitchen representing the back and the dining-room the front of the house for Goffman. The front was where the "play" was put on, while in the back the players could relax and in some sense be more true to their actual personae. In the case of the Shetland kitchen, it was "backstage" that local eating manners and habits were followed, while in "front" the players presented what they believed acceptable to their British diners. In the kitchen, when meals were taken, "Forks and knives were sometimes grasped fist-like, and tea was served in cups without saucers ... the kitchen portion of the food was prepared in the island manner, with little stress on individual pieces and cuts, and more stress on a common source of servings" (Goffman 1959: 117). Furthermore, it was only the "appearance" of freshness and cleanliness that was performed in the frontstage: "Pats of butter, softened, misshapen, and partly used during their sojourn in the dining hall, would be rerolled to look fresh, and sent out to do duty again" (p. 118). Such telling dissonances between front- and backstage continue to ring true, as in memoirs such as *Kitchen Confidential* (Bourdain 2000). The notion of performance has been applied by numerous scholars to the work of restaurants, and in particular to the server–customer interaction (see, for example, Crang 1994, Finkelstein 1989; Martens and Warde 1997).

The first published ethnographies of restaurants written by anthropologists appear in the 1970s and 1980s. James Spradley and Brenda Mann's *The Cocktail Waitress* (1975) and Gerald Mars and Michael Nicod's *The World of Waiters* (1984) represent breakthroughs as full-length treatments of restaurants, based on anthropological concepts such as kinship, exchange, rites-of-passage and joking relationships. *The Cocktail Waitress*, subtitled "Woman's Work in a Man's World," is set in a bar that serves food in "a large Midwestern city." It focuses on the symbolic and social construction of gender as it plays out in status hierarchies within the bar, server–customer interactions, practices of buying rounds of drinks, categorization of customers, and many of the other micropractices of the everyday functioning of the bar. It also provides detailed character portraits of the women servers, their different social statuses and life choices, and how they find different ways to perform "woman's work in a man's world," concluding that: "In Brady's Bar sexual identities were defined and expressed as people asked for drinks, took their places in one part of the bar or another, joked and talked, paid their bills, and greeted old friends"

(Spradley and Mann 1975: 145). Mars and Nicod, by contrast, work in the all-male context of hotel waiters. They focus on the power dynamics of restaurant service, with particular attention to the "fiddles" or the many ways that servers may attempt to cheat customers, or, more often, the restaurant itself, in pursuit of various benefits: "The enormous range of fiddles we found have a common feature: they are acts of dishonesty which the people involved do not consider dishonest. What underlies this notion is an unwritten code, not easy to discern: it sets out the limits beyond which it is considered inappropriate for a particular person in a certain situation to benefit from fiddling" (Mars and Nicod 1984: 116). To recognize this is to recognize that in Goffman's sense "teams" are quite fluid in the restaurant setting, and waiters may cross over to the customer's "side" as often as stay on their own (cf. Crang 1994: 690).

Studies of restaurants begin to take off from the mid-1980s, with a number of full-length ethnographies and articles pushing research into new aspects of the restaurant scene and proposing new theoretical approaches to restaurants. Warde and Martens (2000) put the customer at the center of their study, using interviews rather than primarily participant-observation to explore the different reasons customers have for dining out, and the different types of enjoyment sought in the experience of the restaurant. Paules (1991) and Gatta (2002) bring new approaches to the study of female servers. Paules' book *Dishing it Out* brings an explicit framework of "resistance" to the exploitative nature of restaurant work in looking at how women find many overt and covert ways to invert the "symbolism of service." Paules also explores occupational structures and why waitresses tend to avoid unionization or "moving up the ladder" to higher positions within the restaurant. In *Juggling Food and Feelings*, Gatta, by contrast, draws on Goffman's "scripts" as well as Arlie Hochschild's (1983) and Robin Leidner's (1993) ideas about emotional labor in service industries to discuss strategies used for "emotional balancing" in high-stress serving situations. She examines the official scripts provided by restaurant manuals and restaurant managers, which largely emphasize a passive process of shrugging off daily workplace dramas, noting that these official scripts "treat servers' emotions as robotic" in the quest to ensure customer satisfaction (Gatta 2002: 51). But she is more interested in the unofficial scripts, the multiple practices used by servers which go beyond the narrow concerns of owners and managers to find emotional balance in ways which "affect an individual's existential being" (2002: 51).[2] Gary Alan Fine's *Kitchens* (1996) provides a phenomenology of the experience of time in the restaurant kitchen, and also breaks new ground by developing an analysis of the aesthetic and sensory aspects of restaurant work. Fine describes the various constraints on "aesthetic production" (p. 178), as well as the ingenious ways that chefs develop to talk about the evanescent aspects of food such as taste and smell, drawing on other aesthetic domains such as music in pursuit of a shared discourse, while recognizing that much must be left to "the tacit practical knowledge that the cook must bring to the stove" (p. 212).

One interesting recent direction has been to shift focus from "performance" to "bodies" themselves, as they move through and interact in the space of the restaurant. Probyn (2004), drawing on Deleuze and Guattari, suggests that to capture the work of restaurant servers we need an "ethology" of movement and flows, giving minute attention to how bodies interconnect through food and sexual desire (cf. Laurier *et al.* 2001). For example, servers are connected to customers through the common practice of eating "leftovers" off their plates, and to other servers through the constant motion of activity. When things "flow" in a restaurant, servers can lose the sense of their individual bodies, taking on the aspect of a larger organism. As the server Wendy Levy describes it, there can be a kind of *communitas* that allows for sexual license in serving work: "You're always in motion, you're physical, plus the heat of the stoves and everything else. Late at night, it's like you cannot be held responsible'" (cited in Owings 2002: 137). Ideas about flows of bodies in the restaurant context could be enriched through comparison with other cultural contexts in which individuals are seen as more fluid and the concern is to control the flow of shared substance among people properly. Thus Liechty's (2005) account of the connection between restaurants and prostitution in Nepal, where a caste system is under challenge from commodification, provides much comparative food for thought, with restaurants providing a greater challenge to the prior social order than sex work.

While these studies are concerned to balance structural approaches with "negotiations," "practice" or "performance," they tend to see *structure* in terms of organizational or occupational sociology, i.e. the structural constraints of the restaurant as business. One recent direction in restaurant studies, however, has been to push the analysis beyond the doors of the restaurant to look at the wider sociocultural landscape in which restaurants are set. At the same time there has been an increasing focus on non-mainstream restaurants, i.e. "ethnic," health-food or fast-food restaurants. Lovell-Troy's book-length *The Social Basis of an Ethnic Enterprise: Greeks in the Pizza Business* (1990) sets the tone for a number of scholars interested in ethnicity and restaurants. Lovell-Troy's study includes an examination of migration patterns, issues of cultural continuity and change, the reliance on kin ties in restaurant work and the structuring of US business opportunities and employment practices. A number of authors have given attention to the ways that culturally-embedded ideas about kinship and gender play out in restaurant labor practices, what Bubinas (2003: 206) refers to as "ritualized forms of socioeconomic exchange" (see Hernandez, Lem and Yano, this volume). Others, drawing on notions of globalization – globalized networks of capital, labor and products – suggest the need to look "beyond ethnicity" (Krogstad 2004: 213) in understanding issues of restaurant migrant entrepreneurship, to the mixed embeddedness of ethnic restaurant labor in "social networks, regulatory issues, market conditions and associations among immigrant entrepreneurs." As Smart (2003) notes, immigrant restaurant entrepreneurs are no longer fully dependent on co-ethnic resources in order to integrate successfully into local communities. They have their own global networks, economic assets and varied backgrounds.

Another productive research focus has been on the relations of "ethnic" restaurants to the surrounding community, with some pointing to the commodification of ethnic identities in Italian restaurants such as *Fazoli's* (Girardelli 2004) and others looking at the resistance of certain ethnic identities to commodification (Harbottle 1997), and still others suggesting that restaurants can create ethnic identities where none previously existed (Wu 2004). Ferrero (2002) provides a complex picture of ethnic commodification, arguing that Mexican restaurants in Los Angeles exist in a diverse socio-economic landscape, from Taco Bell, to "authentic" restaurants in "bad" parts of town, to upscale venues. She further suggests that many of these restaurants act to transgress stereotypes and assumptions about Mexicans: "Mexican food becomes the catalyst of a behavior that challenges stereotypical concepts about the ethnic other and class and social status" (2002: 203).

Building on this approach, some analyses look to examine the larger networks, "scapes," and sociocultural practices in which restaurants are set. These approaches are influenced heavily by social geography, as in Pillsbury's early (1987) mapping of the "location dynamics" of over 2000 restaurants in Atlanta (cf. Milbaeur 1990). They also draw explicitly on recent literature on globalization in suggesting wider sociocultural processes such as homogenization, flexibility, individualization, multiculturalism and nostalgia as driving forces in creating the current restaurant "experience" in many parts of the globe. Turgeon and Pastinelli suggest that ethnic restaurants in the urban landscape of Quebec City could be thought of as "deterritorialized ethnosites," which they describe as "microspaces" for intercultural contact where the "foreign is made familiar and the global miniaturized" (Turgeon and Pastinelli 2002: 247ff). Zukin (1995) suggests that the local can "reterritorialize the global." In New York City, she notes, restaurants cluster together by type, eventually becoming neighborhood institutions such as "Little Italy." Zukin also explores the job segmentation of restaurant work, according to ethnicity and class, in New York City, where new ethnics compete with artists, actors and students for restaurant positions and, in so doing, help frame the perceived "authenticity" of ethnic restaurants (Zukin 1995: 172). Zukin frames restaurants within a larger "symbolic economy" of the city that the restaurants help shape: "The restaurant is both theater and performance. It serves and helps create the symbolic economy" (1995: 156). Bell and Valentine advance the project of mapping this symbolic economy, noting the way that cities have evolved into "centres of consumption" (Bell and Valentine 1997: 143), with food as an increasingly important part of urban culture. Bell and Valentine suggest that restaurants provide consumption experiences that are as much about identity – of places and people – as they are about the serving and consuming of food.

Homogenization, or "McDonaldization," in George Ritzer's (1991) coinage, has been central to debates about globalization. Ethnographies of McDonalds and other fast-food venues have, indeed, been an important component of recent work on restaurants. Some have suggested the loss of diversity in eating habits as reflected in the spread of fast-food and related practices throughout the world, even in that bastion of culinary distinction, France (Fantasia 1995; Ritzer 2002). Others argue for the "It's OK, they've appropriated it" approach; Watson's volume *Golden Arches East: McDonalds in East Asia* (1997) being the most important example (cf. Stephenson 1989). Watson's volume is significant not only for its fascinating discussions of the different ways that McDonalds has been "localized" throughout East Asia – since burgers lack rice, McDonald's is recognized as a "snack" rather than a meal – but also because it is the first collection of articles on restaurants in non-Western settings. Focused ethnography allows the authors in this collection to suggest the ways that McDonald's is transformed from fast-food into "slow food": "In Hong Kong, middle school students often sit in McDonald's for hours – studying, gossiping, and picking over snacks; for them, the restaurants are the equivalent of youth clubs... Suffice it to say that McDonald's does not always call the shots" (Watson 1997: 7). However, other authors have used ethnographic tools to suggest a globalized homogenization of labor and food-supply practices, with horrendous human and environmental consequences in terms of deskilling of labor, Fordism and Taylorism in production, clear cutting of forests and attendant pollution (Barndt 2004; Leidner 1993; Reiter 1997; Ritzer 2002).

Another approach is suggested by Waters (2002), who sees the McDonaldization process as producing its reverse, a response represented by the search for heterogeneity and what he calls the "aestheticization of production ... decreasingly susceptible to McDonaldization" (Waters 2002: 219). In terms of restaurants, this aestheticization has been analyzed in the context of the growth of "slow food" restaurants in Italy and elsewhere. Miele and Murdoch (2002) explore aestheticization in a rural restaurant in Tuscany, parsing it into "organizational aesthetics," or the way that the restaurant brought craft skills and traditional knowledge to the fore and an "aesthetical ethics" of typical foods linked to *terroir* or the local ecosystem, as well as to human networks of exchange. While they note that such aestheticization developed in conscious reaction to perceived McDonaldization, they also suggest that it doesn't simply represent a virtuoso choice, as with Fine's chefs, but reflects a "practical aesthetic [that] animates the labour process in ways that work with, rather than against, tradition and typicality" (2002: 323; see also Parkins and Craig 2006; and Trubek's and Mars's chapters in this volume). The contrast between slow and fast, which calls up the familiar binarisms of tradition and modernity, *Gemeinschaft* and *Gesellschaft*, community and alienation, however, is perhaps too stark to capture many of the complexities of the contemporary world. We need to be attentive to the much more subtle and complicated temporalities, the projections of memory and nostalgia, and notions of progress and decay, that animate restaurant imaginaries (see Beriss, Hubbert and Yano, this volume).

This debate about slow and fast food in relation to terms such as "globalization" and "de- and re-territorialization" may sound familiar; it has certainly been extended by anthropologists and other scholars to many other contemporary processes and practices. Food has become a key symbol in these discussions of culture and history. Studies of particular commodities – sugar, cod, salt – have provided insights into both local social development and transnational processes (Kurlansky 1997, 2002; Mintz 1985). The loss, recovery, and invention of food traditions has been central to discussions of national identities, gender, and globalization (Belasco and Scranton 2002; Long 1998; Ohnuki-Tierney 1993; Wilson 2005). Analyses of food policy and food production and distribution and of consumption patterns have been similarly significant in understanding public health, the nature of urban life, and global inequities (Bestor 2004; Watson and Caldwell 2005; Kulick and Meneley 2005; Lien and Nerlich 2004; Nestle 2002). The studies that follow examine many of the ways in which restaurants stand at the center of global trends involving food production, exchange and consumption.

On the Menu

Restaurants are global. The practice of eating out has spread across many societies in recent decades, and with it some restaurant chains have also expanded to most of the world. Restaurants participate in this expansion in a variety of ways, from participation in global supply chains, to the diffusion of organizational models, cooking styles and the circulation of workers. Yet even the global restaurant is, in the everyday sense, a local practice. The studies in this book work to demonstrate the ties between local practices and global context. Restaurants are total social phenomena precisely because they provide a privileged context through which many of the central research questions confronting contemporary societies can be usefully explored.

We start, then, with three ethnographic vignettes that point to the themes of the longer chapters that follow. Designed to set the stage for the rest of the book, these essays bring us inside the life of particular restaurants. Karla Erickson asks readers to think of a restaurant as a kind of ritual space for kinesthetic analysis. Her analysis suggests that workers and customers use the restaurant space for a great deal more than just serving food. Michael Hernandez takes readers inside the restaurant kitchen, suggesting that becoming a cook in a particular restaurant can be similar to becoming the member of a family. Through learning food practices and sharing food in the restaurant, Hernandez acquired the "shared substance" that is kinship in many societies across the world (Carsten 1995). Amy Trubek focuses on the efforts of one Wisconsin chef to create and define a *cuisine de terroir* where none previously existed. Each of these chapters uses ethnography to illuminate the world contained in a restaurant while, at the same time, pointing to the way those worlds reflect and highlight many of the central issues that run through life outside the restaurant.

Questions of authenticity and hybridity, nostalgia and contested memory come to the fore in several of the chapters that follow. Christine Yano explores a recently closed eatery in Hawai'i. It is one of a dying breed of restaurants called *okazuya*, Japanese American take-out delicatessens with their roots in pre-war, plantation-based Hawai'i. Yano analyzes *okazuya* through the lens of nostalgia, discussing ways in which these take-out restaurants have become emblematic of the past. *Okazuya* are seen as an alternative to American "fast food" such as McDonalds, and the asocial spaces these latter restaurants represent. In an interesting contrast, Derek Pardue looks at the way sound and décor are used in the design of American chain restaurants – he examines the case of a casual dining restaurant in central Illinois – to create both nostalgia and community for diners. Pardue shows how chains draw on local memorabilia and particular kinds of music to design a space that refers to an idealized past. Jennifer Hubbert looks at a more obviously political form of nostalgia, represented through restaurants that recreate the aura of Mao's Cultural Revolution in contemporary China. Cultural Revolution theme restaurants allow patrons an opportunity to recapture the experience of the late Mao era, serving fare that reflects the "bitter, sweet and sour" of China's past. Hubbert considers the link between memory and commodification, exploring what happens when places of pleasure (restaurants) turn to an era noted for pain (the Cultural Revolution) to satisfy the demands of consumer capitalism.

The relationship between ethnicity and dining out runs through many of the chapters collected here. Krishnendu Ray provides an anthropological history of the relationship of ethnicity and restaurants in the United States, tracing both changing tastes and distinction strategies that led from preferences for French *haute cuisine* to the Americanization of Italian food and the rise of other ethnic cuisines. Ray uncovers a pattern of "ethnic succession" in the restaurant world, linked in interesting ways to patterns of migration and to changing classifications of cultural difference. Eve Jochnowitz explores Russian Jewish immigrant restaurants in New York City as sites of spectacle and venues for culinary tourism. Unlike the *okazuya,* or even the Cultural Revolution restaurants, these restaurants tend to be openly hybrid spaces. For Jochnowitz, restaurants are the theaters in which the recently formed Russian-Jewish communities perform the values they cherish most. However, these performances seem to be focused less on authenticity than on a self-consciously ironic play with tradition. By examining the interactions in the restaurants of Russian Jewish New York, Jochnowitz teases out the changing relationship between these Jews and their Jewishness, as well as their influence on the culinary and cultural landscape of the larger Jewish community in New York. A related kind of rethinking of ethnicity occurs in Winnie Lem's analysis of family-run Chinese restaurants in Paris. Lem explores the ways that the "thesis of Chinese culture" has been used to explain the success of ethnic entrepreneurship. However, she goes beyond her criticism of this work to show the ways that Chinese restaurateurs adopt such theories to explain the success of their values. This "self-orientalizing" (Greenhalgh 1994) provides restaurateurs with an effective ideology to secure the labor of family members, but also has consequences for the lives of women, who are often marginalized as a consequence of their devotion to the family business.

Defining ethnicity is only one of the many social questions that are worked out in restaurants and that define how restaurants work. David Beriss shows how the firing of a waiter in a prominent New Orleans restaurant sparked debates about the impact of tourism on the city's cultural identity. While tourists may allow a restaurant to remain profitable, many city residents argue that, without significant local clientele, chefs, managers and owners will lose sight of their putative responsibility to reproduce the local culinary culture. Restaurants provide, in this case, a framework for public conflicts over what constitutes cultural authenticity as well as over what, in a context saturated with debates about class, race, and gender, might constitute the proper way to speak about such issues. Gerald Mars examines the relationship of restaurant practices to a changing socio-economic milieu in a high-end family restaurant in Northern Italy, revealing a variety of tensions. Here, as the family shifts from sharecropping to running a restaurant, new tensions develop, especially around gender, that lead to a rift among its members. Even as the restaurant's success is linked to the way it represents the fruits of one set of cultural ideals, another set, redefining gender roles, redefines the way people think about the practices that make a restaurant work.

In our final ethnographic study, David Sutton argues that the tip is, in the end, a Maussian gift, laced with the ambiguities of freedom and obligation, spontaneity and compulsion. Sutton goes beyond a purely Maussian approach, however, suggesting that the tip partakes of both gift and commodity. Tipping, he argues, is not simply an interesting topic in the holistic understanding of the running of restaurants, but is the kind of marginal practice within American society that helps us to analyze some of the contradictions inherent in the culture of capitalism.

These chapters cover quite a quantity of ground, from the production, distribution, and consumption of food within restaurants, to the role restaurants play in creating nostalgia born of globalization and of debates about cultural authenticity. We examine the way restaurants trap people in ethnic and gender roles and how they provide people with ways to redefine those roles and identities. We show how both the kinds of restaurants people encounter and the way restaurants are run reflect and provide insights into the transformation of the broader society in which they are found. Yet precisely because we see restaurants as ideal total social phenomena for our postmodern world, many aspects of restaurant life and its relationship to that world remain to be examined. We would argue that this relationship deserves to be analyzed with the diverse tools and methodologies that anthropology provides. These accounts are by no means meant to be inclusive or definitive; there remains much to be done on the anthropology of restaurants. Rather, in reflecting anthropology's diverse methodologies and perspectives, we hope this collection will provide an initial stimulus to further scholarly exploration of the multiplex ways that restaurants can be situated in our contemporary world.

Notes

1. For an early overview of the state of the post-Katrina state of the New Orleans restaurant industry see Beriss 2006a,b.
2. Leidner's book (1993) provides some ethnography of work in a fast-food restaurant, and includes interesting discussions of the divergent experiences of "routinization," both positive and negative, in service work. For a review of Gatta, see Sutton 2004; for further discussion of Paules, see Sutton, this volume.

Small Plates

1

Tight Spaces and Salsa-stained Aprons

Bodies at Work in American Restaurants

Karla A. Erickson

When you go to a restaurant for the first time, you have to figure out the rules of the space and how things are done. You must quickly decipher clues to the mood and ambience from the decorations and lighting to the behavior of the clientele, and decide how you feel and how you will act in that environment. A restaurant is a stage for service. But the decorations and flavors are only the backdrop to the show. Here, I ask the reader to forget what he or she knows about restaurants as businesses and places to eat, and begin to think of the service exchange as a dance.

Examining service as a dance extends the research on service work by high-lighting the carefully orchestrated second-to-second negotiations of workers' bodies and demeanor as they move about the restaurant. Dance is defined as "a way of expressing emotions through movement, moving nimbly or merrily to express pleasure by motion, and the performance of prescribed or improvised steps and gestures" (*Webster's Dictionary*). I use "dance of service" to describe the rhythm, energy and enticement produced by the repetitive and spontaneous use of bodies in service work. The dance of service is a performance that includes interaction with the customers. What does the dance of service tell us about the role of restaurants in American culture? Drawing on my ethnographic study of a Tex-Mex restaurant I call the Hungry Cowboy, I examine the sorts of relationships and exchanges that are possible, encouraged or dissuaded by the staging of bodies in the restaurant space.[1]

The Dance of Service

Imagine the restaurant like a stage; the line between back and front is demarcated not by a curtain but rather the place where kitchen tile turns into dining-room carpet.[2] Deep in the belly of the kitchen where steam rises and grills hiss, cooks and dishwashers move expertly behind the line. Customers huddle, tightly packed, in the entryway, then later spread out, claiming their space once seated. Servers pass in and out, front and back, negotiating the stage of the restaurant with elbows, words and balance, hundreds of times each night, several times each minute.

Now, imagine this restaurant scene as like a dollhouse with the roof removed, so that you could look down upon it, watching how the actions at the back and the front interlace, like those of a dance.

Act I: The Night Begins

Backstage

5 o'clock The last servers to arrive rush in the back door; wisps of cold air follow them, cutting through the wet heat of the kitchen. Jessica wraps her apron around twice, tying it as she walks, and greets the cooks and then the waitresses. She seems to survey the staff, checking out who's there for the night, while Julia rushes toward the manager's office, deep in the bowels of the building, to explain that her car didn't start and that's why she's 20 minutes late. She punches the clock and rushes up front.

Frontstage

Passing into the restaurant, she straightens up, tugs on her shirt, pins on her nametag, consults the seating chart and begins wiping down her tables, adjusting the condiments, and stocking up her work station with napkins, ice and water.

Backstage

In the back of the house, the kitchen begins to hum. Beth fills plastic cups of salsa while chatting with Patty, while the cooks interject jeers and puns into their conversation. The servers who have guests in their sections keep asking those who lean on the prep area to move to the right, "I need some chips." The conversation continues, interwoven with comments from workers as they push their way through the cramped kitchen space. The manager on duty rushes through, shoots a look at the servers who are leaning and drinking coffee, announces the special for the night, and walks out, passing the hostess, Katie.

As Katie enters the kitchen, she looks more frazzled than the relaxed waitresses: "Patty, you have 3 at 5, 4 at 16. Jessica, you've got 2 at 7 and 5 at 23, and there's a table in smoking that needs to be watered. We've got a party of 8 coming in."

As the front of the house fills up, the dance accelerates. Lisa goes to the cooler, takes out the trays of salsa and sour cream prepared in advance, opens up the lid to the large condiments, and fills the chip drawer. Billy sneaks past her to grab some chips while she's filling it, reaches over her for the napkins, and across Alex to get plates. As the tickets come in, the cooks start yelling orders: "All day, that's two chicken enchiladas, three burgers, one no mushroom, double fajita combo and three buffalo wings." The cooks chop and fry, stir and sear in response to a steady stream of orders, shouting orders in a mix of Spanish and English. The sound level rises, the prepared plates start to pile up, ready for delivery. Lisa grabs plates out of the window, yelling behind her to the preparation area, which has suddenly come alive: "Julia, you're up, Tammy you're up, Billy you're up." Billy grabs a tray from her, adds the chips, twists around Julia, who is grabbing dressings for her salad, and raises the tray up – "Tray out!" – over Jessica, Betsy and Meg, who are all pressed together at the soda machine. With deft maneuvers the three fill eighteen glasses on three trays, talking the entire time about last Saturday – Who was it that passed out, again? Their arms move up and down fast: glass tray out, glass on tray, scoop of ice, fill up the soda, reach for the water, reach up for the straw, down for the lemons, across for children's glasses, butt to one side, elbow to the other, turn, duck, exit.

Frontstage

In the front of the house, the chaos continues. The inadequate lobby has in a few short minutes overflowed into the restaurant. The busser fills the ice bin and sweeps the floor. The manager and hostess grab menus and crayons and booster seats as fast as they can, take down names, send customers to the bar to wait. The booths fill up, and waiting customers have now spilled into the service area. Julia pushes through, tray held high: "Excuse me, I have to get through." Betsy takes one look at the gridlock in the entryway and turns on her heel and takes the alternative route. Servers line up at the computers, waiting to place orders, and tap their trays at the service bar, awaiting their drinks. Out here customers are everywhere, so even as servers duck and weave, twist and lift, they must look competent not flustered, deft not tired, cheerful not irritated. Julia lifts the margaritas, spins, keeping the tray steady, and uses her free arm while grabbing cocktail napkins to move a customer firmly out of her way. She delivers the drinks, waits for the appetizer order, checks on the family munching on nachos, refills some water, removes dirty plates, and glides smoothly in, "Tray in!"

Staging Service

Every night begins like this, the rising heat and energy of bodies arriving: the customers in the front door and the staff in the back. They meet at the table. All of the work done in the restaurant culminates at the table. As the bodies stream in both doors, their behavior is guided by the rules of the space. The space for the customers, who are the audience to the staged service, is subtly delineated from workspace, where workers put the show together. This particular geography is one example of what Philip Crang describes as the "sociospatial relations of consumption" (1994: 677). The restaurant is designed to define movement, permitting use of certain pathways and forbidding others. The entryway to the kitchen must blend with the front stage of the dining room, yet must be distinct enough to prevent customers from accidentally accessing the behind-the-scenes space. Imagine a member of the audience sneaking behind the curtain in the middle of a scene change. Customers are such a disconcerting element in the backstage area that when customers do accidentally or intentionally enter the prep area, all motion stops. One by one, as servers recognize the intruder, they stop and turn to look, waiting until the offending trespasser recognizes they have overstepped their allocated space and the intrusion ends.

The behind-the-scenes of the restaurant is constructed precisely to hide the evidence of workers' labor. Customers are meant to see as little of the work that goes into their meal as possible, and the division allows for this. As much as this space is intended to confine servers' behavior, it also protects them, providing a space not of rest, but of relief, where they can be themselves and where their work is acknowledged and visible. Behind the scenes, servers collide and swear, tell stories and holler. While servers' partial confinement to the backstage of the restaurant and the subsequent obscuring of much of their labor contributes to their servile status, the backstage also protects them from the critical eye of the customer.[3] Servers use the backstage to assemble food and beverages, but also to drop character, if only for a few seconds. The backstage is where the work gets done, where workers go to forget they are at work, to hide from customers, and to "have fun," all of which often include physical and sometimes sexual maneuvering.

Salsa, Sweat and Pork Juice: Bodies and the Work of Waiting Tables

Bodies are intimately engaged in and necessary to the work of waiting tables. My interviews with servers at the Hungry Cowboy are seasoned with physical language and references to bodies. Jessica explains the intensity of the workplace by saying, "I think that in the restaurant industry there's probably more people in one spot all the time." Her comment reflects how the restaurant brings together many bodies in a limited space. On a busy night, not only are the forty-two tables in the bar and restaurant peopled time after time, but all open spaces are packed with people waiting to be seated.

To be a good server, you have to be quick on your feet and able to maneuver the small spaces and crowded passages of the restaurant. The dance of service is part of what gets servers "hooked"; they like the challenge of a busy night, but they also come to value the physical contact and the closeness in space that the job requires. When I asked Billy what he liked about his job, he said, "I like the physical aspect of serving. I'm not the kind of person that can sit down. As I get older, I can sit down more, but I like the physical aspect of it." Skillful use of the body is necessary to this work: a staff that communicates well will eventually get so accustomed to passing each other, switching places, transferring trays, sharing space and helping each other that words no longer are necessary during the busiest parts of the evening. A waitress who calls herself Alex says, "Yeah, I do like it because you're always aware of people around you, and that's another thing, it's an incredible degree of awareness, you have to touch people all the time, and you communicate through a simple touch, it's amazing, by just touching someone lightly on the back they know exactly what they need to do and think about it, you're maneuvering between these tight spaces." The tight spaces draw bodies into contact so routinely that the physicality and even sensuality of this work plays a significant role in the occupational atmosphere.

Turning the Tables: Customers as Players on the Front Stage

The table is the spotlight of the restaurant drama; it's the reason that everyone arrived for the show. On the stage of the restaurant, every player has their role, and a designated area of their own. Customers are the most confined spatially. For example, customers who are not greeted upon entering a new restaurant may feel unwelcome, and unclear as to what they are allowed to do, or where they can move. Once customers have been assigned a table and been guided there by an employee, they settle in by establishing a territory that belongs to them for part of an evening. Waitresses refer to this when they speak of customers who stay a long time as "paying rent" on the table.

Even though customers are primarily limited to their table and the pathways down which they are escorted, customers are still actors in the restaurant drama. Like servers, their attire, demeanor and movements are observed and subsequently affect the service exchange. Some customers insist on sitting in a particular area of the restaurant that makes them feel more central to the action, or hidden away where their table is protected from the sound and activity of producing food and service. Customers mark their space by stretching out, laying out jackets, papers, or photographs, moving around items on the table, or rearranging chairs. Adult customers' degree of comfort and sense of ownership of their space varies greatly. Some customers appear to perch in their seats, apologize for getting in the way of workers and are quick to leave once the official business of eating is complete. Other customers take off their shoes, put their legs up, hold hands, kiss or put their arms around their tablemates; some shout out to other customers they know, turn to talk to the people at the next table, or motion to the manager to come over just for a chat.

In addition to functioning like a territory, the customers' assigned table or booth is also like a seat in a theatre: it determines their vantage point on the dance of service. As consumers, customers have enhanced power owing to the fact that the restaurant is supposed to satisfy their consumer desires. While servers have greater access to the front and back stage of the restaurant, and must act as the liaison for communicating and retrieving the items customers desire, customers are encouraged to view the entire restaurant as their own space. Yet workers spend more time in the space, know all the nooks and crannies and the location of items, and have access to places to hide away and escape. Subsequently, servers feel a sense of ownership and view the restaurant as their space.

The volleying for control over space plays out in service exchanges. In response to loud noises from the kitchen, an item they are informed they can't have, or slow service, customers often ask, "What is going on back there?", thus pointing to the limits placed on their own movement and gaze. Regular customers often use their privileged access to information to find out about dating habits between employees, secrets of food production, or other private workplace interactions. In asking such questions, customers acknowledge that they are only audience to a portion of the action in a restaurant and recognize servers as workers for whom the interactions at the table are only part of the larger story of their lives. Questions about workers' lives outside the restaurant break through the staged performance that requires servers only to be servile and friendly, absorbed by the need-fulfillment of their customers. Over time, interactions between regular customers and servers begin increasingly to resemble friendships or other private relationships, rather than the scripted and predictable exchanges of role functions. For example, "What can I get you to drink tonight?" is replaced by "How was your weekend?"

The Public Meets the Private and the Front Meets the Back

Space can be read like a text. Entering a new space, we scan the landscape for signs and indications of the rules that govern the space. Restaurants are carefully managed stages for the exchange of cash for food and service. But restaurants are also more than that. In the process of going out to eat, we enter a social world, taking part in a play of sociability within the confines of the marketplace. Certain customers become so comfortable in the Hungry Cowboy, that they start to treat it like their own living room, walking shoeless to the bathroom, or greeting servers like old friends. Restaurants work hard to make customers feel at home. What happens when customers start to treat a public space like their home? What does it mean for workers' identities and workplace culture when servers willingly trade on private personal characteristics like their sexual appeal to make more money or have more fun at work?

Too often service work is studied with the same analytical tools as those applied to factories or offices. Thinking carefully about the restaurant as a stage where movements of bodies and the use of space affect how each player acts and reacts within the service exchange, reminds us that there is more taking place than a business exchange. Restaurants inhabit a peculiar space somewhere between the public world of the market and the private realm of home and family, and the moments in the dance of service when these two realms blend encourage us to reconsider how we play our roles as producers and consumers in a service society. For now, I hope only to lift the curtain of the serving life enough that paying to be served in restaurants can no longer be approached as an uncomplicated exchange.

Notes

1. This chapter is one part of a larger study currently titled *Sweat and Salsa: Working at the Hungry Cowboy*. A previous version of this chapter was published in *Space and Culture*, vol. 1, issue 1, February 2004. I am indebted to Jennifer Pierce, Thomas Augst, David Sutton and the *Space and Culture* editors, specifically Rob Shields, for their advice and suggestions while revising this work.

2. Ethnographic research for this article was conducted at a Tex-Mex restaurant in Minnetonka, Minnesota, where I worked for ten years, conducted participant observation for two years, and held intensive interviews with employees and staff. I refer to this restaurant throughout as the Hungry Cowboy. The Hungry Cowboy opened in 1991 and promises to serve up Tex-Mex food with Southern hospitality. It is located in a second ring suburb of Minneapolis, in a strip mall. Despite its unassuming location and interior, the Hungry Cowboy manages to draw in a devoted regular clientele who routinely wait for half-an-hour on the weekend to eat there. The Hungry Cowboy is staffed by thirty-five employees. More than ten of the employees have been working there for six or more years. The quotations included in this chapter are taken from interviews with servers to whom I refer by pseudonyms. The serving staff is predominantly female: as a result, the majority of interviews, quotations and impressions are taken from waitresses explicitly referred to as such. At the time of the interviews, only six of the twenty front-house staff were male.

3. I use "backstage" in keeping with Erving Goffman's theorizing of backstage/frontstage personas. I situate my research within the tradition of symbolic interaction and what has been called the "sociology of the everyday." Erving Goffman's research on roles, role distance, interaction ritual, backstage/frontstage and presentation of the self inform my study of the dance of service.

2

Forming Family Identity in an American Chinese Restaurant

One Person's Transformational Process

Michael D. Hernandez, Jr.

Over the past few years I have become very alarmed that researchers and workers in the fields of nutrition and food have constantly inundated symposia, conference sessions, and chat rooms with claims that the notion of the family is being divorced from food. The one thing that many individuals tend to forget, consciously or unconsciously, is that the definition, formation, and practice of family is ever-changing to fit a person's or group's needs at any particular moment. The following work is an example of the process an individual, myself, undergoes to become a part of a family in a Chinese American restaurant. This process, reinforced through embodied practices, creates a sense of discipline, honor, and loyalty that allows an individual to create and maintain their identity as a family member. I will focus on the social processes of constructing and maintaining extended family identities within Carmen's China House through food preparation, eating, and discipline.

My research at Carmen's China House first began as a project that looked at the relationship between family and cultural history and the means by which this history is passed on to subsequent generations. Over the first few weeks of my initial research, I became aware that Carmen was not only teaching me to cook, but was also beginning the process of incorporating me into her family.

After my project began, I became very intrigued with the topic of restaurants and the community identities that are formed within them. Since the 1980s, a growing anthropological literature has addressed the ways that food, across a broad range of societies, is used to create the "shared substance" that forms the basis of kinship. Food is one of a number of possible components – in addition to biology, genes, time, and labor – through which people express their sense of interrelatedness (Bodenheim 2000; Carsten 1995; Weismantel 1995; Weston 1995). Little information has been published on the anthropology of food/restaurants, and even less on the formation of identities within the restaurant setting. With the help of my colleague David Sutton, I came across a reading entitled "Commonwealth of Food" by Gary Fine (1996). In Fine's work, he describes the formation of community, or more particularly "family building," within a restaurant environment. "Restaurants as small organizations are communities, often consciously. With the modest number of employees found in most restaurants – rarely does a restaurant have over one hundred employees – workers know each other's biography and interests through personal narratives and shared experiences and see themselves as linked" (Fine 1996: 112). The key to understanding this organization of culture is through the metaphor of a family within enclaves of the restaurant: wait staff, cooking staff, bar staff, etc.

In January 2004, I began working for Carmen as a cook's assistant. For five months I worked both weekday and weekend shifts. I learned how to do food preparation, inventory, cooking, and table waiting. During this time period I also video-recorded fourteen hours of cooking footage and thirty-six hours of interviews with employees, and spent seven national and international holidays at the restaurant and uncountable hours with Carmen's family at their home. During this time I was slowly introduced into the processes of becoming not only an employee but also a member of Carmen's family.

Carmen's Background Information

Carmen Fang, a native of mainland China who fled Communism with her family when she was a child, immigrated from Taiwan to the United States in 1973 to attend school at Southern Illinois University Carbondale (SIUC). Before immigrating to the United States, according to Carmen, she lived in a traditional Taiwanese patriarchal family with a strong matrifocal component. According to Carmen, "Mother was my parent, she taught us, she supported us, and she guided us."

From the start, Carmen found it difficult to both run a restaurant and maintain her family in a traditional Taiwanese family structure. Her husband suggested that she get assistance from her family. She brought her mother to the United States to help care for her three children. Because of a limited visa, her mother had to return to Taiwan. Soon afterwards, Carmen's husband, unhappy in the United States, also returned to Taiwan. Carmen, believing that there were better opportunities for her children here in the United States, decided to remain in Carbondale. Realizing that she could not keep a traditional Taiwanese family environment, she began to modify her family structure. A local friend helped her with the baby while her other two children began to work in China House as order-takers and as translators for their mother. Over the next twenty years the children – with help from friends – were raised at the restaurant.

China House Family Formation

How is the family identity formed in China House and how are traditions carried over from her biological family to the China House family? Carmen has incorporated Taiwanese/American family traditions in the structure of China House. Before one can explore the formation of family at China House, one needs to understand Carmen's view of family: how she defines and constructs her understanding of what "family" is. During my first interview I asked Carmen what the concept of "family" meant to her.

> *Carmen*: Family is very important, back from my home or even here. Family is like ... when your are tired you can relax, when you are sad or you hurt from outside from anyone or from work you can come home and relieve pressure at home, you can talk to your mother and talk to your father ... and let the father and mother be with you be it happy or sad, you can be happy or sad and they can be with you to share. A mom is always there to take care of you, cook your food for you, and there is nothing like mother cooking. At home the family is so important. Even now here, I believe that my family back in Taiwan, my three brothers and one sister, still contact each other.

Going on, she also explains that her notion of what family is changed after she began working at the restaurant and her biological extended family could not stay and help to raise her own children. In this portion of the interview, Carmen explains how and why she modified her concept of family. By using this new framework she has been able to live and succeed in the United States.

> *Carmen*: In American family, I do not have any. But definition now, since I have been live 31 year here in America ... yes that the Chinese family that I had when I was growing up was so important and unique but yet I am here. I do not have an American family but I have American friends. But the friends are like family ... it's like when you have a problem and you have to ask them then to help you. And that is what mom always tell me if you had stayed at home family is your first priority, but when you are not at home away from your country the only family you have are your friends. You have to have friend it is your friend that are your second family.

Carmen explained that over the years, without her new American family, the restaurant would not have survived several years of hardship, her children would not have gotten help with their schooling, and she would have had no emotional support to get through her life. "Without my new family, we would not have made it."

Chinese Cooking/Food

Traditional Chinese cooks believe that food selection, preparation, and presentation is a means to create *fan*, or a balance of opposites. Margaret Visser in *Much Depends on Dinner* explores the balance of Chinese food. "'Fan' is part of the ancient and elaborate system of yang versus yin by which traditional Chinese thinking divides up the universe" (Visser 1986: 164). Some of the most common divisions thought of when one talks about yin and yang are "male and female" as well as "hot and cold,"

Figure 2.1 Carmen at work. Photo credit: Michael Hernandez.

Figure 2.2 Carmen at work. Photo credit: Michael Hernandez.

but there are a number of other categories. These categories are not in opposition, but rather are complementary pairs that create balance or bring things into balance (Anderson 1997; Legge 1996). According to Carmen, food itself, with its many qualities, has balancing properties. These properties are color, texture, and flavor.

As a customer of Carmen's China House I would order sweet and sour chicken without carrots and each time the dish would come with carrots. Why was this? After I began working for Carmen, I assembled the vegetables to be added to the sweet and sour chicken I was going to take home. She placed the vegetables on the chicken and then walked over to the preparation table and grabbed a handful of carrots and laid them on top.

The next day, I walked into the kitchen and started to cut the vegetables for that day. I got to the carrots and remembered the meal I had the night before. I turned to Carmen and asked her why she placed the carrots on the sweet and sour chicken.

> *Carmen:* You needed it; you have to have the carrots, it good for you. Did you eat them?
> *Michael:* NO.
> *Carmen:* Why? You need them they are good for you. Without it, it could be bad. Next time you eat them [pointing at the carrots in the preparation bin]; here, eat one.

I picked up a sliced carrot and ate it.

> *Carmen:* You like them. No face. Eat more. Why you don't like carrots?
> *Michael:* I like carrots. I just do not like carrots with chicken.

Carmen placed her hands on her hips and gave me a funny look. Throughout the day Carmen would point out every ingredient in each dish.

Over the next few weeks I noticed that certain foods were paired with each other. After weeks of preparation, it became second nature to combine food items such as dofu [tofu] and mushrooms, bamboo and bean sprouts, carrots and chicken, pork and onions.

Family Meals

Along with the *fan* of food, activities also have a yin and yang. Carmen and I would often talk about my workday and school. Many times I told her I had worked all day on my research, or had worked all night writing a paper or preparing for the class I was teaching. She was concerned that I was not getting any off time or fun time. She would explain that everyone needs both as part of their life. "Here at China House we work when we need to and we rest and eat when we can. We always do this. If we do not rest we make mistakes, and I make mistake, and they [the customers] are not happy. That's bad."

Towards the end of each night everyone working would sit down at the "family table" in the restaurant to rest and eat a meal. This table was located close to the kitchen. Carmen would take the leftovers or the overstock food and make a large family meal. These meals would be made for the more traditional Chinese palate by leaving out the salt and sugar added to the dishes she makes for her customers. As we ate she would tell us stories about the food and her family. She would point out the ingredients in the dish and what they meant in Chinese history. Then she would ask what we had done at school or at home that day

I realized that Carmen believed that the family meal was very important to her family identity. During the interview, I could see that there were many parallels between how Carmen described her biological family and the China House dinners in which I had participated. I wanted to know how Carmen viewed the meals we had in China House in relation to her family meals.

Michael: Is it important to eat dinner at China House?

Carmen: Yes. Very important.

Michael: Why is it important?

Carmen: Because everyone is hungry. You can't expect everyone that work there [China House] not to eat. If they do not eat, they do not do a good job. If they eat they do a good job.

Michael: What happens when you eat together?

Carmen: If there is something they need to do or prepare, or they make a mistake you can tell them. You can tell them that you did this wrong and help fix it. Just like a family. I tell them that I am not perfect and I make mistake.

Michael: Do you talk to the kids at the restaurant about what is going on in their families?

Carmen: Yeah, I ask them how your family is, what you are doing; I basically like to understand their family.

Michael: Do you talk about problems with your kids at the restaurant?

Carmen: Oh yeah, we talk about everyday problem. I ask them about school. We work out our problem: I ask them if they need help. That what a family is. I care about them, they are like my own kids.

Discipline

One factor contributing, according to Carmen, to successful Chinese cooking and being a part of a family is discipline. During my time at China House, I was trained to prepare the ingredients used in the dishes to be made that evening. I started by cleaning all the vegetables, and then I would chop and dice carrots, onions, broccoli, mushrooms, cabbage, pea pods, and peppers. I would drain and rinse the bamboo, watercress, and sprouts. At the end of my time at China House, I had become efficient at this task; however, at the beginning it was a different story. My second day at

Figure 2.3 Carmen oversees her son. Photo credit: Michael Hernandez.

China House, I was peeling carrots and cutting the ends off. Carmen walked over to me and pulled a carrot out of my hands. "You're doing this all wrong, you're wasting it. You need to take off the top [layer] off." I thought at first I was wasting food, and on reflection I was, but then I realized that I was not conforming to her standards. James, her youngest son, came to help me. I watched him peel and cut. He did every peel and cut the same way. He held the small end of the carrot and peeled the big end first. Then he turned the carrot over and held the big end and peeled the small end. I asked him why he peeled that carrot that way. "It works better. Your hand does not slip this way. If you peel the small end first and then the big end your hand will slip." After all the carrots were peeled I had to cut the carrots in uniform slices. I picked up a large knife with a curvy blade. I began to slice the carrots. After I had finished I asked Carmen what I needed to do next. Carmen walked over to the preparation table and grabbed a handful of carrots. "This is not right. Too big. You need to do this again. If we use this the food will not be right." She picked up the knife I was using and sliced them smaller. "Like this," she said. She handed the knife to me and told me to try. I re-sliced the carrots. She watched and guided me through the process until I had finished. This was repeated with all the vegetables we used.

After the first week I wanted to start cooking. However, Carmen wanted me to master the preparation table. I was getting tired of just chopping and peeling. I walked into the kitchen and I began to work. I was becoming very bored with this task. She handed me a cup of tea and asked what was wrong. I explained that I wanted to cook.

She said, "You have to get to know the food and understand how to be part of China House. You have to do this right first, then you cook." I asked how long that would be. She told me "First you do this right and second I will tell you." I began to work really hard to please her.

I started to show up before my shift to start work. The other workers would come in and compliment my work and encouraged me by telling me that they believed I was almost ready to start cooking. They would say things such as "Your cuts are getting better, the food is really looking good, and you're almost as good as Carmen." This would make me work even harder.

Looking back on my notes, I realized I was being disciplined by her and by the workers, and that the harder I worked and the better I got the more I was accepted into the China House family. As I was being accepted into China House, Carmen began to implement other forms of disciplinary action. One day, a waiter and myself were taking a break and we were smoking outside the back door. Carmen came out to find us. The door flew open and she just stood motionless. In a disappointed voice, she asked us to come in and help because a number of customers had come in together. The waiter walked by Carmen with his head down and went to wash his hands. Carmen blocked me and asked me what I was doing. "You smoke? You smoke? Why you smoke? You know that bad for you. You should not do that, you need to quit." She stepped to the side and I walked into the kitchen, washed my hands and began working again. After the rush, Carmen cornered me. "Why you do that? You know you're hurting you, and you hurt me. I hate smoke. My son Ping smoked. It is bad. You not hurt just you, you're hurting China House. I help you. If you do not stop, I stop talking, you go home." I was stunned. I had to promise not to smoke the rest of the day as well as quit smoking altogether over time.

During an interview that took place after the smoking incident, Carmen confronted me. I asked her why she reacted in that manner. She stated, "Family is important to me." She explained that she did not want to see anything happen to me. She went on to explain that her middle son Ping smoked and it really hurt her.

She began telling me the story. According to Carmen her son Ping was about eighteen when he began smoking. "I did not know at first."

Carmen: One summer Ping had asked if he could move his room to the basement [of their home]. A few months later I caught him.
Michael: You mentioned that your son smoked ... how did you find out?
Carmen: I often smelled something smoking. I questioned him. *"Did you go to the bar or are your friends smoking?"* I smell some smoke. He said Oh ... he lied to me. He

said Oh, Jonathan, his good friend and he smoke, Jonathan I picked him up and he was smoking something. So I thought that was true. One day I smelled some smoke and I do not understand because I did not cook and I don't smoke. I questioned him [Ping] and he said no, no one smoke. Ping said maybe it is my clothes because I went to the bars. So I said O.K.

Later in the summer Carmen decided to air out Ping's mattress in the basement. "I flop the mattress ... oh boy I saw a whole bunch of cigarette butt." She left the room as she found it and waited at the front door until Ping got home that afternoon. Ping walked through the door and Carmen took him downstairs.

Carmen: So I pointed to it down there [butts in the bedroom]. "What is that?" And I said "Who did it?" He said, "I did". I said "When you start smoking?" And he said about a year ago. And I said "WHAT!"

According to Carmen, discipline is a severe but necessary means to keep the family together. This reinforces family loyalty, health, and obligation. Carmen asked her son why he had lied to her. He replied that he did not want her to get hurt. She replied, "Now I did not get hurt?" Carmen confronted Ping's about his loyalty to her and to the family. Carmen described how Ping hung his head and did not say anything through this process. "I told him that I could not tolerate this. I told him ... kid you need to move out."

Before Carmen made Ping move out, she told him that when he quit smoking and "cleaned up" he would be welcomed back to the family and to her home. Ping moved away for two months before returning. Carmen explained that when he came back it was never mentioned again. "I love my son. I do not want anything happen to him. Like you, you're a part of my family. I want you to live a good life and I want you around for long time."

Conclusion

What about smaller restaurants that are not large enough to form enclaves? Unlike Gary Fine's family model that used small enclaves within larger restaurants to form and reinforce a family structure, Carmen's China House family structure is constructed and reinforced through Carmen herself. In my observation and through my participation within China House, Carmen occupies the role of a matriarch or mother, rather than an owner/manager. The people who work for her become her children rather than employees. Her treatment of her biological sons and her employees is the same, and her expectation of behavior and loyalty does not change. Carmen uses food, meals, and discipline to construct a framework to transform and incorporate individuals into the China House family. For Carmen, food itself is an example of balance and is used as a tool to illustrate one's place within the

China House family. Meals are used to establish cohesion between individuals. Not only are meals used as means of balancing a lifeway, they also tie everyone together through shared experience and emotional needs. Discipline is a process that addresses loyalty and family role adjustment. Discipline is not a negative force; rather, it is a reaffirming action that brings one back into the family system.

Carmen is seen as a mother to the China House workers. Carmen believes that China House is a family. This can be seen in her use of descriptive terminology. For example, she rarely uses the term "employee." During our interview sessions, and while working at the restaurant as well, I never heard her use this term. Rather, she most commonly to refers to these people as her "kids." "Restaurant" is another example of a word used by neither Carmen nor the kids. This term is rarely used during interview sessions and never used in the China House; she always refers to the business as "China House." China House is her family and her home, and now it is mine.

Note

1. These numbers come from a volunteer survey conducted in June 2001.

−3−

Tasting Wisconsin

A Chef's Story
Amy B. Trubek

Introduction

Perhaps I am a naïve culinary optimist. I know that Wal-Mart, McDonald's, Olive Garden and Sysco dominate our culinary landscape. I know that many Americans, when confronted with an office party in New Mexico, Illinois or Kentucky, will as often as not end up buying a box of frozen, prepared appetizers from Cosco. How can I possibly believe that in the era of global convenience cuisine there is also emerging a modern *cuisine du terroir*, with fidelity to place and season?

Appropriately enough, because of something I ate in a restaurant. Although we tend to assume that cooking and eating take place primarily in homes, restaurants are part of our everyday life: we spend fifty percent of every food dollar on food that has been prepared outside of the home.[1] Restaurants no longer represent just a traveler's necessity or an anniversary event; now restaurants are the answer to that oft-asked question, "What's for dinner?" (or for lunch, or for breakfast). Scholars have linked cafés and restaurants to the increased importance of the public sphere in the West since the eighteenth century as a new space for promoting dialogue and marking distinction.[2] However, restaurants, and the people who labor behind the scenes to transform the raw into the cooked, have also created new ways to experience and think about food.[3] It is often assumed that the food prepared in restaurants *reflects* a culinary tradition, but what if, instead, this food *creates* one?

Why are some chefs championing their knowledge of ingredients at the same time that almost all consumers know less and less about where their food comes from and also have less and less direct access to local food?[4] A connection exists between the consolidation of choices for Americans as to where they buy their food, what they can buy, and the turn towards local by these chefs. This connection occurs because of the way Americans *think* about food, or the way perceptions frame choices. Two models for understanding and acting dominate in our attempts to procure ingredients and cook dishes: the inevitability of modernization and the quest for an agrarian utopia.[5] The "inevitability of modernization" model rests on the assumption that an industrialized, globalized and consolidated food supply is the unavoidable consequence of our modern ways. The "quest for an agrarian utopia" model rests on the assumption that in our past the food supply was knowable, based in communities and in some sense more pure.[6]

Most often these are seen as incompatible: you must reject the one to embrace the other. The story of chefs building regional cuisines in restaurants allows for the examination of a third way, or perhaps a middle way. This way exemplifies what Esteva and Prakash call "grassroots postmodernism," a response to modern conditions focused on "rooted local thinking which inspire[s] local actions."[7] And the results are an emerging model of food that combines social values with entrepreneurial activities.

I came to see the importance of restaurants and chefs to any contemporary American regional cuisines via an engagement with my own senses. This was several years ago while eating dinner at Odessa Piper's restaurant, L'Etoile, in Madison, Wisconsin. I still remember, during dessert, the surprise of cutting through the layers of baked filo to find only small nuts nestled in a simple brown-sugar *penuche*. I was expecting more – maybe fruit or chocolate. I took a bite and was stunned. The nuts were hickory, and they tasted like an intense cross between a pecan and a walnut. Combined with the *penuche* they reminded me of maple–walnut ice cream, but the flavor was more complex, with something of a smoky campfire. In texture, these nuts were more delicate than either pecans or walnuts, almost flaky.

"What are these hickory nuts?" "Where did they come from?" I asked the waiter. "Oh, they are a local tradition, from here, Wisconsin." Now I was amazed.

I grew up in Madison. The foods I remember from my childhood came from the state's ethnic groups: German bratwursts, Cornish pasties, Norwegian lutefisk. My family ate at L'Etoile on special occasions, but I hadn't been there for years. After I was seduced by the hickory nuts, I realized L'Etoile combined local thinking and local action. In my hometown, of all places. hickory nuts were just part of a full range of regional ingredients being used by a sophisticated chef, Odessa Piper.

The historian Warren Belasco sees American regional cuisine over the past fifty years developing in two directions: elitist and populist: "While elitists craved the perfect smoked wild turkey with fiddlehead ferns, populists pursued the perfect sub with fries."[8] The more populist fare, for example Cajun popcorn shrimp and Buffalo chicken wings, he argues, became part of the mass, consumer food system.[9] Belasco cogently describes what happened when the counterculture first created and then battled with the mainstream food world over "healthy," "natural" and "organic" foods; and the story of regional foods reflects the larger story. He values the efforts of those involved in building, as he puts it, a countercuisine, rejecting the industrial and capitalist methods favored by the "logic of modernization" model. Nevertheless, he wonders if, in the end, their efforts to change the way Americans think about food resulted in American regional foods becoming a "museum" or part of a "multicourse postmodern menu."[10] Odessa Piper's story reveals the perils he outlines, but also the possibilities for another ending to the story.

Piper is one of an increasing number of American chefs who defy the inevitability of modernization when they cook. She thinks first about where she lives. She takes her inspiration from Wisconsin's bounty, and her cooking is firmly located there. Her dishes, however, are not inherited from the past. Hers is not your mother's cooking.

Recently I spent time back home in Madison, talking with Piper, working as a prep cook in her kitchen, and visiting some of the farmers who supply her. I wanted to understand how her cooking – what she calls a "regionally reliant cuisine inspired by the creativity of necessity" – came about.[11] I wanted to participate in the everyday rhythms of the restaurant.

A Chef's Story

Piper, now 56, owned and operated L'Etoile for 28 years, a rare feat of longevity in the restaurant business.[12] Little about her story is usual. Unlike many chefs who care about regional ingredients, her culinary origins aren't high-end, but hardscrabble, back-to-the-land, and political. Before she began her restaurant career, she lived for two years on a self-sufficient commune in New Hampshire and then two more years on an organic farm in Rolling Ground, Wisconsin.

JoAnna Guthrie, owner of the organic farm in Rolling Ground where Piper lived, was Piper's mentor. Guthrie was a world traveler, a member of the Theosophical Society, the esoteric, eclectic religious group founded in 1875, and a woman intent on cultural change. Guthrie believed the true way to transform American culture was through farming organically and the "little arts" of cooking, serving and dining. "She didn't treat me seriously; she treated me like a wild child," Piper says. "Her influence caused me to clean it up. JoAnna Guthrie was a cultured lady."

Guthrie, however, was not a trained chef. In fact, she never worked on a farm or a restaurant before she started one of each in Wisconsin in the early 1970s. She was a social visionary, an early exponent of New Age spirituality.

Guthrie also decided Americans needed to be educated about the "art of living," which included making and eating good food. Thirty years ago, fresh ingredients and French food were practically unknown in the nation's heartland. In 1973, Andrea Craig opened Andrea's Restaurant on the Capital Square, just as the Dane County Farmers' Market was beginning to take hold there (she later sold it to Piper, and it became L'Etoile). Craig recalls trying to make *coq au vin*, or chicken stew, in the early 1970s, and having great difficulty finding any fresh mushrooms anywhere in town; only canned button mushrooms were available. She ended up begging (literally) her food purveyor to hunt down fresh button mushrooms, an ironic turn of events since Wisconsin is a state well known (by foragers at least) for its abundance of wild mushrooms.

In 1972, Piper was one of those who helped Guthrie open the Ovens of Brittany, the first bakery in Madison to produce French-style pastries and breads from scratch.

The early workers were all Guthrie disciples: "We cooked for her. She was our palate and tasted everything we made," Piper said. The bakery was not a traditional business. "There was a huge amount of personal investment. We were so identified with what we were cooking."

In those early days, everyone working at the Ovens of Brittany was a disciple of Guthrie, committed to her new age philosophies. No one really thought of it as a business, Piper says. At first it was difficult to get unsalted butter from the local distributor, so Piper and her colleagues went to nearby supermarkets and bought all the unsalted butter they could find. They never concerned themselves with costs, only pursuing fresh and high-quality ingredients.

According to Guthrie, restaurants and bakeries committed to these principles would introduce people to the true art of living. Guthrie wasn't interested either in managing people or in making a profit. Her goals were saving the land, making great food, civilizing Americans, and creating peace. Her vision still propels Odessa Piper and L'Etoile.

Foraging a Local Cuisine

Piper's cooking is not typical of the Midwest that I knew. Rather, it reminds me of French *cuisine du terroir*, "cooking from the land," meaning with ingredients cultivated in the surrounding region. The phrase also embraces wild foods, and those, too, are found at L'Etoile: plums, crabapples, black walnuts, ramps, purslane, watercress, clover flowers, mushrooms, and, of course, shagbark hickory nuts.

Piper grew up near Hanover, New Hampshire, where her thrifty Yankee parents foraged for mushrooms and other wild foods. As Piper puts it, "I was blessed with life choices knowing what was happening in the wild." Her grass-roots approach to ingredients was further solidified when just after high school she joined the Wooden Shoe commune in Canaan, New Hampshire. The goal at Wooden Shoe was to raise and grow all their own food, and she recounts that "an image from the time at the commune is of us trying to grind the wheat to make our own flour." There were times when they did not have enough food; thus foraging was not just nostalgic but necessary.

Since self-sufficiency through farming and foraging for their own food were pivotal tasks both at Wooden Shoe and Phoenix Farm, Piper's cooking apprenticeship truly focused on the ingredients first, and only later on techniques and traditions.

When she opened L'Etoile in 1976, she heard about shagbark hickory nuts and she began to ask where she could buy them. Eventually, a vendor at the Madison farmers' market brought her some. Now L'Etoile purchases 200 pounds of them a year, and they are a central feature on the menu.

"They are the nobility of nuts," Piper says, "what the black truffle is to mushrooms." Shagbark hickory nuts have "more flavor ... more snap, more tooth-feel than either pecans or walnuts." Unlike most nuts, they require toasting to intensify their flavor and create the shattering texture that makes them unique. Each meal at L'Etoile begins with a hickory-nut shaman, a crisp, light cracker made of chopped hickory nuts, flour, and butter. The cracker is garnished with fresh goat's-milk cheese, a seasonally varying selection of chopped herbs (including thyme, rosemary, and sage), and half a hickory nut. Piper says, "I really want to get the miracle of this place into everybody's mouth right at the start."

Shagbark hickory (Carya ovata) is a relative of the pecan and a North American native, widely found in Ohio, Indiana, Illinois, Wisconsin, and Iowa. It's hard to miss because the unique bark peels away from the tree in thin strips from six inches to four feet long. The trees are often found along roadsides. On the small dairy farms that still dominate the rolling hills of southern Wisconsin, the cornfields and cow pastures mingle with stands of oak and hickory.

Today, the main place to find shelled shagbark hickory nuts for sale is at farmers' markets. At the Madison farmers' market, the stands that sell the nuts are run by longtime farmers or retirees. Harvey Ruehlow of the Nut Factory says, "The old guys are dying off, and the young people don't have time." He and his wife, Beverly, learned to forage and pick from Harvey's dad, who loved to eat cinnamon rolls topped with chopped hickory nuts (old-timers use hickory nuts only for baking). Most of the nuts are bought by chefs and gourmet home cooks.

Shagbark hickory nuts are central to Piper's regionally reliant cuisine. This cuisine, like France's regional cuisines, develops in relationship to the surrounding geography. In France, specific places are known for their distinctive foods, which serve as a building-block for the regional cuisine. In *The Food of France*, Waverly Root famously divides the entire country into the domains of butter, lard and oil and then creates seventeen regions. He says there is an "ecological relationship, I suppose you might call it, between geography and cuisine."[13]

These efforts have always been conservative, in the literal sense. In Bordeaux, Cabernet Sauvignon grapes are the traditional variety and now they are mandated as part of the A.O.C. system. In Provence, olive oil, goat cheese and olives are long standing and celebrated ingredients. The downside of protecting of traditional foods and practices in France has been to turn *produits de terroir* into artefacts in a living history museum. Innovation and change are frowned upon. Such conservatism can also be seen in the often timeless quality of the food served in restaurants there.

A modern American *cuisine du terroir* has to be more forceful. Most of Wisconsin's citizens do not interact with the land on a daily basis. Our recent history revolves around trampling on rather than preserving the agrarian landscape. Thus many are skeptical about the existence of *terroir* here, for we have lost our culinary linkages to a place (if they existed in the first place). If nurturing and responding to the bounty of a region define a *cuisine du terroir*, ours must be intentional. Ingredients, recipes and dishes that reflect Wisconsin are not the lucky accidents of times past.

The French foodview, however, was part of Piper's unorthodox training into the restaurant business. When JoAnna Guthrie started the Ovens of Brittany, she decided to use two operating principles: one, to look to France for ideas about cooking techniques and dishes to prepare, and two always to cook from scratch. Piper says that in the early days, "We were literally cooking out of *Mastering the Art of French Cooking*."[14] Their countercuisine was inspired by both the forests and farms of Wisconsin and the regional French dishes they used to guide them.

The regional foods that make up a *cuisine du terroir* taste of the land from which they come. Certain plants and animals are adapted to a particular spot – its soil and rock and climate – and draw out a distinct flavor. Among foods from a locality, strong harmonies can occur. Historically, such foods developed slowly, and generations living in one place tended to favor what worked well and tasted best, other things being equal.[15]

In many ways, Piper is inventing a Wisconsin *cuisine du terroir* from scratch. Her ingredients reflect the triad long promoted by Europeans: geographic specificity, artisanal methods, and locally adapted varieties and breeds. But equally important for her are "communities and cultures. Terroir is something that arises out of the relationships between artisans and the land." She doesn't work alone. She says she is committed to the "love that brings something out between people and agriculture." Piper combines respect for past agricultural practices with an openness to supporting new inventions and ingredients.

But Is It Just a Restaurant Cuisine?

Does it reduce the significance of the achievement that this modern Wisconsin *cuisine du terroir* depends so much on one professional chef cooking in one restaurant? No – not if we consider the importance of restaurants to our everyday decisions about where and what to eat. Today, rather than from mother to daughter, information about ingredients, techniques, and dishes is more likely to be passed from chef to customer. Most people first taste and learn about hickory nuts, pasture-raised beef, radicchio, or cloth-bound cheddar in restaurants. A regional cuisine in our postmodern era must involve both the domestic and public spheres, for we cook and eat in both arenas.

When chefs buy local food, they also educate by exposing American diners to unexpected flavors and preparations. "The taste of place is very much an acclimatization of the palate. That recognition does not occur naturally," Piper commented. When chefs feature local foods, they become teachers, introducing their customers to the importance of freshness and season. Each L'Etoile menu begins with a short paragraph detailing the Wisconsin ingredients used that week, ending with these lines: "Some of the finest foods produced anywhere in the world are available here in the Midwest. We thank you for supporting the farmers who supply L'Etoile and valuing their commitment to these patient arts."

Also, chefs have purchasing power. They constantly seek variety. They want distinctive flavors and unusual dishes. Small farmers respond by diversifying what and how they grow.[16] Challenges arise when an entrepreneur is guided by a social mission. Piper readily admits that she never used a classic restaurant business plan: "It always felt like a highly personal mission or obligation. It was my turn to carry the torch for a while."[17] This sense of mission kept her going, even during difficult financial periods. Eventually she was able to make L'Etoile a viable business, paying her workers good wages and taking a salary for herself, as well as paying her dozens of farmers, foragers and others for their products. She was not taking emblematic regional dishes and placing them on a menu full of standard restaurant fare (prime rib and mashed potatoes, lasagna). She developed her menus using her *vision*: Piper was an agrarian utopian when she *thought* about her food but along the way her taste of Wisconsin became part of a modern, market-driven business.

The "middle way" of American regional cuisine certainly possesses contradictions. Most restaurants' kitchens are small and cramped. Workers are always fighting for adequate space, and L'Etoile is no exception. Restaurants rarely keep foods over periods; I've never heard of one with a cold cellar. In a cold northern climate like Wisconsin's, this means buying locally in the winter is difficult. Putting large amounts of food by in the harvest months is not always feasible.

More and more restaurants across the United States are buying locally and regionally, but their use of these ingredients drops off sharply in winter, and higher costs often limit the amount that restaurants buy at any time. A pound of hickory nuts costs around $17; a pound of pecans, $8. No matter how much chefs in Wisconsin love hickory nuts, most use them rarely. Piper's idealism and imagination have made her purchases of regional ingredients unusually large and consistent, but even for her Harmony Valley Farm's carrots tend to be showpieces on the plate, while for stock carrots from California will do. She does distinguish herself from other chefs also committed to purchasing local food in several ways: the extensiveness of her direct buying; the starring role these ingredients play in her menus; and her responsiveness to their characteristic flavors in the creation of each dish.

Meanwhile, regional ingredients and foods don't make it into the average home because in these times they are not widely available, they are frequently more expensive, and they are sometimes unfamiliar or intimidating. If a shopper looks at a display of frisée or Jerusalem artichokes and wonders what exactly you do with them, he or she is likely to move on. But the same home cook may take on the challenge if the raw materials are put into a context, say in a dish eaten at L'Etoile, or in the form of a story shared by the grower, or in a recipe from a friend who shops regularly at the farmers' market. At Madison's year-round farmers' market, each purchase, each personal exchange affirms the connections necessary to sustain a *cuisine du terroir* in the years to come.

And Piper's cooking has a widening influence. Shoppers who come by the Harmony Valley stand at the market often say, "We ate this at L'Etoile – how can I cook it?" Piper holds regular cooking classes and offers popular tours of the market. Harmony Valley Farm also sells to other restaurants that stress regional ingredients, including Harvest in Madison and North Pond in Chicago. The Harvest's two owners worked at L'Etoile before opening their own restaurant two doors down and right across the street from the farmers' market.

Impressively, Piper believes many people have already begun to recognize a Wisconsin taste in the ingredients from the region. She speaks of "a newly arrived polyglot cuisine starting as people settle in and familiarize themselves and cook." She says, "We're patterning and imprinting."

In southern Wisconsin, with passionate believers like Odessa Piper and with the thriving Dane County Farmers' Market, I see hope for a countercuisine built as much on the relationships of people with each other as with the land around them. Unlike Old World cuisines, the emerging regional cuisine in southern Wisconsin isn't based on allegiance to the past but on nurturing each and every ally. One of L'Etoile's hickory nut suppliers told me, "Odessa has been a big influence on us keeping at this." According to Piper, "All we did is pay attention to the relationship between artisans and the land, and now we have a beautiful cuisine."

More than forty years ago, Elizabeth David in *French Provincial Cooking* commented on France's *cuisines du terroir*, which she saw even then as threatened: "Recipes alone are not enough. A flourishing tradition of local cookery implies also genuine products; the cooks and the housewives must be backed up by the dairy farmers, the pig breeders and pork butchers, the market gardeners and the fruit growers, otherwise regional cookery simply retreats into the realms of folklore."[18] She realized then the necessity of a network of people, working in concert with each other, to any vibrant regional cuisine, in order that all the possible ingredients, tastes and recipes are available.

And for David, chefs and restaurants play a crucial role, promoting "dishes derive[d] from peasant and farmhouse cookery."[19] Like Piper, however, she did not think their job was to invent a culinary heritage museum; rather, "the professional cooks and housewives adapt the old methods to changing tastes ... [and] chefs develop new dishes based on the old ones but still using the essential ingredients."[20] Restaurants have long created vital spaces for a *cuisine du terroir*: spaces of collaboration, of imagination, of commensality. As we rely on the public sphere for where to cook and how to eat, those chefs, restaurants, cookbook authors and others are more important than ever to any cuisine. For better or for worse, the constraints of the marketplace in a dynamic tension with agrarian ideals may create the new boundaries for American regional cuisines.

In Madison, bratwursts and Cornish pasties are still standard fare, especially on football Saturdays, when 70,000 people have tailgate parties before they head to the football stadium to watch the University of Wisconsin Badgers play. But now there is another version of regional cuisine in the making. Piper, her over eighty purveyors, L'Etoile's customers, and shoppers at the farmers' markets all look to the land as their inspiration and for their livelihood. As Esteva and Prakash put it, "Without the tending of human hands, top soil is being blown away, along with the stories, rituals and practices that make 'cultural soil.'"[21] Like Elizabeth David, Piper and all her allies take to heart the importance of regional ingredients as they create a thoroughly modern taste of Wisconsin, combining a savvy understanding of the rationales of the market with a commitment to utopian ideals. And so a contemporary American *cuisine du terroir* is created.

Notes

1. National Restaurant Association (2003).
2. See Habermas (1989); Bourdieu (1984); Spang (2000).
3. See Fine (1996); Trubek (2000).
4. Heffernan and Hendrickson (2005).
5. See Belasco (1989); Levenstein (2003a); Ray (2004); Berry (2002).
6. Concepts of purity play an important role in both values and practices related to the American food system. Many regulations related to food safety created in the twentieth century imagine a "pure" food supply.
7. Esteva and Prakash (1998: 10).
8. Belasco (1989: 230–2).
9. Ibid.
10. Ibid., p. 248.
11. All the remarks by Odessa Piper were recorded during October 2003.
12. Piper sold the restaurant to Tory Miller and his sister Tracy in 2005. She still serves as a consultant to the restaurant.
13. Ibid.
14. Interview, October 2003.
15. What will probably always remain missing from any new cuisine du terroir is a group of dishes commonly known in the area, as in a traditional cuisine.
16. Elsewhere (Trubek 2004) I consider in detail the relationship of Piper and L'Etoile to local area farmers' markets.
17. Interview, September 2005.
18. David (1960: xi).
19. Ibid., p. x.
20. Ibid., p. xi.
21. Esteva and Prakash (1998: 53).

Mains

–4–

Side-Dish Kitchen

Japanese American Delicatessens and the Culture of Nostalgia

Christine R. Yano

Sagara Store. The simplicity of the name evokes an earlier era in Hawai`i, before ubiquitous talk of branding, fast food outlets, and endless meal choices made the question of where or what to eat a ponderous issue. To get to Sagara Store from downtown Honolulu one has to take the H-1 freeway past the Honolulu International Airport turnoff, through middle-class subdivisions that creep up mountain ridges. One then takes a fork in the road to the H-2 freeway that plows through former pineapple fields toward surfing beaches of world renown. After several miles, one

Figure 4.1 *Okazuya* in downtown Honolulu. Photo credit: Christine Yano.

Figure 4.2 *Okazuya* in downtown Honolulu. Photo credit: Christine Yano.

takes another major fork in the road that veers away from those surfing spots toward the sleepy plantation town of Waialua and beyond that, to the end of the paved road. Waialua is about as far away as one can get from the hotels of Waikiki on an island where tourism rules. Sagara Store in Waialua is the eatery where locals go. In an unmarked wooden building (directions: "across from the high school"), Sagara Store has been serving its version of home cooking since 1922.

This chapter examines Sagara Store and other similar eateries called *okazuya* (literally, "side-dish house/business"), Japanese American take-out delicatessens in Hawai`i.[1] The food that Sagara Store serves has its origins in rural southwestern Japan; but the menu has expanded to meet the needs and appetites of the evolving local clientele in Hawai`i. I analyze Sagara Store and other *okazuya* as sites of nostalgized discourse, discussing ways in which these take-out restaurants have become emblematic of the past and the distant in highly specific ways. Sagara Store may be considered, in the words of Kathleen Stewart, a "space on the side of the road," both literally and figuratively (1996). Related to Stewart's concept is Svetlana Boym's notion of "off-modern," which she describes as a "critical reflection on the modern condition that incorporates nostalgia. ... The adverb *off* confuses our sense of direction; it makes us explore sideshadows and back alleys rather than the straight road of progress"

(Boym 2001: xvi–xvii). The side-road space and back alleys are not narrative or architectural ones, as in Stewart's or Boym's study, but culinary sites. Through interviews with owners, workers, and customers at several *okazuya* in Hawai`i and archival research, I analyze *okazuya* as "a gap in the order of things" that produces both an alternative to mainstream American society, and also its intensification through issues of nostalgia and sense of home (Stewart 1996: 3). Furthermore, the "sense" of which I speak carries the double meaning of general feeling and bodily impression. Home, therefore, adheres often specifically through sensate mnemonics. It is the smell and the taste of *okazuya* food that evokes home (typically conflated with the past) for many customers. In this chapter, I intersperse the ethnographic specificities of Sagara Store (in italics) with more general discussion of *okazuya* as what I call "side-dish kitchens," culinary sites in Hawai`i akin to a "space on the side of the road."

Okazuya Primer

Okazuya arose in the early twentieth century in Honolulu and other semi-urban (and in the case of Sagara Store, small town) areas of Hawai`i as a direct response to a largely blue-collar population. With homecooked meals for lunch as a Japanese model, but without women in the home cooking those meals in working-class Hawai`i, a niche developed for the birth of *okazuya*. For its proprietors, opening an *okazuya* became a humble means to own a small-scale business, "build up social networks and new social spaces, and to improve his or her position within a dominant system" (Ferrero 2002: 198–9). The humbleness of the business is often reflected in its physical plant: at their most elementary, some *okazuya* even today are strictly take-out establishments, with little more than a counter where food is displayed.

It is important to note that *okazuya* do not exist in this exact form in Japan. Instead, there are establishments in Japan known as *sōzaiya* (delicatessens) that sell numerous ready-to-eat dishes primarily for busy housewives to create or supplement a meal. Although some of the dishes may overlap, in their format, as discussed below, these *sōzaiya* are not *okazuya*. Rather, *sōzaiya* offer dishes in multiple serving portions to be shared by a number of people. *Okazuya* thus constitute a local Hawai`i adaptation – its own kind of "space on the side of the road" *vis-à-vis* Japan – of a take-out delicatessen.

In the 1920s, persons of Japanese ancestry constituted over 40 percent of the population in Hawai`i, including thousands of former plantation laborers who left the fields for the urban center of Honolulu. Even as many left the fields, still others remained in plantation towns to fuel the sugar and pineapple industries that were the rural economy's mainstays. The birth of *okazuya* catering particularly to the needs of Japanese American urban male blue-collar workers is reflected in their hours, menus, and types of service. The extension of clientele to include persons of different ethnicities, white-collar workers, and females has not altered the fundamental structure of *okazuya*.

The current hours of operation are typically from 6:30 a.m. to 1:00 p.m. (or until the food runs out), six or seven days a week. [2] The opening hours reflect the early start of work and school in Honolulu, where construction crews gather at 6:30 a.m., offices open at 8:00 a.m., school starts at 7:30 or 8:00 a.m., and morning rush-hour traffic extends from 6:30 to 8:30 a.m. Some early-morning customers buy food to eat for breakfast, while many others purchase food to eat later for lunch. Some *okazuya* close as early as 11:30 a.m., while others stay open as late as 2:00 p.m. The early closing hours explicitly place these eateries well outside the service of dinner, or even a late lunch.

Sagara Store opens at 5:30 a.m., five days a week. Its closing hours depend on whether or not school is in session – in the summer when there is no school the owners close their doors at 1:00 p.m., but during the rest of the year it stays open until 2:30 p.m. to accommodate students who might want to pick up an after-school snack. Whereas it was once both a general store and an okazuya, the general store half of it has closed. In the dimly lit room, the shelves of the general store section lie empty; footsteps produce a faint echo on the bare concrete floor. The empty shelves reflect in part the shrinking population of former plantation towns in Hawai`i. With the closing of sugar plantations in the 1990s, towns such as Waialua have seen significant depopulation, especially among the youth. But even the youth have more options and travel more easily than in the past, and may choose to drive to the neighboring surfing town Haleiwa for a range of fast foods. The customer base for Sagara Store is thus shrinking by both numbers and preferences, as well as growing older. Supplemented by the occasional tourist who wants to see the end of the road or an errant surfer scouting for big waves, the store manages to stay afloat through a small but steady clientele.

The food that *okazuya* serve typically does not change during the day. As is true with many Asian cuisines, specific foods do not mark particular times of day. In delicatessen style, *okazuya* food is all ready-made and portable. The fact that the day's entire menu must be available by the *okazuya*'s opening means that food preparation and cooking begins in the middle of the night, for some as early as 1 a.m., for others as "late" as 4 a.m. The arduousness of the work for which *okazuya* are known lies not only in the long hours, but in the early (or middle of the night) hours. Because *okazuya* workers toil while others sleep, their labor is seen as particularly difficult.

Work at Sagara Store begins at 1:00 a.m. with cooking and food preparation in time for the store's opening. In talking to the yonsei *[fourth-generation Japanese-American] sister proprietors on a languid Friday morning in August 2003, the elder of the two leads the conversation. In the dim light of the store, she speaks wearily of the daily grind, her head often resting against her outstretched arm. To my surprise, she is a prep school graduate who left Hawai`i at eighteen to study social work at Colorado State University. She never expected to be running this family business,* *but finds herself, along with her sister, at its helm for the past ten years. This is a far cry from her dreams of a career, but she say she has gotten used to it. Nevertheless, in the lull before the lunchtime rush, a pause in her busyness gives her body time to wind down, and all she would like to do right now is to sleep.*

Okazuya do not necessarily place ethnic boundaries around food: in general, proprietors cook whatever they think will sell. The food thus constitutes a culinary-based social history of immigration to Hawai`i centered on Japanese-Americans.[3] Each customer selects from an array of dishes to create a customized plate that always includes rice (sticky Japanese rice) and some combination of *teriyaki* chicken or beef, "butterfish" (Japanese-marinated and grilled cod), *nishime* (Japanese stew), *namasu* (marinated vegetables), and other Japanese-based dishes. Most *okazuya* also serve Chinese-style stir-fried noodles, reflecting the long history of Chinese laborers in Hawai`i that predates the Japanese immigration. Some *okazuya* offer foods based in other ethnic groups' cuisines, such as *kal-bi* (Korean short ribs), chicken or pork *adobo* (Filipino vinegar-seasoned stew), and sweet and sour spare-ribs (Chinese). American-based dishes have also become staples of the *okazuya* menu:[4] potato-macaroni salad, grilled hot dog, luncheon meat, corned beef hash patties. The inclusion of processed and/or tinned meats reflects the American milieu of Hawai`i, as well as the Pacific island location, where the emphasis lies on imported meats with a long shelf-life. These foods also reflect the overall blue-collar base of *okazuya* and their clientele.

Sagara Store presents its food in bowls, plates, and pans on a counter. There is no steam tray or refrigerated display in sight. Instead there is simply a glass-encased wooden cupboard with two shelves. It evokes pre-war pragmatism, with little thought given to presentation. The quantities of food that are taken out at any one time are not huge, and spoilage does not seem to be a concern of the proprietors. The food is typical okazuya *cuisine and does not differ much from pre-war offerings. The exception is one of the most popular items among younger customers – Spam* musubi *– a grab-and-go favorite that appeals to the local taste for rice and salty meat.*

Rice at *okazuya* is a staple, as at other Japanese eateries. But one cannot typically order a scoop (or two) of rice. Instead, rice is served as finger food in the form of sushi or *musubi* (rice balls). What distinguishes *okazuya* is that it is specifically for take-out, rather than what one would eat at a sit-down restaurant.[5] Therefore, it may be classified as picnic or "lunch-box food" – portable food that may be served either hot or at room temperature. The *Japanese concept of obentō (a ready-made meal packed in a container)* shapes the *okazuya's* food offerings. In *obentō*, rice is accompanied by dishes that can be served at room temperature. *Obentō* is typically eaten not at home, but outside the home when traveling or at school or work (see Allison 1997).[6] So, too, the food served at *okazuya* is meant to be like that from home, but eaten elsewhere. This is reputedly home-cooking, rather than "restaurant" food. In fact, the dishes served at *okazuya* have become sufficiently codified for it to constitute its own genre of cuisine – "*okazuya* food" – not restaurant food, but labor-intensive foods associated with the Japanese American home in Hawai`i.

Further evidence that *okazuya* cooking is not necessarily food that is found in homes lies in the fact that in some cases, owners had to learn how to cook "*okazuya* food." For example, the proprietor of a now-defunct establishment explains: "My mom [the original *okazuya* owner] didn't know how to cook *okazuya* food. ... All she used to cook [when the *okazuya* first opened] was beans – lima beans, kidney beans. Gradually, the customers started telling her to make other things, like *chow fun* [=*chao fen*, a Chinese rice-noodle dish]" (quoted in Ohira 1999: A4).

Most *okazuya* serve only individual portions. One walks up to the counter and faced with an array of dishes on display, orders specific foods from a server. Portions are flexible rather than fixed, within limits. Therefore, one server may scoop a large portion while another may dish a smaller quantity, depending on the vagaries of whim, mood, generosity, and personal relationship with the customer. Furthermore, one server may opt to select prime pieces of meat or chicken, for example, while another may pick at random. Yet another server may know a customer's preferences and cater to these. (All this is done without any tipping.) What results is a variable plate of food that reflects a specific social relationship (or lack thereof) at a particular point in time and space.

The *Okazuya* as a Site of Sociality

What these practices suggest is that *okazuya* are not only businesses, but more importantly sites of sociality, whether biologically based or interactionally constituted. The sociality exists on both sides of the counter and in the transactions between them. For one thing, *okazuya* are primarily family-run operations. The biggest problem that *okazuya* currently face is a lack of family members willing to take over the business. When confronted with this problem, *okazuya* owners prefer to shut down rather than sell to non-kin. Particularly with an ethic of a family business, the reputation adheres as much to the name of the establishment (often with the family's name being a part of it, as in "Sagara Store") as to its products.

In the early days of *okazuya*, all or nearly all workers were family members. Today, most larger *okazuya* hire non-family workers, especially to service the counter, clean up, and do elementary food preparation. But the central feature of the *okazuya* – the food and its making – is typically only entrusted to family members. The cultural rationale given to this is that the food served at an *okazuya* carries with it the "flavor of the family," entrusted to the succeeding generations through treasured recipes.

Sagara Store's current proprietors are two yonsei *sisters in their forties, the great-granddaughters of the store's founder. They work with the part-time assistance of their retired parents. The store was handed down along female lines – great-grandmother to grandmother to mother to the two sisters – even if some of the workers and cooks have been men. Learning the trade of Sagara Store took place incrementally: while growing up the sisters helped out at the store whenever it was busy, but they didn't do actual cooking until much later. The transition between mother and sister owners has been gradual. Mother and father still pitch in and help prepare food in the morning, and the sisters keep cooking and replenish the foods throughout the working hours, often with the help of the younger sister's husband. The sharing of responsibilities is both clear-cut and flexible, like choreographing an improvisational ensemble: each one knows what she has to do because of an overall structure, but if one needs help, the other one fills in, often without being asked. This kind of adaptable kitchen requires mental, emotional, and physical coordination that people say is achieved best or most "naturally" within the family. There is no contract that specifies duties and responsibilities; instead there is an unspoken agreement on the overall goal of the enterprise and a commonly shared pact and understanding as to what it takes to achieve that goal.*

Relying on the "flavor of the family" extends to other aspects of the business. In interviews with *okazuya* owners, several of them comment that they cannot place responsibility for day-to-day operations on anyone but the family. Using "blood-is-thicker-than-water" idioms of expression, several of them mention that by virtue of being in the same family, a person possesses the following kinds of characteristics: dependability, trust, long-term knowledge, quality control, diligence, commitment, and easy familiarity. For example, one *okazuya* owner explains:

The family members that worked [in the old days], they were around it for so long that they knew what [to do]. They kinda had a head start, I guess. They always made sure that things were done properly, quality-wise. Now you gotta watch more [with non-family employees] to make sure things are coming out the way you want it.

Okazuya owners draw such a clear boundary around family in terms of the workplace that the kin group becomes a trope of positive qualities and a source of nostalgia. One trusts kin; by contrast, one must approach non-kin with caution and constant vigilance. This kind of talk further dismisses uncooperative family members as mere exceptions, while praising exemplary non-family workers as "just like family."

Nevertheless, family-run businesses come with their own set of problems. As an enterprise run outside contractual business procedures, the family-run business stands in danger of exploiting its worker-members. Thus, *okazuya*, at least in the past, had a cadre of flex-workers who worked on an as-needed basis, often receiving little or no pay. One retired *okazuya* owner recalls:

During the generation before, in my father's time and aunt's time, we had lots of relatives. There were so many people they could call [to work], and they were willing to come and wanted to come. Many, many, you know, [came to work when called] – the elderly Japanese ladies. They were willing to come to roll sushi [specifically *makizushi*], like that. ... But now, nobody, especially of Japanese ancestry... The elderly Japanese people, they go to classes, and they do other things. ... The relatives were so many, but now there's not too many.

According to this former owner, the labor problems of *okazuya* stem from the following points: (1) ties to the extended family are diminishing, and therefore the labor pool of relatives is shrinking;[7] and (2) family members are involved in their own individual activities and have less time or willingness to commit it to the family enterprise. Furthermore, this owner extends the family more broadly to persons of Japanese ancestry, manifesting not only a kin preference, but also a racial bias preference for workers. In doing so, she subtly implies a cultural knowledge that comes from growing up within a Japanese (American) household (i.e. an achieved awareness) and possessing Japanese blood (i.e. an ascribed awareness). Successfully running an *okazuya* relies on both.

To the above labor problems of *okazuya* one might add the passing of generations and the disinclination of younger family members to engage in the hard work, long hours, and early rising that *okazuya* ownership demands. The younger generations' dismissal of *okazuya* work comes in part as a result of higher education (although one Sagara Store owner is an exception), especially since, proportionally speaking, Japanese-Americans have attained post-high school education in increasing numbers. Thus parents – though some may be *okazuya* owners themselves – do not necessarily encourage their offspring to engage in this kind of work. According to them, they have sent their children to college specifically to avoid the *okazuya* lifestyle of hard labor. One *okazuya* owner looks to his long workdays and concludes that he would not want his children to take over the business: "It's better if you work regular jobs with eight-hour days and weekends off" (quoted in Oi 1999b: D1).

I ask the elder sister, "What do you see for the future of your okazuya?" *She pauses, the air hanging heavily. Then she responds in a halting monotone. "I don't know ... I don't even know ... We don't even know if we want to keep doing this like my grandmother did, 'cause it's hard work. I really don't know. But I told my daughter, 'You better not do this, because it's...'. People always say, 'Oh, you folks make a lot of money.' That's what they think. But there's not a whole bunch of money in it and the work is really tiring. It's long hours.... We'll see how long we can last." She gives a half-hearted smile and leaves her last sentence dangling in mid-air.*

Within a family business, workers who are relatives often have little recourse for complaint and must interact according to family dictates. In this sense, a disgruntled family-member worker stands to lose his status within both the company and the family if things do not go well. Employee relations thus take on a different sense when family is involved. One young female *okazuya* owner in a brother–sister team explains: "A lot of people tell us, 'It must be hard to work with your brother.' Of course we fight and stuff, but you know how they say, blood is more forgiving afterwards than having it out with a friend." In this way, the blood-is-thicker-than-water dictum provides stability within the company even though it may restrict options for its workers.

Among the *okazuya* I visited, several were small operations that only involved family members. In the case of the brother–sister operation, it was only the two of them (one to do the cooking, the other to man the counter), with another (unpaid) sister handling the accounting. When asked if they would hire additional workers, the sister-owner replied, "If anything, it would be relatives that we'd hire. It wouldn't be somebody, just put in an ad, and have somebody come out here [to work]... It's trust, yeah. We cannot be watching them every time." Her brother added, "Especially not for work. I don't think I would let anybody touch the cooking part [of the business]."

In these small-scale businesses, the load of responsibility falls squarely on everyone's shoulders, not only to conduct business, but to do so while maintaining workable relations. The traditional Japanese *ie* (household) serves well here as a model of a corporate household, rather than a biological unit.[8] Although the *ie* may be easily interpreted as a family (a kin group of parents, offspring, and other "relatives"), in day-to-day functioning it included non-kin elements of a household, including outside workers. In Hawai`i *okazuya* embrace some of the problems of the *ie* model by insisting that persons related by blood or marriage maintain positions at the helm of the business, but forgo the pragmatism and flexibility of past *ie* management in Japan that included non-kin members. *Okazuya* also differ from a strict *ie* model in the relative gender-neutrality of work roles. In contrast with the strong patrilineality of the Japanese model, the Hawai`i business is run with some gender flexibility. Therefore, although some *okazuya* are headed by male cooks (as is signified in their names, such as George's Delicatessen and Masa's Foods), others have female cooks, such as Sagara Store (as well as Caryn's *Okazuya* and Ethel's Delicatessen).

Owner/worker–customer relations form an essential component of the sociality of *okazuya*. The fact that *okazuya* are generally small and none are franchised means that the owner is not a distant head, but intimately involved in day-to-day operations. Customers thereby have the opportunity to establish a relationship with the owner/worker. Furthermore, the owner is often the cook, so that the customer's relationship with the owner is not only social and transactional, but also gustatory. The customer knows the owner/worker/chef through their cooking. That culinary relationship is often longstanding. Each owner I interviewed proudly mentioned "regulars" – customers who have frequented their establishment for years, exhibiting loyalty that often extends to succeeding generations. One retired *okazuya* owner recalls:

> The same people come every day, some people almost every day. ... I mean for years and years and years. And then their relatives come, too. So there's this kind of bond or

something. I hardly go in there [now], but if I go in today, I'll see the same people and say, "Oh, how are you? How you been?" The same people are there. And they'll come and eat.

The sociality of *okazuya* rests in the culinary habitus of customers.

*The proprietress of Sagara Store explains, "The secret to staying in business for so many years is good, loyal customers. The community is one big family. Some people come to visit us straight from the airport" (quoted in Dela Cruz and Chai 2002: 20). In other words, for "regulars," eating the food from a place such as Sagara Store establishes and affirms the fact that they are home. In a one-*okazuya *town such as Waialua, "regulars" and "the community" are one and the same, creating "one big family" centered on the* okazuya *and its foods. Sagara Store is thus coterminous with Waialua town, its resident-customers bound together by the fact that they share food from the same kitchen.*

Several customers note the close association between *okazuya* and a sense of home (or hometown). One litmus test of "home" lies in considering what one misses when one is away, and concomitantly, what one wants to do or where one wants to go upon return (cf. Hannerz 1996: 27). As Susan Kalcik points out, "food links people across space and time, so that it helps create a bond with past members of the group as well as between living ones" (Kalcik 1984: 59). It is this bond that is expressed in the airport reference given above. One former resident of Hawai`i who now lives in Seattle talks about her favorite *okazuya*: "'I love this place. When I came home [to Hawai`i] on vacation, this is the first place I came.' ... In her one-week stay, she's eaten there twice and will likely be back for another dose before flying back to the mainland" (Oi 1999b: D1).

Fans of *okazuya* talk about favorite establishments. In other words, they are fans not of *okazuya* food so much as of specific *okazuya*. When the question of what to have for lunch comes up, customers choose between their favorite *okazuya* and other fast-food establishments, not from among *okazuya*. The competition for *okazuya*, then, is not with other *okazuya*; rather it is with other genres of fast food. Where *okazuya* win the competition may lie not so much in the food itself, but in the close relationships between owner/workers and customers. One *okazuya* owner explains:

> You know it's much more expensive [to eat at an *okazuya*] than eating like in McDonald's. So there must be something else about it that they [customers] like. ... The clientele, it's a personal relationship. ... It's a little personal touch, I think, that is there. It's not just a business thing.

One customer of a now defunct *okazuya* explains: "When you came in, they were always smiling. The chow fun [Chinese rice-noodle dish] was the best, not oily or greasy. And Flora's mac salad with onions, celery and cabbage was really good. I'm missing it already" (quoted in Ohira 1999: A4). The food – and the appeal – then, are not generic, but specific: not macaroni salad, but "Flora's mac salad." The "regular" comes back to *okazuya* within the context of a longstanding relationship with both food and people. Choosing to eat at an *okazuya* for a "regular" means purchasing not only food, but also the guarantee of a greeting, a familiar face, and the ease of intimacy.

The longstanding relationship between owner/worker and customers is part of what makes the job satisfying. One *okazuya* owner explains, "It's hard work but when you see people who enjoy our food, people who always come back, that's what keeps you going" (quoted in Oi 1999b: D1). One worker says, "You know what I enjoy most? It's greeting the customers, because you know they say I'm always smiling." The owner of an *okazuya* that closed in 1999 remarks, "We'll miss our customers, but there's gratification knowing that they enjoyed our food all these years. I was the cook and could never miss a day of work. I'm thankful that God took care of me and let me do this for so long" (quoted in Ohira 1999: A4).

As it gets closer to 11:00 a.m., the number of customers at Sagara Store gradually increases. They are all locals of indeterminate ethnic origin (Japanese, Chinese, Filipino, or mixtures of these). The lunchtime rush at Sagara Store translates into older men, women, and children wearing t-shirts, shorts, rubber slippers, shuffling in singly or in groups of twos or threes. They barely constitute a line, even at the peak of busyness. The sisters know pretty much what these folks will order. The customers' pace and rhythms are slower, gentler, softer than mine. They are greeted by the sisters with a slow smile that is not effusive, but quietly sociable. McDonald's corporate perkiness is nowhere to be seen. Occasionally conversation in the store picks up around tidbits of news: so-and-so getting married, so-and-so diagnosed with cancer, so-and-so hitting it big in Las Vegas. Gossip is served up as a side-dish to the food, which, like the talk, does not shout but beckons quietly with its familiarity. The children, too, are old friends of Sagara Store, since the walls and servers have borne witness to them even before they were born.

What "regulars" gain by their loyalty is the special treatment of an intimate. In some cases, the worker dishes out only the customer's favorite pieces of chicken, for example, or parts of a stew (for example, "no carrots"). In other cases, the worker knows that a female customer may be on a low-carb diet, dishes out smaller portions, and charges accordingly. One *okazuya* owner says, "You kind of know who to give plenty and who not to give. Like the guys who work around here, you know they like plenty, right?" Another *okazuya* owner explains, "After awhile you kind of know who's the one that likes certain things ... like not wanting the gravy touching the rice or the salad." Yet another *okazuya* owner declares, "We have some customers who come in every day. The people on the counter – when they see them coming – they get their plate ready [filling it with the customer's favorites even before the customer orders] so by the time they get to the window [*okazuya* counter], their food is ready to go" (quoted in Oi 1999b: D1). This kind of empathic knowledge derived from long-term interaction simulates the environment of home rather than of business. In fact, it is the inculcation of a "home" atmosphere that becomes the model of *okazuya* operation.

For one, most *okazuya* display an array of food, but no prices. Some *okazuya* post prices, but I have never seen these placed near the foods to be served. Furthermore, even where prices are listed, it is often not made clear the quantity of food that might be served for a particular price. The ambiguity retains flexibility in the transaction, especially for foods that do not come in discrete units. I have also rarely seen a local customer ask the price of an item. Based in the ethos of familial trust and intimacy, the customer selects and the server dishes out, no questions asked. As one *okazuya* owner explains, "Nobody really questions our pricing." (The typical cost of a full plate at an *okazuya* is from \$4 to \$7.)

Second, *okazuya* workers – kin and non-kin – generally show considerable loyalty to the business. There is not a high turnover rate of workers, as is the case with many fast-food establishments. *Okazuya* workers tend to be older, long-term residents of Hawai`i. In fact, workers (kin and non-kin) often develop familial relations with each other through daily interaction. One newspaper article describes the overlapping dialogue of two unrelated *okazuya* workers: "The words fold over each other so it's unclear who said what. This is typical of conversations with them. After a decade or so on the job, they move and talk in a rhythm to which both are tuned" (Oi 1999a: D6). With such long-time workers, a customer can expect to see the same workers at a particular *okazuya*. The customer's experience is thus one of familiarity, not only in the food that is served, but also in the workers.

Third, *okazuya* food is interpreted as "homestyle cooking," even if this is not food that is typically made at home these days. Rather, it is food more closely associated with young people's parents' or even grandparents' generation. One proprietor recalled a woman in her twenties peeking into the store and commenting, "Oh, that's the kind of food my grandmother used to make." Thus, the sense of home invoked by *okazuya* may not be one's actual home, but a nostalgized sense of kitchens past and the grandmothers who inhabited them. This is associative memory tied up in food.

Fourth, learning how to make *okazuya* food is done primarily by observing other previous cooks within the family, helping out in the kitchen as an informal apprenticeship, and sometimes consulting recipes that have been passed down through generations. In my various interviews, I have yet to come across an *okazuya* cook who had formal training (in fact, one might say that boasting formal training might detract from the "homespun" quality of the food). Instead, most watched their parents (or other relatives), helped at the business, and gradually picked up the trade in what David Sutton calls "embodied apprenticeship" (2001: 126). They learned incrementally through bodies and bloodlines, rather than through cookbooks or formal lessons (as at Sagara Store). Learning in this way teaches the basics of a family's version of *okazuya* food. At the same time, each individual cook may put his or her own stamp of flavor upon the dishes or introduce new items. Thus, what one eats at *okazuya* bears the stamp of a family's cooking, even while allowing for individual expression, variation, and sometimes innovation.

Seeing the customers arriving, I thank the sisters and gather my things to leave. Again, the older sister speaks up, motioning to the food. "Okay, what do you want to eat?" Without waiting for an answer, she takes it upon herself to load a plate with sushi, nishime, namasu, kimpira gobo, and shoyu chicken, wrapping the plate with paper and securing it with a rubber band under which she inserts chopsticks and a napkin. It is one of the more assertive acts from either side of the counter that I witness while visiting Sagara Store. In true okazuya style, the paper-wrapped plate of food looks much as it might have seventy years ago in pre-war days. Of all the okazuya I visited on O'ahu, the owners of Sagara Store, with their warm-hearted, low-key, country ways, are the only ones who would not take any money for my food. I drive a short distance to the closest beach. It is an empty stretch of glittering white sand, lava rocks, and lapping waves. Removing the paper wrap, I uncover the plate of food, smell the intermingling aroma of soy-sauce-laden dishes with vinegared rice, and taste Sagara Store's version of "home."

Nostalgia's Kitchen: Side-dish Memory

In the 1980s and 1990s and into the 2000s, Japanese-American family-run businesses in Hawai`i have closed in rapid succession. Newspaper articles detail these closures as evidence of passing of an era. The era to which they refer is the pre-war and immediate post-war establishment of businesses, many by *issei* (first-generation Japanese-Americans). A significant number of these closing or threatened businesses are eateries, prompting a flurry of "last-meal" patronage. Closing restaurants (especially *okazuya*) in particular come laden with poignancy, because of their association with food and "home." Newspaper accounts of these closings show the kind of discourse surrounding *okazuya* and their placement within American life in Hawai`i. For example, one article from 1999 begins:

> Naka's *Okazuya* in Kalihi is gone, leaving hundreds of regular customers with only fond memories of Nancy's chow fun [Chinese rice-noodles], Flora's macaroni salad, and the Nakasone family's famed cone sushi [*inarizushi*]. The last official day of business for the little hole-in-the-wall *okazuya* ... was Christmas Eve. (Ohira 1999: A4)

Okazuya in an article like this are depicted as a dying breed, a relic from the past. "Nancy's chow fun" or "the Nakasone family's famed cone sushi" are foods emblazoned with the personal touch of a maker, rather than created through an impersonal industrial process. The food is part and parcel of a social relationship (even if this is sealed through an economic transaction). The article depicts Naka's *Okazuya* as a "little hole-in-the-wall," off the main track, perhaps difficult to find, whose location and food set locals apart.

This "space on the side of the road" creates a community of "regulars" who don't need signs identifying places or portions doled out in pre-set measure or prices attached to those portions. The fact that many *okazuya* are, indeed, "hole-in-the-wall" establishments in terms of size, location (not in shopping malls, but in older urban or small-town areas), and lack of distinguishing physical features makes their existence part of insider knowledge. Few *okazuya* advertise, and some have only minimal exterior signs identifying their establishment (Sagara Store has none). One non-local resident in urban Honolulu says he drove past a building for thirty years before realizing that it was an *okazuya*. He says that the building was so nondescript that he thought it was a catering office, rather than a place to purchase and eat food. *Okazuya* may not be deliberately hidden, but, by their lack of signage and seeming disregard for attracting unknowing foot traffic, they contradict all principles of "modern" business. They are invisible – the opposite of eye-catching, colorful, come-on attractiveness. What the *okazuya* "space" reifies is not visual branding, but human relations associated with a pre-McDonald's era.

Okazuya food itself boasts a pre-industrial legacy in its making. One customer marvels, "They chop the onions and celery by hand, so tiny. ... I tried to learn the secrets, but it doesn't come out [the same]. It's just so hard and time consuming" (quoted in Ohira 1999: A4). What is involved in making *okazuya* food and appreciated by customers such as this is not only skill (for instance, the ability to chop vegetables very finely), but also effort ("hard and time consuming"). Laments one former *okazuya* worker, "Everything now is done by machines. ... To me, when you make sushi by hand, it's better than a machine" (quoted in Ohira 1999: A4). For some workers, the years of cooking have left a patina of experience not only in their bodies, but also in their equipment. When Naka's *Okazuya* closed in 1999, the owner refused to sell the company's beloved wok. One customer explains: "The wok they used has years of sweat in it, and anything you cook in it comes out good" (quoted in Ohira 1999: A4).

What is significant is to examine the eateries that are positioned as the obverse of *okazuya*. The most commonly mentioned are global fast-food businesses, such as McDonald's, Burger King, Pizza Hut, and Subway. There are other local fast-food businesses as well, such as drive-ins, hamburger stands, and plate-lunch wagons, which serve food overlapping with that of *okazuya* menus.[9] One customer "laments that the modern fast-food industry has taken over Honolulu. 'All the small places like this [*okazuya*] are disappearing, ... and it's too bad. There's nothing more fun than finding a good, local hole-in-the-wall place'" (Oi 1999b: D1). The imagery of this kind of nostalgized account is based in part on size, with its implications of power, temporality, and location. On the one hand are large, global, "modern," industrialized companies taking over Honolulu. On the other hand are small-scale, local, pre-industrial *okazuya*. This becomes a battle of the global versus the local, the industrial giant versus the little guy, fast food versus home-cooked food.

But there are other kinds of contrasts listed by journalists, such as high-end, cutting-edge gourmet cuisine: "In a time when fusion and Pacific Rim flavors get the buzz and when food design has become equivalent to feats of architectural balance, the plain and simple okazu-yas [*sic*] remain a mainstay of food lovers in Hawaii" (Oi 1999b: D1). It is the notion of "plain and simple" – whether in food, social relations, or general lifestyle – that lies at the heart of the nostalgia surrounding *okazuya*. This nostalgia is class-based, as well as temporally and spatially constituted. What is being glorified by the nostalgized discourse surrounding *okazuya* is working-class, plantation/urban culture – "plain and simple."

As with many nostalgias, the reality of the class-based, past, distant life may not be as wonderful as is assumed. The "plain" may have indeed been painfully plain, and the "simple" may not have been all that simple in economic terms. The actual experiences of people's lives under those conditions now being nostalgized were engulfed in economic privation and physical hardship. The education level was low, with many *issei* going no further than an eighth-grade education (often forced to quit school in order to work and contribute to a family's income). Pay was likewise low and family life difficult, especially with the large numbers of offspring in the second generation. The focus of the nostalgia, however, looks beyond material goods and conditions to a reconstructed emotional resonance that *okazuya* evoke. According to a nostalgized reconfiguration of the past, what made the "good old days" good was the close friendships and relationships between people. The flex-plate of *okazuya* allows personal relationships to dictate the end result. The server calling a customer by name, anticipating his needs, and providing a dish accordingly transforms emotional resonance into culinary reality. The nostalgia of *okazuya* assumes that the smile that comes with a plate of *okazuya* food differs from the programmed cheeriness of a McDonald's server, derived as it is from a manual of customer relations.

The space on the side of the road of Sagara Store and other *okazuya* is defined primarily by class, place, and time, and less so by race/ethnicity and gender. Although *okazuya* are Japanese-American in origin, their menus, clientele, and even workers have outreached any narrow boundaries, and comprehend the amalgam of Chinese, Filipino, Hawaiian, and American influences that makes up local culture. As Kalcik points out, "regional and ethnic foodways are often intertwined," the ethnic coming to stand for the regional (1984: 39). *Okazuya* thus straddle and encompass local culture even as they retain Japanese-American associations, so that they are both at the same time. The shift from Japanese-American iconicity to local symbol is transparent and partial: *okazuya* are local institutions by virtue of their retention and manipulation of Japanese-American foodways.

As David Bell and Gill Valentine cleverly intone, "We are where we eat" (1997: i; Narayan 1995: 64). The "side-dish memory" of *okazuya* creates an identity based in the "local" that is both fragile and resilient. Threats to the local come from outside forces of fast-food globalization and gourmet cuisines, but they also come from within. Younger eaters often select meals from fast-food chains over *okazuya*. These chains offer cheaper food that seems more familiar in a global world of the present and future. *Okazuya* cuisine is the food of grandmothers, at least in the pool of meanings given it by many people in Hawai`i. Educated offspring of *okazuya* owners show little interest in taking over the family business; owners themselves do not want their children to engage in a lifestyle of such hardship. These threats to the continued existence of *okazuya* give the nostalgia that surrounds them a panicky tone.

Here is where the resilience of the space on the side of the road lies. In spite of these numerous threats, at least some *okazuya* survive. In fact, new ones are being opened, sometimes by fourth-generation Japanese-Americans who see in them the opportunity to explore an interest in the food business within this particular niche market to which they feel some kind of ethnic entitlement. Perhaps what these new *okazuya* will create is a newly drawn space that reconfigures a sense of the past with fresh energy. They will have to deal with *okazuya* as marketably nostalgized institutions, something of which their grandparents never dreamed.

The irony of *okazuya* lies in the fact that what constitutes their side-of-the-road space is nothing less than center-of-the-road "home." *Okazuya* occupy an idiosyncratic position as both marginal (distant, past, old-fashioned) and mainstream (nostalgized by media, source of comfort food, emblematic of "home"). This is not home as lived so much as imagined through the lens of nostalgia. What people mean when they call *okazuya* "home cooking" is that the food serves as a mnemonic for meals made at home, not that it tastes quite like the food of one's home (or even one's grandmother). The notion of people visiting *okazuya* directly from the airport suggests that eating this food assures them of the completeness of their return, of the seemingly unchanging nature of the food, of the timelessness of this "side-dish kitchen."

Postscript

On July 24, 2005, a week after this article was written, Sagara Store served its last meal. After 83 years of operation, family members decided to retire the business, the name, and themselves. Like other stories of *okazuya* closings, this one made the newspapers with an article entitled, "Store Bids Aloha to Waialua" (Bernardo 2005: A3). Like many *okazuya*, Sagara Store gave the impression of venerability. Therefore, its closing – as reported in the newspaper – came as a shock to customers: "Kathy Yamamoto's jaw dropped when she read a handwritten note posted outside a popular *okazuya* store in Waialua notifying customers that it is closing tomorrow. 'I can't believe it,' said Yamamoto. 'Wait until I tell my husband. He's going to fall on his face'" (Bernardo 2005). It is the shock, expressed as "falling on one's face," that shrouds the closing of this *okazuya* and others with a sense of panic. The fear of losing one's signposts in terms of foodways, businesses, and more importantly, community, colors this space on the side of the road with heartfelt poignancy. As one customer says, "'They're like family to me. ... I love them. I'm gonna miss them'" (Bernardo 2005). The space thus grows smaller as the passing of one *okazuya* marks an era ("the olden days when there was a Sagara Store in Waialua") and its people ("those who ate food from Sagara Store"). Sagara Store's closing prompts nostalgic musings that challenge the concept of home, "side-dish" kitchens, and identity rooted in a sense of the past.

Notes

1. In Japanese cuisine, rice is considered the staple and *okazu*, including fish, tōfu, and vegetables, are considered "side dishes." In a shift in culinary classification systems (Douglas 1997), the meaning given rice and *okazu* has changed somewhat for Japanese-Americans, who regard *okazu* as the main dish and rice as the starch that accompanies it.
2. According to the listings provided in *The Okazu Guide*, the earliest opening is 4:30 a.m. (listed at five establishments). The earliest closing is 11:45 a.m. (listed at one establishment).
3. American missionaries first arrived in 1820. Chinese contract laborers began arriving in 1852, followed by Portuguese in 1878, Japanese in 1885, Koreans in 1904, and Filipinos in 1905.
4. Dishes may be local variants of those found in other parts of the United States. One example is potato–macaroni salad, a mayonnaise-based mixture of both potato salad and macaroni salad. Another example is teriyaki hot dog, which is a lightly fried hot dog basted in a teriyaki sauce.
5. Increasingly, *okazuya* have extended into the catering business, which tends to be more profitable and desirable for its predictability.
6. Note the difference between contemporary, urban, middle-class *obentō* in Japan as Allison describes it (1997: 298–300), and the *obentō* eaten by immigrants to early twentieth-century Hawai`i coming from rural, peasant backgrounds in Japan. Whereas the one is the source of maternal fussing to produce a virtuosic display, the other is plainly functional, pragmatic, and filling.
7. Extended families are not shrinking in numbers, but the closeness with which extended families interact is interpreted as diminishing.
8. The *ie* officially no longer exists since Japan's constitution of 1945 dismantled the institution. However, the notion of *ie* remains in symbolic form in Japan as a trope of "families."
9. A plate-lunch wagon is a truck with a portable kitchen that sells plate lunches and drinks. These wagons can be found at construction sites and near office buildings, schools, and beaches.

–5–

Familiarity, Ambience and Intentionality

An Investigation into Casual Dining Restaurants in Central Illinois

Derek Pardue

Let me begin with two scenes:

Scene 1: Friday night, strip mall parking lot wet from a recent downpour, we zoom into the "family" restaurant. The televisions located in the four corners of the restaurant, around the bar "island," and above the reception area for incoming customers, all are tuned into the local high school football game. After a valiant attempt at a comeback, the local squad falls short. A game-ending missed field goal precedes the familiar consoling phrases: "We'll get 'em next year. We gave it our best."

As customers leave and employees clean up and prepare the restaurant for the next day's business, we see flashes of sports jerseys, trophies, and team photographs – a comfortable, sepia-filled feeling of nostalgia and tradition. The floor manager signals the end of the day by turning off the main lights and makes his way to lock the front door. Just then comes an engine sound and the image of an old, chartered bus pulling up. Exhaust steam rises and local boys get off the bus only to see that the restaurant lights are indeed off. "Ah, they're closed too." "Hey, how do you feel Susie. Whattaya say Joe?" the manager asks. "Sure, I don't mind staying. Let's go" the server and cook reply. "Come on in boys; I bet you're hungry. Whatta game, huh?" We zoom back out with a reassuring phrase: "One more way Applebees plays an active role in the community."

Scene 2: April, 2000 – Kelly,[1] a bartender at the local Cheddar's up on North Prospect Avenue, remembers an evening shift from the previous year. "There was an early warm spell. Something, you know, with the cold and warm air front meeting and we had an early Spring rain and thunder storm. No big deal for the restaurant. Customers were happy to come in, have some food, and enjoy themselves as the storm passed. I remember I was pouring drafts and the satellite went out. You know, interference and we had no music. It was silent. You know, at first I didn't mind, because I never much cared for Steve's [the general manager's] taste, you know, for selecting the music channels. Too much 'classic rock.' Our younger customers think it's kind of hokey, pretty boring. Anyway, I quickly realized that silence was bad. The customers got on edge; they were nervous, because they felt like everyone could hear their conversations. They certainly weren't comfortable. People were looking around waiting for some tunes to come back on. Time seemed to stand still. I felt really bad for the servers. The 15 minutes or so that the satellite was out of service seemed like 2 hours."

The first scene is a descriptive paraphrase of a television commercial aired on Fox network during the 2004 Major League Baseball playoff series. And the second scene comes from my field notes – an interview with a "casual dining" restaurant bartender in April of 2000. What is evident in both "scenes" is that restaurants are in the business of serving not only food but an experience. With regard to the curious genre of restaurants labeled "family" or "casual dining" restaurants, consumers (especially women), are quite sensitive to the dining environment, and corporate executives and general managers respond to this with particular approaches to design.

I take "design" as my keyword of inquiry into making sense of "dining out." In this paper I analyze the construction and maintenance of "community" and "the familiar" within the "casual dining" restaurant franchise.[2] This is a process of commodification, one that turns the feeling of comfort into a valuable product; and, thus, involves human acts of intention and reception. More specifically, I argue that a significant aspect of the meaning of "casual dining" can be located in the intentional practices of sound production and visual decoration. In this manner I distinguish my approach from current scholarship by directing my analysis not to the more or less genuine "appearance of pleasure" or to the potential democratic possibilities of mainstream public dining but rather to that micro-level material that creates familiarity among restaurant customers and employees.[3] In essence, I investigate the elements of a "good time" and a "good place" for eating out.

I ask the question: how do sound and image within the larger scheme of restaurant social design become part of the formation of "community." In this case, "design" refers to the dynamic techniques and strategies, which take visible and sonic forms, present in a popular genre of restaurants in the United States. These restaurants, while they differ slightly in approach and in material, represent a contemporary move towards a common idea of group identification (i.e. the "community") and place (i.e. the "neighborhood" or "our eating place"). I argue that in order to better understand this phenomenon one must pay attention to the details of design present in the specificities of décor and sound.

Methodology

In 2000 and again in 2004 I interviewed servers, bartenders, managerial staff, and kitchen staff in three "casual dining" restaurants in central Illinois. In 2004, after a frustrating period of dealing with bureaucracy and what I have interpreted as corporate suspicion of outside researchers, I was able to distribute a simple questionnaire to customers during lunch and dinner shifts at two of the three restaurants on weekday and weekend sessions.

While the focus of my research was on "intentionality," or the intentional construction of space and community through restaurant design, the questionnaires helped me evaluate the reception of such cultural design from the consumer's perspective. I asked a range of simple questions in an effort to analyze to what extent customers recognize, appreciate and evaluate the features and intent of the sound and image design. I supplemented these fieldwork findings with archival research regarding the new "place" of "North Prospect" and basic corporate discourse around design issues.

Theorizing Ambience in Restaurant Studies

Consumers and corporations have transformed not only food but also the situation of eating into a commodity. For their part, cultural critics and social analysts have broadened their perspectives accordingly and have gone beyond the food in and of itself to assess meaning and have investigated the complexity of food "situations" and human perceptions of "eating out."[4] Restaurants, then, are the points of articulation, where tastes and experiences are engineered and consumed in the public sphere.

Many food scholars have argued that the restaurant is, in fact, a "simulacrum of sociality" (a borrowing from Baudrillard 1994), where productive community-building is difficult if not impossible (Finkelstein 1989). Within our multicultural world, according to this line of analysis, we are practicing the consumption of experience without any durable substance. We buy scenes, just as we purchase cuisine, with a dash of Tabasco here, a spot of baby spinach off to the side, or a garnish of tamarind chutney there. The contemporary consumer connects food and culture through the following ubiquitous phrases: "I don't do Chinese; I had Indian last night." In this sense, both "ethnic" and casual dining are simulacra. Correspondingly, "exoticness" and "familiarity" are purchased scenes, in which food and eating experience play a significant role. These are, of course, generalizations based on aspects of design, the focus in this text, and thus involve certain assumptions about the consumer.

The present dominance of "casual dining" restaurants in new US commercial places such as North Prospect complicates the notion that contemporary consumption necessarily thrives on the desire for the unbounded and uprooted. Locality and identity (often glossed as "community") remain a challenging link corporate managers contemplate as they compete for brand recognition and customer loyalty. This is an issue of social design – the scripting and engineering of human intention into material (décor) and sound (music) for the creation of a productive atmosphere of exchange. Restaurants, in general, are a rich source of what Tia DeNora calls the "cultural material though which 'scenes' are constructed, scenes that afford different kinds of agency, different sorts of pleasure, and ways of being" (DeNora 2000: 123). In the case of casual dining, the key elements of such design are familiarity and comfort.

Familiarity is perhaps the most powerful force of attraction, one that provides a theme for the routinization of restaurant architecture both in sound and image. I am interested in the micro-level of hegemony by turning my attention to the design of familiarity. Hegemony in this context refers less to relations of power and domination *per se* and more to the fashioning of "common sense" with regard to customers' "natural" associations among sound, image, and place within the concept of "casual dining."

Logically, the "casual dining" restaurant comes to the fore as a primary site of inquiry into this process. This category of restaurant is interesting, because it lies in-between, in a "happy medium" (as most Americans consider themselves – middle-class, neither powerful nor powerless, doing just fine).[5] The "casual dining" restaurant is not part of what has been termed the "hyperaesthetics" of fast-food, where convenience determines all facets of food production, consumption, and distribution (Scapp and Seitz 1998: 8). Nor is it the epitome of nineteenth-century bourgeois aesthetics, in which the beauty of the dish and the experience stands above and outside of the consumer. The "fine dining" category represents the culinary version of the lingering "art as autonomous" or "art for art's sake" aesthetic that maintains a socio-economic market. By contrast, "casual dining" is about sit-down "fun," where food is intended as one element in a coherent system of entertainment based on comfort and recognition over utter convenience or verbose pretension. With regard to the latter, "fine dining" situations are ones that assume a level of knowledge and etiquette, which often is exaggerated or an inflated version of the real. For example, menu descriptions, such as *Mussels à la Portugaise*: Prince Edward Island mussels steamed with garlic, plum tomatoes, chorizo and white wine and served with baguette slices," often contain references to "noble" places ("Prince Edward Island") and multiple cultures (French, Mexican, Portuguese, New England) in one dish. Such pretension is ubiquitous within the fine dining world. Managers, employees, and customers consider such information "common knowledge."

The form and content of aesthetics relates to the construction and performance of locality. Actors in all three restaurant categories implicitly invest in locality as they negotiate the marketing and identity factors of distinction and familiarity. A vital part of the dining "situation" involves the creation of atmosphere through sound and decoration. Both in corporate propaganda and academic scholarship, it is more often than not the "fine dining" or the fast/"junk" food establishment that embodies an "architecture of desire" (Finkelstein 1989: 3–4). In the following I address a gap in the literature by focusing on the social design in the case of "casual dining."

The Design of Locality and Fictive Kinship

"The décor of each [X] restaurant reflects its local neighborhood by displaying photographs and memorabilia highlighting hometown heroes and history, area schools, and local police and fire departments... Our vision is becoming the world's favorite neighbor. In 1986, the name of the concept was changed to '[X] Grill & Bar' to reflect the [owner's] original concept of a place 'people could call their own.'"

These excerpts come from the corporate website of one of the restaurants I studied during 2000 and again in 2004. The juxtaposition of globalization and neighbor in the phrase "world's favorite neighbor" is an example of how multinational corporations attempt to market apparent contradictions of place and community. The concept of "world" is the opposite of distinction; its connotation is one of extensive presence, power, and success. On the other hand, "neighbor" is not only a reference to a unique person or place of proximity but also a particular feeling of social connection. What makes this oxymoron effective as a discursive marker of attraction is the concept and structure of "familiarity." In my fieldwork, I found that consumers and corporate producers agree that the phrase "world's favorite neighbor" and other similar mottos are successful in bringing the global and the local together, because they evoke familiarity and, more specifically in the case of "dining out," comfort.

The other two excerpts describing the decorative memorabilia and the feeling of attachment to a restaurant as one's "own" expand the notion of familiarity to include social intimacy. The articulation of "family" to a public dining restaurant is a remarkable semiotic and marketing achievement. The target of families as clients is a long-standing goal of corporate restaurants.[6] In what follows, I will explore how multinational corporations try to situate their restaurants as "our own neighborhood restaurant."

Contextualization of Place

"A new town is rising from the cornfields of East Central Illinois." The *News-Gazette* staff writer J. Philip Bloomer's opening line from the 1994 article "Champaign's northern fringe goes to town" was indeed prophetic. This "new town" would by 2004 include roughly 2,500 acres, approximately a third of the area of Champaign, Illinois.[7]

In May of 1990 Mathew Stamey, member of the Stamey family, who controls a significant portion of farmland in Champaign County in East Central Illinois, stated that "I think the days of farming in that area are past."[8] Over the next decade large landowning families, such as the Stameys, the Kaufmanns, and the Fawcetts, would enter into negotiations with the City of Champaign, usually *vis-à-vis* developers such as the Atkins Group (see Figure 5.8), to organize the spatial design of what would become known as "North Prospect."

Figure 5.2 Construction sign posted in North Prospect area for further commercial construction in 1996. Photo taken by Champaign News Gazette staff.

One of the most successful entrepreneurial ventures in "North Prospect" has been the public dining place. In particular, "casual dining" restaurant franchises, such as Applebees, Cheddar's, and Chili's, arrived in 1995 and 1996. A new eating "place" was created out of razed cornfields and acres of soybean crops. The emergence of "North Prospect" was not the creation of a little Italy or a Chinatown or even an Amish marketplace, following the lead of several central Illinois towns in their spatial

Figure 5.1 Aerial view of "North Prospect" area during the early construction years. Photo taken by Champaign News Gazette staff.

reorganization of "main streets." Rather, it was and continues to be an example of the platitudinous phenomenon of suburban commercial sprawl in the contemporary US landscape. "North Prospect" is hardly recognized as a new place for consumers to become familiar with "exotic" or "other" cultures through "foreign" cuisine. Nor is it a place to remember the local, although a number of locally-franchised businesses, even corporations with several thousand locations across the United States, Europe, Asia and Latin America, advertise a "neighborhood" feel. On the contrary, North Prospect is the attractive new home of a great American pastime – community-building through consumption of the familiar. But what constitutes commonplace recognition so that customers and employees feel comfortable? In the case of "casual dining," this question becomes: what makes eating out easy and thus attractive?

General Categories of Design

Changes in design are part of all corporate restaurants, even the most well-recognized establishments. For restaurant corporate managers, "design" entails visual decoration and layout style (interior design), corporate logo, menu items and appearance (graphic design), and musical atmosphere (sound design). This sort of identity maintenance is not only vital to keep up with current trends, but also an issue to monitor, as today's globalized world corporate restaurant executives worry about brand protection.

According to local managers in North Prospect, there are two basic categories of design, "updates" and "remodels." Updates occur approximately every three to five years. Importantly, the restaurant need not close its doors to the public. These include small interior design changes such as menu and memorabilia layout arrangements. Remodels are more permanent and require the establishment to suspend business for a period of time. They include more structural changes such as carpets, wallpaper, or interior color scheme changes.

Not surprisingly, managers from all three restaurants claimed that their restaurant was the leader within the local "casual dining" niche. Certainly, there are some differences in appearance. Various level managers and many employees of Applebees and Cheddar's highlighted their décor as particularly local. In contrast, Chili's manager Marlon, who has been "in the business" since 1979, explained that while Chili's targets local issues and tastes as part of its overall design, Chili's does not "overdo" it but rather prefers to appeal more universally. Marlon took the opportunity to historicize his claim by reviewing contemporary US "family" – or what he now refers to as "casual" – dining establishments. Marlon started professionally during the early days of what he termed as "theme" restaurants such as Fuddruckers. He joined Chili's in the 1980s and became a managing partner, because, in part, "they [we] understood that the downfall of the 'theme' restaurant was due to its hokey-ness. The 'themes' got old and got overplayed. Part of that you see in the lesser casual dining places. Like some of the places here in North Prospect."

For Clarence and Sheila, managers of Applebees and Cheddar's respectively, locality could not be emphasized enough. They stressed that quantity is important. From an outside perspective, Applebees seems most preoccupied with filling up every little nook and cranny with memorabilia. This concern is represented discursively in television commercials such as the one paraphrased at the beginning of this article. Cheddar's manager Sheila stated that what made Cheddar's unique was its "mix" of the local paraphernalia (*à la* Applebees) and the trademark icon of the huge bamboo rattan ceiling fan located above the center dining area.

However, while the managers spoke of distinction in "style" and thus clientele attraction as their principal asset, I found nothing significantly different that would warrant such sweeping claims of "dominating" the local scene. Chili's managing partner Marlon implied in our interview that Chili's, in fact, needed a "remodel" or at least a serious "update," because "too many of the kind of restaurant that was inspired by us uses these style of menus. There's too many menus; too much for the customer. Too messy. All the stuff on the wall. Too much clutter. I think we're going to clean it [the design] all up. You know, go for a 'clean' look. See, we're always looking ahead. Simple is fresh. It'll be nice – new minimal carpets, color scheme. I really think it'll happen soon. And this unit [North Prospect] is often a pilot model for the rest."

Why do managers such as Marlon, Sheila, and Clarence worry about the micro- and macro-level layout of their restaurants? According to the responses in the survey, customers ranked music, decoration, and temperature almost evenly as most important to "atmosphere." In the following, I describe and analyze informants' comments about what they take to be the role of décor in the everyday life of the "casual" dining scene.

Décor and the Power of Memorabilia

"What the hell do you do over there at U of I [University of Illinois, Urbana-Champaign]? Does someone pay you to do that? Geez Louise." This was the initial reaction of Robert, the franchise manager of the North Prospect Applebees, in the Spring of 2004. He sneered and chuckled at me and my project when we first met.

After a couple of months of frustrating back-and-forth, I decided to try my luck and arrive unannounced, hoping to steal a few minutes from the floor manager and a few representatives from the wait, bar, and kitchen staff. I strategically targeted 3:00 p.m., a "down time" and a potential opportunity to strike up a conversation with local employees. I pulled up on a hot, sweltering day in early June 2004. Surrounded by parking-lot asphalt, I couldn't help but recoil from the onslaught of the reflected heat. I was worried about entering the corporate world (even at the local, "friendly" level), and had made sure I showered and wore a formal, collared shirt with dress slacks. In the 30 seconds it took to walk to the front door, I was already sweating profusely. From the hot asphalt desert, I could hear the tinny timbre of the 1980s British pop/new wave band Duran Duran's "Rio" (1982) over the mid-afternoon traffic on the main thoroughfare Prospect Avenue. I remember feeling a hint of relief: "I'm almost there and there are a bunch of people in there already. I won't be walking into a totally empty place." In fact, three customers remarked on the survey that they liked hearing the music from the outside speakers as they arrived from the parking lot. This was a "little thing" that "makes a difference" with Applebees.[9]

Clarence was a young, twenty-something male, fresh out of managerial training. He was a welcome change for me during my fieldwork with Applebees. We sat and discussed visual and sound design for 30 minutes. He then directed a number of his staff over to "my booth" for 15–20 minute conversations. After a few minutes of awkwardness and suspicion about my presence, the employees opened up and related several stories about the role of music and memorabilia in the restaurant.

"In a place like Champaign, décor is about *spirit*." Clarence paused and looked me in the eyes to make sure I understood "spirit" as a keyword. "College and high-school spirit is how we bring in the community," Clarence continued. I pointed to the reprint of the 1989 U of I (University of Illinois) Final-Four men's basketball team and the U of I football helmet circa 1940. We briefly discussed the "Chief" and the little "Indian" icons visible on the old university sports memorabilia.[10]

Yeah, I think the customers get a kick out of the odds and ends on the walls. You know, what I've noticed is that the women really notice it and often point them out to the guy. On the way to the restroom, you see kids asking the dad questions about the pictures. Like, 'look at that tall guy, who is he? Did he go to our high school? The dad doesn't know and makes up something. None of us know stuff like that, but it doesn't matter. It gets customers talking and they like to see the old-timey pictures. They like to see stuff with local names, things they recognize as part of their dining experience. And, that's what we provide. That works well for most of our customers.

In this narrative Clarence implicitly connects the concepts of "family" and "community" to the restaurant decoration. According to Clarence, and this was echoed by other managers at Chili's and Cheddar's regarding their respective restaurants, Applebees obtains the items on the walls through donations from beverage distributors, chambers of commerce, and some local organizations.

Chris, a member of the wait staff (a "server") for over eighteen months, replaced Clarence in "my booth." I asked Chris about the role of the "local" paraphernalia and the images of the Wright Brothers, next to Betty Boop and Marilyn Monroe, down the way from images of Albert Einstein and Groucho Marx, juxtaposed with black and white cityscapes of Paris, New York City, and the "Great Chicago Fire" of 1871. "What is the purpose of these?" It was no doubt a difficult question.

> Well, I don't know. I mean, I see a lot of couples come in for dinner, or they meet for lunch during the week. Some customers don't really pay attention, but some they see the posters and they start talking about their childhood or their mother or aunt and watching old movies. They quickly move to talk about their own kids and how much TV they watch or they see Groucho Marx and talk about what was funny now and back in the old days. I mean, I guess all that stuff is just another way to get customers to feel comfortable and give them something to talk about, so they don't get uptight about waiting for food and drink. The local paraphernalia works that way too but in a different way. The Hollywood and other stuff gets people reminiscing ... remembering stuff, and that makes them [usually] feel pretty good. You know, the music works the same way. It makes customers feel comfortable. It's all stuff they know.

In his observations, Chris articulated the concepts of family and community through the force of memory. Customers pick up on glossy snapshots of famous icons and blurred sepia reprints of local and national glory and connect them to random snippets of trivial stories of family outings or Father's Days gone by. "You know, whatever, little small talk like that," as Chris recalled. This is the process by which the intentionality of Applebees and local consumers reckons the near (images of locality) and far (images of national and international stars, important historic figures, places, and events) as familiar, so that by extension the restaurant becomes a "good place" for dining out and having a good time.

"Music Should Match the Atmosphere": Sound Engineering and the Provision of Trivial Grooves

As Chris mentioned, music plays a significant role in the social design of "casual dining" restaurants. Business consultants and music psychologists have long known that aspects of this, such as the music's tempo and volume, lead to changes in customer turnover rate and clientele profile in general. Jonathan Sterne asserts in his work on programmed music and consumer culture in US shopping malls that "music becomes part of the consistency of that space [malls]; [it] works as an architectural element of a built space devoted to consumerism" (Sterne 1997: 23, 25). Furthermore, in her studies of small-city English shops, DeNora arrives at similar conclusions. "Each shop is engaged in structuring agency though its attempts to create a sense of occasion and a type of scenic specificity" (DeNora 2000: 139). For her part, the server Kathy from Cheddar's related to me that her previous experience as a salesperson in a young adult clothes and skateboard/surf shop was "all about pumping the volume to attract the right customers... We had to compete with other mall stores, and music was one way we brought them [customers] in."[11]

Since their beginning in North Prospect, both Cheddar's and Applebees have utilized satellite radio services for their music. According to Marlon, Chili's until very recently produced and circulated its own "approved and protected cassettes and CDs." The CDs are labeled: "Happy Hour," "Slow Time," and "High Volume," referring to the number of customers in the restaurant, thus implying the need for more "upbeat" music. "Music should match the atmosphere" is part of what Marlon continuously referred to as Chili's managerial mantra – "LAMA" (lighting, air, music, and ambience). "A Chili's song is a fun tune; it's a comfortable song."

Satellite radio is the most common option for restaurant music. Currently, according to Clarence, there are 120 stations to choose from. "Selecting a station is one of the first duties of the floor managers before opening up for business," Clarence explained. Unlike conventional radio, "selecting a station" in satellite radio does not translate into call letters (WKRP) or numbers (Rock 95.3 FM), but rather it means deciding a musical genre for the period of time.

When asked about this decision-making process, all managers cited "family orientation" quickly followed by "fun." Whether it's a "Chili's song" or an "acceptable song" for Cheddar's clientele, "family" and "fun" music included the following genres: "80s listening," "easy listening," "soft rock," and sometimes "classic rock." Stations that focus on "urban" or "alternative" are avoided.

The interpretation of the concepts of "family" and "fun" is both routinized and personalized. Sheila from Cheddar's was most articulate about this balance of the individual and corporate structure.

Yeah, me and my staff, we don't squabble too much about music. We know it's there; it provides a background for the customers. It gives us rhythm to go through the day. It's like there [important] and not there [trivial]. It's there and I have to choose this on my morning shifts. Many times I don't think about it; I know it has to be a certain kind of music for our customers. You know, women pay more attention to the music. It has to be appealing to a broad range of people. But, you know, I like to express who I am every now and again. I want to make sure me and my staff are happy working, because that spills over into how we interact with customers. In the end, décor and music are part of a larger dynamic, what I call "micromanagement vs. autonomy".

Sheila felt that there should be a balance between corporate standardization and familiarity ("micromanagement") among customers with personality. The locality is more evident in the images, but with sound there is a sense of autonomy related to volume control and choice of channel. Much of this, as Clarence, Sheila, and many servers and bartenders explained, is influenced by the kind of clientele present in the restaurant. As Marlon described the situation, "a manager should always be gauging the customers for satisfaction and comfort level. With regard to music, you have to adjust to what you perceive out there on the floor. You have to smooth out the smirks you see and the complaints you hear and smile to the head bobbing and lip synching customers do throughout the shift."

Sound Design Clashes: Knowing Your Crowd

According to Sheila, music contributes to the atmosphere because "it breaks up the monotony of the work environment, gives rhythm to work, and covers up kitchen noises." However, as Marlon implied, a manager has to "know the crowd" and, for casual dining establishments such as Applebees, Cheddar's and Chili's, "crowds" and sound design depend significantly on the time of day and time of year. Servers, bartenders and managers are keenly aware of the type of customer and most, when asked, point to age and gender as the most important variables in the make up of the "crowd."

Age-group changes intersect with the time of day and year. Late mornings and mid afternoons tend to be times for an "older crowd." "Old," of course, is a relative term. For Danny, a 22-year-old server, "old" means the age of his boss Robert. "I don't mind. You know, I get a lot of older people on my shift during the week. Just like Robert, they like the 'classic rock' stuff. Robert keeps the music usually on that stuff. Sometimes he even goes to the 'oldies' station [on the satellite]. I mean, for us [other servers] that is old. We don't know it. It can get boring. But, Harley is usually the manager on Friday night and he knows that he can't play that stuff ['classic rock'] all night. It's more exciting in here then. People want a little more pop. That's definitely more fun for us and, I think, for them [the customers]."

For the managers at Cheddar's, time of day is similarly important, but what stand out [and thus have to be remembered by managers] are the particular rules of Sunday. Sheila explained, "we get a lot of churchgoers, so we make sure they feel comfortable. To do that we play only classical music on Sundays. No lyrics. Just mellow, soothing music... In general, we get a more mature crowd, so we don't get into all the trends of pop and some of the other things that some restaurants do. I guess we're more down to earth and the music reflects that in some way."

For places such as Applebees and to a lesser extent Cheddar's and Chili's, time of year can play a significant role in sound design. As Clarence described this, "one way to think about the year around here is by season, with football season as number one." In terms of sound design this means that on "game days" Applebees managers frequently broadcast not only the images but also the sounds of the University of Illinois football games during Saturday afternoons in the fall. While Chili's manager Marlon attested that sound broadcast of games was "frowned upon" for "casual dining" restaurants, he agreed that understanding the importance of local teams and game schedules is crucial information for managers. For Marlon, games should be watched, not heard. "I don't want Chili's to be a sports bar. We are different." The issue of sound design thus goes beyond the purview of music and includes the "micromanagement" decision of whether or not to include the sounds of local events such as sports in the eating-place atmosphere.

Conclusion

In this chapter I have analyzed some of the meanings of corporate intentionality present even in the most routinized spaces of food consumption. Corporate managers and customers desire familiarity, because the feeling of the familiar engenders conversation, memories, and other everyday practices of identification. People associate familiar experiences with places, i.e. locality and community, and thus tend to choose one restaurant over another on the basis of such feelings. The production of familiarity so that such choices become "natural" or "easy" is a common objective among casual dining restaurants.

What the evidence from my fieldwork shows is that managers, other employees, and customers from different "casual dining" restaurants approach the issue of locality and design in various ways. Styles of design not only become personal, according to Sheila's notion of managerial "autonomy," but often translate into the purity or blurring of restaurant genres, as in the opinion of managers such as Marlon. There is no doubt that a sociology of food and restaurants must include analyses of the social differences and hierarchies present in the structure of labor, as well as the dynamics of class and ethnicity as they inform the definition of tastes as part of national ideologies. However, one must not lose sight of the micro-levels of how such social structures and ideologies are made manifest in the graphic and sonic design of public places of food consumption. Such material processes are the essence of what I have referred to as the construction and maintenance of "community" and "the familiar" within the "casual dining" restaurant franchise.

Notes

1. All employee names in this chapter are fictitious.
2. See Martens and Warde (1997) for a discussion of the "sociability" of public eating in England.
3. See Finkelstein 1989; Sennett 1976; Shelton 1990. The text quote comes from Martens and Warde's critique of Finkelstein's 1989 ethnography of eating out (Martens and Warde 1997: 145).
4. See, for example, Sidney Mintz's (2002) short, cogent essay on this issue.
5. See O'Keefe (2005: 64–7) and his discussion of the "average American."
6. See *Restaurant News* (2004).
7. See Bloomer 1994.
8. See Pressey 1990.

9. Applebees is not the only "casual dining" restaurant that employs this music technique, but, at least for these three consumers, they associated this "scene" with Applebees as an asset of familiarity and comfort.
10. For more on the "Chief" controversy and the constructed ways whites from Central Illinois forge "community" through their associations with the "Indian," see Spindel (2002).
11. See also "Smart bite" in *Prevention,* May 2004, p. 84, regarding the effect of hearing the music of Britney Spears and faster eating habits.

Interviews

Chris, server at Applebees. June, 2004.
Clarence, local manager of Applebees. June, 2004.
Danny, server at Applebees. June, 2004.
Kathy, server at Cheddar's. June, 2000.
Marlon, local manager of Chili's. June, 2004.
Reynaldo, kitchen employee Applebees. May, 2004.
Robert, local manager of Applebees. April, 2004.
Sheila, local manager of Cheddar's. May, 2000.

−6−

Serving the Past on a Platter
Consuming the Cultural Revolution in Contemporary China
Jennifer Hubbert

It is food that stirs the imagination of her thinkers,
Sharpens the wits of her scholars,
Enhances the talents of those who work by the hand,
And enlivens the spirit of the people.

F. T. Cheng[1]

The Day the Fish Died

It was a late fall evening, back in the mid-1980s, when I found myself in an expensive private restaurant in Kunming, seated at a round table that was draped in decorative linens. The late Chairman Mao, renowned for his anti-entrepreneurial inclinations, had died a decade earlier, and private restaurants were cropping up in myriad forms throughout China. Kunming, located in the remote southwestern province of Yunnan, had experienced less of the rapid economic growth characteristic of China's eastern seaboard, and upscale dining establishments remained a relative novelty. My host, a teacher and administrator at a technical university, had arranged this exceptional occasion, and I looked forward to tasting the local delicacies.

Situated near a large lake, Kunming is well known for its piscatorial delights, and this evening was to feature one of them known as "twice-cooked fish." This entrée was distinct both for its unique flavors and a preparation technique that involved the sequential cooking and consumption of different parts of the fish. After hearing the particulars of the feast, my colleagues and I gathered around the live fish tank. There we indicated our evening's prey to the chef, who extracted it and returned to the kitchen. According to protocol, the chef was to re-emerge with the fish on a platter, surrounded by assorted garnishes and steeped in a delicately flavored sauce, but with only the back half cooked. Ideally, diners eat the cooked back half of the fish, while the head, eyes peering at its predators, flops around on the plate. After the first half is consumed, the chef takes the fish back to the kitchen and cooks the remainder.

One can imagine my relief, and the chef's chagrin, when he appeared at our table, looking decidedly morose, to announce that in fact the entire fish had perished in his frying pan.

This evening was significant in its ability to encapsulate experientially the myriad functions of food and eating. Food's most fundamental role is of course as nutritional sustenance, and despite my misgivings at consuming the half-cooked dead fish, I ended the alimentary endeavor thoroughly sated. Yet, as many anthropological accounts of eating have explored, food's significance extends beyond its caloric composition, acting as a semiotic reflection of cultural practices and social organization.[2] Certainly Mary Douglas's (1976) classificatory schema of the food restrictions found in various cultures enables us to make sense of both my squeamish reaction to the thought of a live fish flopping on my plate and my slightly duplicitous carnivorous habits that allow me to consume meat so long as I do not have to be involved in the death of the animal that supplied it. Yet, as I would like to suggest, food is not only a "key to culture" (Kugelmass 1990), but also a key to politics, and specifically the kind of cultural politics that are involved when fish die in restaurants with tablecloths in post-Mao China.

Food and eating have long occupied a central location in the realm of Chinese cultural politics, the composition of and manner in which one consumes food connoting a complex configuration of moral and political imperatives and social hierarchies. Indeed, Confucius once remarked, when asked about military tactics by the Duke Ling of Wei, "I have indeed heard about matters pertaining to *tsu* [meat stand] and *tou* [meat platter], but I have not learned military matters" (Chang 1977: 11; Yue 1999: 33). Mao himself often used food metaphors to explain politics, arguing that "If you want to know the taste of a pear [have reliable knowledge] you must bite into it" (Farquhar 2002: 79). At the most fundamental level, Chinese food mirrors classificatory notions of *yin* and *yang*, which order both nutrition and the universe into a structure of difference and value (Simoons 1991: 22). Such concepts, and their implications for food and eating, extend metaphorically to larger social affairs, figuring predominantly in the social and cosmological realms (Farquhar 2002: 48). One of the most prominent gods in the popular Chinese pantheon was traditionally in fact the Kitchen God, who demanded elaborate offerings around the Chinese New Year. Extravagant banquets that mark social occasions from birth to marriage to death are a mechanism through which food becomes the vehicle for both the discernment and the creation of social relationships, with social standing indicated by the dining company and by the number and type of dishes offered to guests at such ceremonial repasts. Such feasting not only reflects status, but also produces it, its instrumental nature only thinly veiled by delectable aromas.

It is within this cultural framework that food has the capacity to represent symbolically the contentious cultural politics of contemporary China. In simple terms of content, the fish that perished on my plate in the mid-1980s was a significant marker of China's modernization project for a number of reasons. For a nation accustomed by economic necessity to a highly vegetarian diet, the consumption of fish represented economic attainment and social status. Yet it was not merely what we ate, but also the historical backdrop that addressed salient issues of national modernity. In the early reform years, many small-scale entrepreneurial ventures were launched by unemployed citizens who occupied politically and morally indefinite spaces in socialist class hierarchies. Predominantly uneducated and lacking cultural capital, these "upstarts" were greeted by intellectuals such as my host with disdain. However, the upstarts' endeavors often provided them with a level of financial comfort unattainable by those with more standard work-unit positions. Such private businesses as the one where I dined were thus ambiguous spaces, celebrated as the means through which China would attain modernity, yet owned and managed by people derided in popular discourse as distrustful and "lacking culture." For intellectuals like my host, living on a fixed income and suffering inflationary pressures, restaurant dining was too expensive for quotidian practice. Yet his knowledge of dining etiquette and food symbolism was a way of situating himself as someone who could mark himself as a member of an international cohort of modern cosmopolitans in which taste could substitute for hierarchies based on social position (Zukin 1991).

While the groundwork for this chapter was served at the table with the dead fish, I must jump ahead a decade to continue the tale, turning to one of the more perplexing places in which the link between food and cultural politics has appeared during that intervening decade: Cultural Revolution theme restaurants. This chapter will address this link, examining what happens when Cultural Revolution restaurants find themselves in the awkward dilemma of producing cosmopolitan delights for hungry capitalists while memorializing a historical era that witnessed the denigration of capitalists, subjecting them to rigorous criticism and food deprivation. Serving fare that reflects the "bitter, sweet and sour" of China's troubled past, such restaurants stand in a synecdochal relationship to a complicated notion of "Chinese modernity," working as a space through which class, authority and ideology come head to head over a plate of wild grass.[3] At once memorials to contemporary gluttony and historical deprivation, these dining establishments mark a new reckoning of past and present, linking leisure to dispossession in a manner that foregrounds the contentious nature of post-Mao political and economic reform.

I begin below with a brief description of two Cultural Revolution restaurants, one in Beijing and the other in Kunming. Second, I situate these restaurants within the politics of Cultural Revolution memory. Third, I offer an extended ethnographic analysis of three of the dominant themes that emerged in my interviews with diners, restaurant owners and former sent-down youth, exploring the restaurants as sites for public memory, spaces for contemporary subject formation and arenas for leisure and consumption. When the past becomes a commodity to be consumed at the dining table, what are the implications for remembering? When a Cultural Revolution restaurant is portrayed as a site of public memory, what does a meal there reveal about a post-Mao modernity project that continues to struggle with the moral and political implications of privatization and entrepreneurialism? When the restaurants are seemingly likened to summer camp, how do the plentiful and delectable offerings reflect upon the hunger and deprivation occasioned during the past of the Cultural Revolution? What emerges from this analysis is a clear picture of the contentious nature of Chinese modernity as experienced at the intersection of food and politics, and how such politics make literally palatable the troublesome nature of the past.

Palate Politics

Black Earth [Heitudi]

The first restaurant under consideration here is the Black Earth restaurant in Beijing. Named after the northeastern Heilongjiang region, where the owner was sent down during the Cultural Revolution, the restaurant's menu highlighted cuisine from that area, while also incorporating dishes reminiscent of standard Cultural Revolution fare elsewhere, such as wild grass and fried dough. The restaurant occupied a multi-storied building with reception areas on the first floor and dining facilities on the remaining two levels. With its central door flanked by tall columns and red dragon lanterns, Black Earth looked like many other dining establishments in contemporary China. Yet, upon entering the restaurant, the first thing that caught one's attention was something not typically found in other restaurants: a tangled mess of business cards stuck to the wall, listing the usual names, addresses and occupations. Yet at Black Earth, handwritten alongside the more quotidian information, was also the location of the farm where the business card's owner labored during the Cultural Revolution. While the cards included a range of occupational statuses, from the vaunted positions of ambassador and joint-venture manager, to the more plebian "office worker," it was the Cultural Revolution work unit that emerged as the key to identity on the wall, the unifying (and leveling) factor in a nation where increasing social stratification has replaced social equality as a defining ideological issue. It was on this wall that two radically different social worlds came together – the Cultural Revolution one in which consumption symbolized immorality, and the contemporary one in which it marks success and power.

The second and third floors of the restaurant were decorated in revolutionary chic, with posters of revolutionary operas adorning and consecrating the walls, sharing space with crude farming implements and Cultural Revolution propaganda slogans. Yet, while the theme was of socialist revolution, the effect was decidedly bourgeois. The interior was tidy – the farm implements displayed at clever angles, the posters vibrant additions to shiny checked tablecloths and plastic flowers. These furnishings referenced the aesthetically austere Maoist era, which decried such efforts as reactionary, yet stood in marked contrast to it, coinciding neatly instead with the ubiquitous outside billboards extolling the benefits of home improvement and interior design.[4]

The waitstaff at Black Earth were dressed in "theatrically proletarian" garb,[5] reminiscent of Red Guard and People's Liberation Army uniforms. Such outfitted bodies represent the possibilities of engaging in proletarian labor, yet reappraise its value in the entrepreneurial context of the restaurant setting. While being waited upon during the Cultural Revolution marked a bourgeois class background, in contemporary China it has emerged as a positively evaluated, public indicator of success. It is the labor of finance, not that of the field, that is marked here as worthy. The vision of the Maoist body remains present, yet it is reclad in the garb of capitalist modernity, proletarian subjectivity aestheticized as radical mod (Chen 2003: 387).

Educated Youth [Laozhiqing]

The Educated Youth restaurant in Kunming, Yunnan province, provided an interesting contrast to Black Earth. Named after the youth who were sent to the countryside during the Cultural Revolution to foment revolution and learn from the peasants, the restaurant featured décor and cuisine from Xishuangbanna in southern Yunnan, where some of these youth were relocated. Xishuangbanna, which is home to a majority of China's Dai minority population, is tropical in atmosphere and culturally distinct from the Han majority areas. Travelogues, artwork and popular conversation represent the area and its people as embodying nature and communal generosity. Its women are commonly portrayed as unconcerned with rigid sexual mores, frequently appearing in films and photos in loosely wrapped sarongs, bathing in local waterways (Gladney 1994; Litzinger 2000; Schein 2000).

Educated Youth was one of several minority attractions in Kunming that included art exhibits, dance performances and theme parks. The most popular of these was the Minority Nationalities Village. The Dai village section of the park included several wood and bamboo replicas of traditional Dai houses through which visitors could move at will. According to local lore, Dai custom forbids strangers from entering the inner rooms of a Dai home for fear of disturbing ancestral souls; thus the park's welcome, like that of Educated Youth restaurant, allowed guests to experience ethnic custom without offending cultural mores or enduring long bus rides to minority-inhabited regions of the province.

The dining experience at Educated Youth was one of exoticized recreation. The restaurant sat on the edge of a small paddleboat-filled lake, amidst an urban park peopled by young couples and the elderly enjoying constitutional activities. The park periodically hosted weekend minority dance performances featuring loud percussion units and brightly clad young women in elaborate headdresses. The restaurant building itself was fronted by thatched eaves and sided with rough-hewn timber. Inside, customers sat on bamboo stools at low-slung tables, close to the earth.

Such placement required that diners tuck their feet carefully beneath their bodies, a position echoed in many popular images of minority women, poised on the ground, encircling luxuriant piles of tropical produce or embroidering festive outerwear. Young female servers offered diners a variety of traditional Dai dishes: tropical fruit curries dished on to banana leaves, purple sticky rice served in pineapple hulls, and potent grain alcohol sipped from bamboo canisters.

Absent from this restaurant were the business cards, propaganda posters, farm tools and army uniforms found in most other Cultural Revolution restaurants. Present instead were verdant landscapes of the subtropical region, ethnic crafts and costumes. The dominant forms of decoration gracing the restaurant's walls were blue and white batiks (sold as authentic products of local minority groups) of lithe, sarong-clad young women carrying heavy burdens gracefully over their shoulders or bathing in the rivers. They labor, but they labor as sexualized beings, rejecting the Maoist degendered form of working subjectivity.[6]

The Politics of Commemoration

Both the Educated Youth and the Black Earth restaurants owed their reason for existence to the same historical era, that of the Cultural Revolution. Yet it seemed at first glance that they offered seemingly antagonistic historical interpretations of this epoch. Such diverse interpretations are rendered possible by a national-level accounting that alternately posits the Cultural Revolution in "excessively romantic" terms, or as a period of loss and chaos, or comes close to pretending it never happened.[7]

Despite the passage of nearly three decades, the Cultural Revolution occupies an ambivalent position in contemporary Chinese national discourse. While the era has been denounced as "ten years of chaos" or ten "lost years," it has also recently been reinterpreted in a manner that figures this chaos/loss less as obstacle and more as the source of contemporary greatness.[8] While some of this reinterpretation has been deeply reflective, offered by those who lived through the era, much of it suffers from a vicarious nostalgia seemingly founded upon popular culture representations that categorize the era in decidedly non-contentious terms. That these latter forms of representation predominate is due to a number of factors that render overtly critical representations of the Cultural Revolution somewhat problematic.

One of these reasons pertains to modes of memory transmission. While people may call for a public accounting for the tragedies of the era, they often remain hesitant to participate. Zhou, an administrator at a local art institute, was one such individual. She spoke profoundly about her experiences as a sent-down youth during the Cultural Revolution when she was relocated to the Burmese border with a group of teenaged women, yet remained silent when confronted by the curiosity of her teenaged child.

The place was very bitter, unimaginably bitter. We couldn't do anything. We had no idea how to grow crops. There was so little food, only rice. This was just when we were still growing. We had no food and we labored all day. At first we cried. Then we began to find ways to deal with life... We really knew that China's reality was so bitter, that the peasants were so poor... We knew first-hand about the extreme backwardness.

Following this poignant description, Zhou mentioned that "People need to remember. So much of what is negative today came from that era." Nonetheless, her subsequent commentary about potential mechanisms of memory diverted responsibility to the public sphere. Mentioning Ba Jin, a famous author, much persecuted during the Cultural Revolution, who called for a national Cultural Revolution museum, Zhou sought a national-level accounting of the past through official channels of remembering. Yet, when I asked how she described the era to her own child, she responded that she met his questions with evasion and cursory analysis. Her explanation implied a modicum of danger in overt criticisms of the era. "The people who participated in the Cultural Revolution are still around us every day. People still hate the Red Guards. I don't like being around them. The leaders of the Red Guards are still in positions of power. It's because their families have influence ... they are in positions of power."

National-level politics also play a role in limiting representational forms of the Cultural Revolution. The Party has assessed the era as a ten-year catastrophe and publicly recognized Mao's role in the upheaval, yet it maintains its authority in part because of its association with Mao and his historical legacy.[9] Divorcing itself from the Cultural Revolution enables the Party to draw upon the Maoist legacy for legitimacy while distancing itself from the more problematic aspects of its revolutionary past.[10] Nonetheless, even though the Party has distanced itself from the era, the governmental structures that enabled it remain extant. Thus, disparagement of the era potentially indicates critique of mechanisms of power that continue firmly entrenched in contemporary Chinese political structures.

This uneasiness with the legacy of the Cultural Revolution was apparent in the official museum of Chinese history in Shaoshan, Mao's hometown, which virtually ignored the Cultural Revolution. In this museum, curators have devoted the first four rooms to a linear history of Mao's family background, his intellectual progress as a student, his revolutionary exploits in Yan'an and those of the post-1949 People's Republic. The fifth and final room featured a larger-than-life-sized photograph of Mao lying in his sarcophagus in Beijing. Glass-encased international newspapers expressing grief at his passing surrounded the photograph. Throughout the museum, no mention was made of the disasters of the Great Leap Forward or the Cultural Revolution. In fact, the only pictures of Mao during the entire ten-year period of the Cultural Revolution attested to China's role as an equal in the international order rather than to the Chairman's complicity in the chaos that was occurring on the domestic front. These included photographs of Mao with the Japanese prime minister in 1972; with Nixon in the same year; alongside Edgar Snow in 1970; and shaking hands with the president of Zambia in 1974.

It is within this disputed context of national memory that Chinese individuals have consumed Cultural Revolution restaurants like Black Earth and Educated Youth, producing their own disparate interpretations. Does the Cultural Revolution, through its ideologies of sacrifice, trivialize the efforts of these restaurants to use exoticization and consumption to memorialize the past? Do the restaurants paradoxically undermine their own entrepreneurial impulses through negative reference to the very ideologies that enable their presence? As we now turn to the voices of restaurant owners and diners, we will begin to examine how memory is employed as a medium through which history and political experience are implicated as referents for reformulated claims to authority.

Consuming the Cultural Revolution

Mr Yang, the owner of the Black Earth restaurant, was sent down to Heilongjiang province in 1969, following three years of Red Guard activism in Beijing. He returned to the capital in 1977, and worked in the logistics department of an electronics company, taking ownership of Black Earth in 1994. Explaining his rationale for running the restaurant, Mr Yang focused on his experience in the northeast and the harsh conditions he and others suffered.

> I run this restaurant for several reasons. I do it to commemorate my eight years of experience as an educated youth and the difficulty of forgetting my life in the northeast. ... The restaurant's tactics are to prioritize the characteristics of what was particular about the era, to express the conditions. It allows us to look back on our experiences when food and drink were scarce.

The trope of food deprivation played a prominent role in Yang's representations of the Cultural Revolution. Like other urban youth who spent years in the countryside, Yang spoke profoundly about the crude foodstuffs he and his cohort consumed, and about the constant hunger and resultant illnesses brought about by unfamiliar foods and inadequate nutrition. He cited the restaurant as a way of both maintaining and validating memories of these aspects of the Cultural Revolution.

Food deprivation has played a central role in defining state–society relations in China in general (Yue 1999: 3; Farquhar 2002). In a nation that has historically been beset by famine, the mere fact of satisfying caloric requirements has remained central to the well-being of the population. From the late Ming deprivations that beleaguered northern China, to the shortages of the 1940s, to the Great Leap Forward, millions of Chinese have starved to death, and regimes subsequently toppled, as a result of both natural disasters and ill-conceived political policy. This has made food and eating a profound matter of both physiological and ideological concern. One of the mechanisms through which Mao established hegemony was in fact the CCP's provision of more equitable access to foodstuffs. Even today, Mao's legitimacy as a socialist ruler is often reflected upon through popular commentary about his "simple" eating habits. Mr Cai, a business manager and former sent-down youth, positioned Mao as having achieved moral authority through this relationship with food: "Mao lived a very simple life. He ate simple food and used the same types of bowls that we use. We really respect his moral character."

Such narratives of culinary goodness are contrasted with reports of contemporary official corruption that, as Ms Wang, another sent-down youth, explained, begins with eating: "To start a business here you have to invite everyone to eat, to a big banquet with many expensive and varied dishes. It [the corruption] is both the system and the culture." Contemporary newspaper articles draw upon similar consumption-inspired, rhetorical tactics, warning a rapidly modernizing nation of the dangers of capitalist excess by highlighting stories of greedy capitalist alimentary overconsumption and waste. Through such tales of gluttony and avarice, food becomes a medium through which cultural and ideological concerns are experienced and expressed.[11]

While Yang was explicit about his desire for consumption at Black Earth to play a memorial role to food deprivation and hardship, he was equally insistent about the necessity of this restaurant's providing a *public* memorial space:

> This restaurant has become really well known among educated youth. They come here and talk about everything in the past. They talk freely with no holds barred. They come to renew old friendships but also to establish new ties, to enlarge their social network. At the same time, it also provides those with the same history an environment in which to recall the past. Lots of educated youth come but also lots of others. But the restaurant gives priority to the educated youth and their experiences... After they enter they go directly to the business card wall and read them and stick theirs on the wall... As a period of history ... it's difficult to forget... You cannot just blot out history. We need to remember what the educated youth went through.

As a memorial to the difficulties of the past, as a space in which remembering happens, Yang envisioned his restaurant as writing a counternarrative to what he called "excessively romantic" depictions of the Cultural Revolution and to official representations of the era that either decry it as chaos or ignore it. He intended the restaurant to serve as a disruptive memory, dislocating sanitized versions of the past from their positions of complacency. At first glance, this would lead one to expect governmental antipathy toward Cultural Revolution restaurants like Black Earth. Yet, when asked about official attitudes toward Cultural Revolution restaurants, Yang declared that the government does not have an opinion. In fact, he continued, "Lots of Party officials were themselves educated youth. The government has neither special support nor opposition to the restaurants. It treats them like any others. But given that they frequently visit, isn't that like approving, like having a positive policy, in fact the best support of all?"

This "positive policy" deserves some attention. In comparing the two "museums" (the official Shaoshan museum and the culinary), we see that the debate is not only over the specifics of history but also over who has the authority to represent that history and the form in which that representation occurs. If well-being is to be transmitted to the next generation, it is not only memory that is important but also the "correct" memory (Povinelli 1993), and the structure in which the correct memory is transmitted. While the Party's current authority is linked to the very economic policies of consumerism and free markets that negate its Maoist premise, these are also the same policies that have enabled restaurants like Black Earth to memorialize that troublesome history.

In fact, as his narrative makes clear, for Yang, Black Earth interrupts a politics of forgetting. However, it does so in a way that privileges a new politics of entrepreneurialism. Food becomes a mechanism that does not instigate remembering merely for sake of remembering, but for building relationships and constructing particular types of entrepreneurial subjects. This next section will begin to explore how Cultural Revolution restaurants make reference to the past in ways that seemingly justify its tragedies as mechanisms for the creation of producing and consuming subjects who embody contemporary narratives of corporate politics as the salvation for Maoist misfortune.

The Politics of Consuming Subjects

While Mr Yang was explicit about his expectation that Black Earth should act as a public memorial, he also linked his Cultural Revolution experiences to his own success in the contemporary world of consumer business, mentioning that the restaurant served over two hundred people each evening:

> While it [the restaurant] is a useful tool in helping to remember the past it also allows me to use the knowledge I have obtained over the years to run the restaurant... Our generation lost so much. But it also gained more than a little. My experiences as an educated youth have had a huge influence on the second half of my life. As a group, we educated youth are bolder. The experiences tempered us, and we can adapt ourselves to fit any environment.

Interestingly, in his narrative, Yang drew upon a distinctly Maoist discourse of self-reliance and adaptability. Self-reliance [zili gengsheng], a key Yan'an slogan that in its Maoist extreme justified national autarky, re-emerged in this context as essential to post-Mao modernity. The Cultural Revolution reappeared not as chaos and loss, but as the inculcator of attributes of success and moral character. Nonetheless, while the restaurant may have provided a venue for old comrades to "talk with no holds barred," the setting was one of service and consumption. Cultural Revolution restaurants thus emerge perhaps as less "era-defining" (Zukin 1991: 215) than market-defining. There, the kitchen becomes a primal scene of global consumption, with wild grass and fried bread representing a basic restructuring of social and market power.

Li, an undergraduate student and Cultural Revolution restaurant diner, similarly linked these eating establishments, considered as a mode of remembering, to contemporary endeavor:

> The policies of the government today are influenced by the lessons of the Cultural Revolution. We cannot avoid facing history, so why not push open the door of the restaurant to remind us of the sweet and sour in the past? This restaurant can remind us of the mistakes that the country made and remind us not to commit the same mistakes. Although people experienced many hardships and lost many particular things, they also gained many things that only people in difficulties can gain. They are more strong and staunch than people in other periods. They are the backbone of China today. We can go to this restaurant both to relive the nostalgia of the past and to find a new start for our futures.

Through such narratives, the restaurant as a mode of remembering was explicitly linked to post-Mao governmental policy, connecting historical, socialist adversity to contemporary, capitalist accomplishment. It is here that the effects of Maoist ideology are refigured as a Weberian work ethic wherein austerity and suffering engender economic success and social status. When one thinks back to the business cards on the wall, what at first appeared to be an ironic juxtaposition now materializes as a mutually supportive arrangement, in which it is the specific history that, rather than negating the present, forms its immediate foundation.

Mr Liu was another former sent-down youth who ran a Cultural Revolution restaurant in Beijing in which the most prominent aspect of its interior was, like Black Earth, a wall of business cards listing the Cultural Revolution work units of visiting diners. Liu's restaurant, named Big Grasslands [*Dacaoyuan*], after the plains of Inner Mongolia where he labored during the Cultural Revolution, was similar in décor to Black Earth, featuring crude farming implements, cafeteria-style tables and a rustic-themed menu. The restaurant occupied about one hundred square meters of space and employed eighteen people.

When the Cultural Revolution began, Liu was in his first year of high school. He joined the Red Guards and began traveling around the country to "exchange revolutionary experiences" [*chuanlian*] with other young activists. Shortly after returning to Beijing, he was sent to Inner Mongolia. "Life there was very bitter. For a really long time I never had meat to eat. I would have to go out into the woods and kill wild rabbits. I almost froze to death out there … I had so many disturbing experiences."

Liu returned to Beijing in 1975, just before the end of the Cultural Revolution. Hoping to go to college, Liu sat for the college entrance exam twice, failing both times. He explained: "When I was in high school it was not very acceptable to study. I was one of those kids who fooled around. Being "red" [socialist and politically active] was more important than being "expert" [in this context, academically successful]. He subsequently worked as a bookkeeper for several years, getting increasingly frustrated with his job as he watched a succession of friends become wealthy by "jumping into the sea of business" while barely managing himself to make ends meet. Finally, he decided to test his own entrepreneurial skills. His first endeavor, buying and selling clothing in Beijing, was fairly successful for a few years, making him "a bit of money," while his next several adventures, trading commodity goods in the Soviet Union and Eastern Europe, "did not lose money, but did not make a lot either." However, when he was in Eastern Europe, he fortuitously happened upon other former sent-down youth who mentioned that several Cultural Revolution restaurants had opened in Beijing:

> I thought about it for a while. I did lots of research and thought it would certainly be successful and earn money. Why? Because there are so many educated youth in Beijing: these people are doing really well, they have really important jobs. So they come to this restaurant. This restaurant can help people get in touch with each other. Do you see the business cards on this wall? They are all put there by restaurant guests... Those who have done well can show others how well they are doing. Those who have not done as well, once they see their old revolutionary friends, how high they have risen, they can then go through the "back door," use these connections to do better. Nowadays, connections are really important... You need to have relationships with these people.

In some ways the narratives of Yang and Liu, both Cultural Revolution restaurant owners, were similar. Like Yang's, Liu's tale began by drawing dramatic attention to food deprivation. Yet the remainder of his life story revolved less around using the restaurant to remember that deprivation, and more around the search for income, with the restaurant figuring merely as one of several similar adventures. Liu, like Yang, also highlighted restaurant dining as a mechanism for renewing social ties. Nonetheless, while Yang placed emphasis on the restaurant as a way to meet people and hash out old experiences, denoting the shared importance of communal historical experience despite upward mobility, for Liu, it served a more instrumental purpose, in which the experience was itself a mechanism to promote upward mobility. Liu's reference to the role of food in producing and reproducing social relationships drew directly upon cultural practices of eating and food symbolism outside the walls of his restaurant. Yet inside, such instrumental practices drew directly upon a historical moment that rejected the premises through which Liu located meaning, appropriating networking practices enabled by a socialist material context for post-socialist forms of identity. Through connections maintained at the business-card wall, the restaurant did not so much reject the past as reconfigure it for present purpose.

Liu's utilization of the Cultural Revolution as a means of cashing in on the Chinese economic boom was not unique to this restaurant. From Mao's hometown, to provincial local flea and antique markets, to Tiananmen Square, Mao kitsch sells. Wang Wenhai, an artist who mass-markets Mao figurines, has recently sculpted a Mao Buddha, a gay Mao, a female Mao and a Mao pillow for those who wish to share their bedchambers with the former chairman (Watts 2003). Even the Communist Party has gotten into the act, recently publishing a four-volume, self-help series on Mao as management guru and entrepreneurial problem-solver. As the columnist Zhang Changlei, in the weekly magazine *China Business*, notes of these volumes: "Mao offers you enterprise management tips you can't get from other business studies" (Zhang 2003: 5). The books use Mao's political strategies as examples of tactics for managing projects, motivating subordinates, overcoming crises and prevailing in business transactions. Li Bo, an administrator at the Party publishing house, reports that ten thousand sets of the Mao-as-management-tool books have already been sold (Zhang 2003: 5).

Drawing upon the kind of Cultural Revolution past highlighted in these Mao-as-management-problem-solver books, Liu told a narrative in which Big Grasslands Restaurant becomes a mechanism through which consuming subjects are understood as produced not in spite of the past but because of it. The Cultural Revolution resurfaces as a resource for entrepreneurial aspirations and successes in the present; it is understood as enabling the production of a consumerist ethic that enhances rather than detracts from the post-Mao project of capitalist production. In this next section we will see how Cultural Revolution restaurants contain the possibility of further enabling what has been so trenchantly labeled "cultural nihilism" (Su Xiaokang and Luxiang Wang 1992) as the politics that get consumed with the sweet and sour entrée move from those of commemoration to consumption to leisure.

The Politics of Leisure

For both Big Grasslands and the entrepreneurial Mao book series, the Cultural Revolution becomes a detached icon, referencing a past, but one largely stripped of its contentious nature. It is a consumable product, offered as a backdrop for leisure and consumption. One evening I dined at Educated Youth with Ms Hu, a 22-year-old graduate student in linguistics. She explained how the restaurant mirrored the experiences of her aunt, who had spent several years in a minority area during the Cultural Revolution. "The stories my aunt tells me about when she was sent down sound adventurous and exciting. The living conditions were terrible; however, their spiritual life was rich. In their spare time they busied themselves reading, singing, dancing. They got on well with each other. They really worked hard to help China."

This image of the Cultural Revolution as a time of recreation was highlighted in the public sphere through a popular television series that aired at around the time that

Educated Youth opened for business, contemporaneously with these conversations about the restaurant and the Cultural Revolution. This television show, an evening serial soap opera called *Unpaid Debt* [*Nie Zhai*], dramatized the adult lives of a group of Shanghai youth who had been relocated to Xishuangbanna during the Cultural Revolution. Each of the youth had formed a relationship with a local person that resulted in offspring. At the end of the Cultural Revolution, these former sent-down youth returned to Shanghai, abandoning both partners and progeny in the deep southwest. The show's storyline obscures the ensuing decade, re-entering the lives of its characters when their discarded teenage offspring relocate to Shanghai to reunite with their lost parents and embark upon life together in an urban setting.

While the Cultural Revolution provided a temporally distant backdrop for the series, it was showcased at the start and finish of each episode through scenes from the movement's early years, as sent-down youth left Shanghai for adventures in revolution. In these segments, the young revolutionaries stand regally in the back of an open-air truck, singing a catchy ditty that belies the significance of the era, "Who can tell me what is right, what is wrong... We were young, we made difficult choices." The title of the drama plays upon the "debt" owed to a cohort of youth, often known as the "lost generation," that missed out on opportunities for schooling and career advancement. Yet, in the context of the drama, the debt is relocated to the realm of personal accountability, situating "repayment" as the responsibility of the individual rather than at the level of state policy. The "wrong" choices involved inopportune personal relationships and disloyalty, not injudicious national revolutionary strategies that rent families asunder, devastated careers and short-changed a generation of students. Against a backdrop of an emblazoned blue sky, these young revolutionaries clasp their arms around one another, smile and laugh in a spirit of joy and cooperation as they head off for what can only be perceived, by the looks of it, as a blissful week at summer camp.

Television shows such as *Unpaid Debt* play into perceptions of the Cultural Revolution as camp or theme park, where alongside outdoor activities, one learns socialist morals and revolutionary ideology with a devoted cohort of activists. For Hu, Educated Youth, with its fanciful décor, exotic cuisine and ethnic artwork, reinforced this possibility. Like visits to camps and theme parks, this restaurant represented a consumable simulation of an era, making it cerebrally "fun" to participate in the Cultural Revolution, sitting on low-slung stools, surrounded by the exotica of a perceived world of romance and difference, both of an era and of a cultural other. The fare, out of the ordinary and sumptuous, in marked contrast to the actual coarse and sparse Cultural Revolution cuisine, prevailed over the prior reality of privation, rewriting the story that is eaten alongside the pickled bamboo shoots as one of impassioned youth marching to collective glory as the prospective saviors of a beleaguered nation rather than one of isolation and deprivation.

Hu's narrative of the Cultural Revolution began as a simple narrative of ludic pleasure, much like that portrayed in *Unpaid Debt*, of singing and dancing, camaraderie and collective spirituality. However, as she continued, her narrative assumed a more complex stance on cultural politics. Leaving singing and dancing behind, it developed into a triangulated story about play, power and ideological certainty, concluding as a parable of power in which students like Hu held positions of authority within the nation-building project. As was mentioned above, Hu was a graduate student in linguistics, destined for a teaching position at a regional educational institution. Up until the mid-1990s, college students were guaranteed post-graduation jobs. These guarantees ensured long-term employment but also locked the recipients into their assigned positions, leaving them little bargaining power should the arrangement not fulfill their career and/or location desires (Hoffman 2001). While several of her fellow graduate students, possessed of highly commodified English-language skills and personal family connections, had obtained positions in transnational joint-venture corporations in big coastal cities, Hu, from a small town in the southwest, on scholarship at the university, had resigned herself to a career in education, feeling that such positions had slipped in the socio-economic hierarchy of the late 1990s:

> Intellectuals don't have a very high social position in China. Due to the development of the economy, money has now become the standard for deciding social position. Successful businessmen are respected, envied by others. Intellectuals are not well paid and their living conditions are not good... Knowledge has become less important than before. In the traditional Chinese value system, people respected knowledge and looked down upon commercialism. Business people had low social status and were regarded as cunning and greedy. Knowledge was respected and people who were knowledgeable were highly respected and had high social status... Today money is respected and knowledge is ignored.

For someone like Hu, facing the prospects of a low-paying job, in a local institution filled with reluctant assignees, reflections upon the Cultural Revolution involved analyses of hierarchies of power. In a cultural context in which even Confucius required seventy years to "harmonize his own desires with that which is right" (Ikels 1989: 112), the reconstitution of authority away from age and toward youth that occurred during the Cultural Revolution was an impertinent rejection of the fundamental underpinning standards held sacred in traditional society. Mao's recognition of students as his personal revolutionary successors figured new spaces of authority for youth. Hu's analysis posed the Cultural Revolution as an era in which a capsized power hierarchy landed youth on the top of the authority heap. While contemporary students like Hu struggled to find "practical" jobs armed only with what she named "impractical" academic lore, Mao's policies during the early years of the Cultural Revolution not only seemingly provided positions of authority but also, in her words, "tempered" those who experienced the era, providing them with moral character, and making them "self-reliant, staunch and strong." For those whose collective hardships involved little of worthy notice, adversity itself became an object of desire.

Lastly, Hu's narrative was one of ideological certainty in which students during the Cultural Revolution struggled for a cause rather than an income: "They had unity, they had beliefs in something other than money." While she recognized the material deprivation of the Cultural Revolution, it was an understanding of deprivation compensated for or even enhanced by the perceived availability of spiritual wealth. It was also an image of selfless pursuit for the national good, passionate beliefs and student camaraderie. She compared the generation of Red Guards and sent-down youth to her own cohort and to her own life as a young graduate student and future college teacher: "They were more independent, we are more spoiled... Their suffering made them strong. My life does not have such passion ... I admire that time period. The youth then were united. They had beliefs." This was an imagined era of Chinese utopianism, not of violence and repression. Its communist narrative was one of justice that provided moral inspiration in ways that the contemporary economy failed to satisfy. Nonetheless, while Hu's commentary was one of value and ideology in the past that reflected a perception of ideological poverty in the present, it was intimately inflected by the realities of contemporary China.

> Some say that money cannot buy happiness; maybe it is true, but I think maybe those who say so have a lot of money... What you learn in university only gets you a little money. You have to give up your dreams and be practical ... go into business. Is happiness to be wealthy but not have dreams or have dreams but no money?

Hu's impressions of the past lacked personal historical context, her nostalgia, uninformed by experience, assumed "real" meaning through representation. Yet, while clad in the ideological dress of the Cultural Revolution past, Hu's pragmatism was born of contemporary, quotidian familiarity and the realization that other citizens who had forsaken education for the marketplace were living far more luxurious lives than she would ever likely experience. Paradoxically, for Hu, in her search for depth and authenticity, these Cultural Revolution restaurants, exemplary sites of contemporary consumption, surfaced as unwitting critiques of the very thing they seemed to epitomize.[12]

Fissures of Modernity and Hegemonies of Form[13]

As did my experiences with the dead fish, so do contemporary Cultural Revolution theme restaurants denote the complexity and conflict apparent in post-Mao forms of modernity, revealing changing standards of social identity, class status and cultural authority. Although such restaurants are places of culinary and consumer "pleasure," the pleasure ironically has the potential to embody the entirety of the Cultural Revolution. However, these establishments act simultaneously as mini-museums that refuse to accommodate an amnesiac nation, and as contemporary meeting-grounds for those who, having shouldered the burden of misguided national policy on their adolescent bodies, reject interpretations of the Cultural Revolution as entirely waste and chaos.

A memorial requires recognizing the traumatic nature of the event. As the Party hesitates to acknowledge past trauma to the extent required for a formal memorial, for some diners and owners, these private restaurants assumed the cathartic functions of public memorialization. However, as sites of leisure and consumption, these restaurants were located firmly within the reform era's stress on the production of capital excess and on an ideal of status defined through the consumption of material products. Even as their form invokes the past, such restaurants satisfy two official projects in the present, that of the circulation of fungible assets and of desensitizing historical trauma.

Cultural Revolution restaurants thus satisfy the desire for authenticity of past, present and future. Yet one wonders whether the form, or the language, becomes the message and the mode of thinking. As temporal and ideological distance foreclose upon other forms of remembering, consumption becomes the space in which the past is present, the space in which memories are consumed as the promise of the future. Black Earth, Big Grasslands and Educated Youth allow patrons to remember the Cultural Revolution, to reveal the fissures of modernity, but within a common structure of consumption in which the dining establishments encourage the production of social stratification through consumerist economic policy, solving the problems of a troublesome past through promises of contemporary pleasure.

Acknowledgments

Special thanks are due to Chih-Ching Chang, Monica DeHart, Lisa Hoffman, Guobin Yang, Mingbao Yue, and my research assistant inBeijing.

Notes

1. Cited in Simoons 1991: 13.
2. For example, Appadurai 1981; Counihan and Van Esterik 1997; Meigs 1984; Sutton 2001; Watson 1997.
3. "Bitter, sweet and sour" was the menu description of a Cultural Revolution restaurant dish. During the Cultural Revolution, wild grass was sometimes harvested by sent-down youth and made into soup.
4. During the Cultural Revolution, efforts at adornment, whether of one's house or one's body, were considered bourgeois and reactionary. Homes were largely

devoid of artwork, save for the ubiquitous portraits of Mao, while men and women alike clad themselves in drab-colored suits (which have since come to be known in English as Mao suits, but are often referred to in China as "blue clothes" [*lanyi*]) or imitation army uniforms. Even one's hairstyle was dictated by these revolutionary norms. Former Red Guards have recounted stories to me of the efforts to which they went to force public compliance with visual uniformity, one woman mentioning how she and several of her cohort waited on the sidewalks for unsuspecting passers-by with long hair, which they promptly grabbed and cut off.

5. The phrase is from Jenner 1988, cited in Chen 2003: 387.

6. This is not meant to imply the lack of gender of the Maoist laboring body, but the refiguring of gender that labor policies provoked. For a more radical critique of the degendering of the laboring body, see M. Yang (1999).

7. A Cultural Revolution restaurant owner used the phrase "excessively romantic." That conversation will be discussed at length below. I have written elsewhere about these debates over the meaning of the Cultural Revolution in a study of Mao badge collecting in contemporary China (Hubbert 2006).

8. This latter interpretation was particularly apparent in the many conversations I held with college students who spoke of the Cultural Revolution experiences of their elders as the reason behind the post-Mao successes of that cohort. See the discussion with Ms Hu detailed below. There is a growing literature on the contemporary significance of the Cultural Revolution. For only a small example, see Sausmikat 1999; F. Yang 1991; G. Yang 2003.

9. It is important to note here the selective nature of state critiques of the Cultural Revolution. While official assessments are highly critical of the Gang of Four, they maintain the continued importance of the era's Maoist ideological lessons. Thanks to Mingbao Yue for pushing me on this point.

10. For instance, while an official Cultural Revolution museum is scheduled to open in Sichuan, its restaurant, decorated in period style, is intended to "bring back the memories of workers, farmers and soldiers eating communally and ridding themselves of bourgeois liberalism" (http://www.chinaartnetworks. com/news/show_news.php?id=2068).

11. Such examples contradict what Simoons calls a "tradition of frugality" in which excessive consumption of food and alcohol was a sign of moral turpitude (1991: 18). Food in China has also played a complex role in political dissent. The refusal of food through public hunger strikes was a mechanism of remonstrance throughout the dynastic years and re-emerged to a global audience in 1989 as pajama-clad, oxygen-sporting college students employed these tactics to force a dialogue with the contemporary regime (Gang 2002; Wasserstrom and Perry 1992).

12. On the relationship between consumption and generation in China, see Hubbert 2003.

13. I borrow this title from Yurchak 2003.

–7–

Ethnic Succession and the New American Restaurant Cuisine[1]
Krishnendu Ray

Introduction

Even casual observers of the American restaurant scene will notice that there are certain niches – such as diners and take-outs – where particular ethnicities predominate. If they have some familiarity with the history of American restaurants they would also know that there is a pattern of ethnic succession over time. Foodwork that used to be done by German and Irish immigrants in the mid-nineteenth century was performed by Italians and eastern Europeans at the end of the century, who in turn were replaced by Greeks, and then by Asians and Latinos at the end of the twentieth century. At least that has been the case for cities in the northeastern United States.

Tastes have changed too. Continental cuisine gave way to French cuisine, which has conceded its place to Italian cooking in America's most expensive restaurants, accented by Asian and Latino ingredients today. Even a new cuisine called American Cuisine has come into being. There is a twofold ethnic succession here: one in the sphere of food served; and the other in the ethnicity of the labor force. The two are shaped by each other in counterintuitive ways.

Observers often notice that kind of ethnic succession, but they rarely try to explain it, perhaps because of the fear that they might be seen as perpetuating ethnic stereotypes. In the process they avoid facing an essential truth about the restaurant business – it is kept afloat by a labor force that is segmented by ethnicity – and as a result abandon us to uninterrogated theories of racial preferences for particular business niches. If so many Greeks are in the diner business, then Greeks must have a natural affinity for it, goes the typical line of reasoning. Even sophisticated academics have fallen prey to such easy generalizations. Joseph T. Manzo in an otherwise impeccable piece entitled "From Pushcart to Modular Restaurant" (1998: 222) notes that one of the reasons for the ubiquity of Greeks in the diner business is "the seriousness which they applied to the business, the added touch of homeyness that developed in diners because family members worked there and the 'openness' with which they shared their feelings and philosophy, the latter two being distinctive of southern Europeans." Is seriousness about business, homeyness, or even openness a peculiarly Greek characteristic?

A common-sense association between race and profession, based on the obvious empirical predominance of particular groups in certain business niches, begins to be read as a sign of racial affinity in the absence of better-developed theories. There can be much better explanations. To develop them I need to do two things: (a) take a few steps back to identify the long-term pattern of ethnic succession in the restaurant business; and (b) restrict the analysis to one segment of the restaurant industry – full-service, fine-dining restaurants – in one place (mostly New York City), so as to make the data manageable. A brief excursion into the history of American fine dining, which I pursue in the first section of this chapter, shows the replacement of French food with Italian, accompanied by a progressive Americanization of taste. Accounting for this process requires a close examination of changing tastes in ethnic food as well as an analysis of changing restaurant labor markets, both of which I undertake in the last two sections. Rather than any primordial affinity for particular professions, I will show that ethnic succession in the fine-dining segment of the restaurant industry can be explained by changing ideas about what constitutes fine dining, as well as by shifts in American labor markets.

A Historical Sketch of Fine-dining American Restaurants

There have been three major waves of restaurant building in the United States. The first wave coincided with the Gilded Age, which not only gave us numerous American restaurants but also the cocktail (Thomas 1862). Delmonico's, established in 1833, arguably the most famous American restaurant of the nineteenth century, preceded this expansive phase. It was followed by venerable institutions such as Antoine's (1840) in New Orleans; Parker House (1855) and Locke-Ober (1875) in Boston; Maison Dorée (1861), Hoffman House (1864), Knickerbocker (1871), Sherry's (1881), Lüchow (1882), Waldorf-Astoria (1899), and Rector's (1899) in New York; Jack's (1864), Palace (1875) and Shroeder's (1893) in San Francisco; Grammer's (1872) in Cincinnati; Rector's (1884) of Chicago; and Bookbinder's (1865) and The Bellevue Stratford Hotel (1902) in Philadelphia. The outliers were Grossinger's in the Catskills in 1919 and Colony in 1921 in New York.[2] When Congress passed the Volsted Act in 1920, to enforce the prohibition amendment to the Constitution, it closed the first chapter on American fine-dining restaurants.

By some accounts, Delmonico's was the only recognized restaurant in New York City in 1833, while there were up to six thousand such establishments by 1876 (Root and de Rochemont 1976: 334). According to Harvey Levenstein, the pre-eminent historian of American food habits, this was the classic period of conspicuous consumption, when a newly rich class sought to establish itself in the realm of consumption as theorized by Thorstein Veblen, who was writing at precisely this moment (2001: 13).

The Civil War and the financial speculation that followed produced a whole new crop of super-rich parvenus, who soon provided a monumental spur to the spread of French cooking in America... As imposing new mansions marched relentlessly up New York's Fifth and Madison avenues, their kitchens, manned by newly-imported French chefs, became major armories in the battle. When daring forays were made out of private homes, the ranks were drawn up at Delmonico's, the Fifth Avenue Hotel, the Brunswick House, and the Hoffman House, all of which served French food (Levenstein 1989: 70–1).

The simultaneous presence of old elites and the newly rich – by one count 84 percent of the rich in the 1880s were newly minted (Stanley and Danko 1996: 16) – made these restaurants the perfect locale for intense status competition by way of showy dinners and restrained manners. By the 1880s the competition for conspicuous consumption had reached absurd limits, with menus engraved on silver plaques, a $100,000 dinner for fifty hosted by Diamond Jim Brady, and a $10,000 breakfast for seventy-two by Edward Luckmeyer, who hosted a banquet with four live swans caged in gold wiring crafted by Tiffany's on a lake carved on the dining table.

The food was stringently haute French. Surprisingly, until the 1870s, "the taste for French food [had] never entered the [American] mainstream," writes Levenstein (2003: 11). He notes that a French chef became a necessity in establishing the new code of dining only by the 1870s:

> The ascendancy of French cooking is evident in many menus that survive from the upper and upper-middle-class hotels of the post-[Civil] war era. In the late 1860s and early 1870s they tended to be mainly English/American in their offerings and language, with only an occasional French touch. By the mid- and late-1870s, however, a wholesale invasion of French terms and French dishes was under way. (Levenstein 2003: 15)

There were a few exceptions, such as Lüchow's (1882) in New York City, Shroeder's (1893) in San Francisco and Grammer's (1872) in Cincinnati, that served German cuisine, while Parker House (1855) in Boston served New England cuisine, but these merely underlined the otherwise wholesale addiction of the elite to French food.

The second wave of restaurant building clusters between the Second World War and the Vietnam War. Le Pavillon in New York, established in 1941 by the staff of the French pavilion at the World Fair, leads this group (Smith 2005). It is followed by Brennan's in New Orleans (1946), La Côte Basque (1959), Four Seasons (1959), La Caravelle (1960), Lutèce (1961), La Grenouille (1962), and Le Périgord (1964), finishing off with the outlier Le Cirque (1974). Interestingly, with the exception of Four Seasons and Brennan's, the names are fervently Francophone – leading the New York restaurateur Drew Nieporent to characterize it as the Le/La phase of American fine-dining (Nieporent quoted in Bruni 2005: F4). This list is also a lot shorter than the one that precedes it in the Gilded Age and the other that follows in the post-Vietnam era.

Chez Panisse (1971) carried the Francophone resonances of the Second Wave, and yet brought a markedly different aesthetic of the Arts and Craft Movement to American cuisine in the post-Vietnam War era. The new focus was on "organic architecture," and a sparse informal style arrayed against the opulence of the Le Pavillon variety. The craftsmanship of bourgeois home-cooking was the new posture, contrasted with the mannered style of French haute cuisine. There was also an explicit critique of the ornate neoclassicism of Delmonico's oeuvre. Rusticity replaced elegance. That went hand-in-hand with the crusade of Alice Waters – the owner of Chez Panisse – on behalf of organic and seasonal produce. She also unlocked the door to the Mediterranean by way of the south of France.

The list of fine-dining restaurants that opened in the United States in the wake of Chez Panisse is impressive. To identify some of the most visible ones we have to include Jean-Louis at the Watergate (1979), Spago (1982), An American Place (1983), Stars (1984), Rattlesnake Club (1985), Union Square Café (1985), China Moon Café (1985), Frontera Grill (1987), Susanna Foo's (1987), Hammersley's (1987), Trotter's (1987), Nobu's (1987), Coyote Café (1987), Citrus (1987), Aureole (1988), Olives (1989), Lark Creek Inn (1989), Biba (1989), etc. The list is interminable both because of the explosion in restaurants and the proximity to our own time, when it becomes impossible to discern between a flash in the pan and a legitimate star with staying power. Perhaps a convenient stopping point would be Emeril's Delmonico (re-opened in 1997), which nicely closes the epoch that opened with Delmonico's in 1833.

Perhaps we are too close to the details of the current expansion to get some perspective, but there is an emerging consensus among American food writers that we are in the midst of a culinary revolution. As proof they point to the explosion in good restaurants in the United States in the wake of Chez Panisse. The disagreement is only about the signal temporal moment. Some date the great transformation in American culinary culture to Craig Claiborne's naming of chefs in *The New York Times* restaurant reviews in the 1960s (Brenner 1999: 79). A convenient date for some is the day in 1966 when Julia Child made the cover of *Time* magazine under the title "Everyone's in the Kitchen." Some date the revolution to 1972, with the publication of James Beard's *American Cookery*, which celebrated American regionalism (Brenner 1999: 194). Some insist on 1976, when Jeremiah Tower, the chef at Chez Panisse, featured the first Californian menu, with dishes such as "Monterey Bay Prawns" and "Walnuts, Almonds, and Mountain Pears from the San Francisco Farmers' Market." Some have argued that American foodies still needed the jolt of June 1976 to free themselves from excessive Francophilia. That was when two Napa Valley wines bested the best of French wines in a blind test, in the over-heated narrative of the time. Freed from too much veneration for things French, Americans were willing to play with their food. Others draw attention to the groundwork done by the birth of *Gourmet* magazine in 1941 and especially the self-assurance with which the Four Seasons, which opened in 1959, described itself as an "American" restaurant – "people had their first cherry tomatoes at the Four Seasons; they had their first baby avocados in the Four Seasons; they had their first snow peas in the Four Seasons… And so there was this emphasis on product as opposed to the emphasis in a French restaurant, which is on 'cuisine' and sauce."[3] Leslie Brenner finds the early Four Seasons menu replete with American regional specialties such as Smithfield Hams, Virginia Blue Crab, California Teleme Cheese, seasonal vegetables and field greens (Brenner 1999: 39–40). We can also take 1982 as the benchmark year, when Zagat produced its first formal survey of New York City restaurants (informally the survey began in 1979). A commercially successful survey is good evidence both of the number of restaurants and its importance to a reading public. Be that as it may, I want to draw attention here to another aspect of the recent explosion of new American restaurants, and that is its relationship to ethnicity in two ways: the ethnicity of the food served and the ethnicity of the labor force.

Ethnicity of the Food Served: The Valorization of Italian-American Food

On December 5, 1881, a *New York Times* correspondent noted, "I have never during many years of discourse on culinary topics, disguised my opinion that the modern Italian 'cuisine' is, next to the Spanish, the most detestable in Europe" (1881: 3). In 1889 when Alessandro Filippini, the chef at Delmonico's, published his cookbook called *The Table*, there were hardly any distinctively Italian recipes in it. More than seven decades later James Beard could still dismiss Italian cooking: "My opinion of Italian cookery is not too high," he wrote from France in 1955 (quoted in Kuh 2001: 61). Addressing what appears today to be the inexplicable disrepute of Italian cuisine, Patric Kuh notes:

> If rusticity was the direction food was to take, then it could easily be thought that Italian food would have had a head start… The problem for Italians was precisely that their best food stood in direct contrast to the aesthetic of refinement that was the ideal throughout the 1940s, 1950s, and 1960s. (Kuh 2001: 180)

Kuh is right. Sometimes aesthetic evaluations of food have nothing to do with the nature of the food or the skill involved in producing it. The Italian misfortune – at least in American eyes – may have been that Italian-Americans were poor and derided, and hence their food was dismissed for those reasons, rather than for any objective evaluation of their cuisine. When American Italians climbed out of the ghetto and into sports arenas, corporate offices, governors' mansions, city halls and movie studios, Italian food was reassessed in the American imagination.

Today, by contrast, Italian food is everywhere, not only in "Italian" but also in "American" restaurants. It is instructive to look at the food at one Zagat-rated, self-described American restaurant, where the chef describes his cooking as a blend of "a variety of international flavors including Asian, Southwestern and Italian, with classical French technique." It is a norm in this class of restaurants to refer to their "techniques" as French, even when pot-stickers and pasta are served. The appetizers are calamari tempura, French soufflé, Vietnamese spring roll, and potato gnocchi. The entrées are olive oil poached salmon, truffled risotto, grilled rack of lamb with a port wine demi-glace. Sometimes the dishes acquire an Asian, Latino or Caribbean twist, such as horseradish crusted ahi tuna with a miso aioli. The food is basically Franco-Italian with an exotic accent.

We can see a similar pattern of change in the menu of the restaurant that has become a paradigm for the Third Wave – Chez Panisse. Italian food and techniques have been incorporated into the canon at this temple of New American cuisine at least since Paul Bertolli. (Although from the very beginning, Alice Waters was drawn to the Mediterranean coast.) In the winter of 2006 the menu included mushroom gnocchi with Parmesan cheese, cauliflower crostini, bresaola with faro, wild rocket, and Parmesan, a few kinds of pizzetta, ricotta ravioli, and side dishes of olives, anchovies and Tuscan olive oil.

As Stanley Lieberson (2000) has shown, in any fashion cycle what follows depends much more on what precedes. Lieberson points out that the new style is never completely different from what went before, because then the new approach would be both incomprehensible and ugly. In identifying patterns of popularity in children's first names, Lieberson detects external and internal dynamics (feminism or black ethnic activism in the former case, phonemic preferences in the latter), both contributing to incremental changes in way names are chosen or invented. One can see a similar incrementalism in American tastes in restaurant cuisine. The American gustatory model for fine-dining restaurants has moved progressively in a geographical arc from Paris, through Marseilles, to northern Italian cities, then to Naples and Sicily, and on to the Mediterranean coast of Spain. By analogy with Lieberson's phonemes, one can also see the gustemic movement – from butter, sour cream and chives, to olive oil, garlic and herbs. Of course, such a change is incremental only when the viewer is peering in from Asia. For locals distinctive differences from neighbors are never incremental.

Changes in the curriculum at the leading cooking school – the Culinary Institute of America (CIA) – point in the same direction. In 2001 "The Cuisines of Europe" was changed to "Cuisines of Europe and the Mediterranean," underplaying the formerly hegemonic Germanic cuisine of spätzle, sausage, pork chops, dairy and cabbage, and highlighted the cuisines of Italy, southern France and North Africa. One special unit in the new curriculum is exclusively focused on pastas – including the making of fresh pastas such as tagliatelle, tortelli, fettuccine, cavatelli, orecchiette, etc. (Rascoll 2004, personal communication). In a presentation on the future of American restaurants in 2005, CIA's President Tim Ryan noted the growth of American, Italian, Latino and Asian cuisines and virtually ignored the French, which is remarkable given that the CIA's curriculum is still structured around French techniques. That is changing too.

Major surveys of American restaurants – such as Zagats – also reflect changes in the same direction. But before I present the Zagat data let me provide some caveats. First, Zagat lists are enigmatic. Zagat-rated restaurants are not randomized. The selection gets filtered through two layers of opinion-makers – the first, tens of thousands of self-selecting surveyors who volunteer to rate a restaurant. Second, the reviews are not analyzed by any scientific statistical method. They reflect the preferences of the editors themselves, who cull the reviews and assign overall scores by no publicly discussed system. As far as we know these are opinions of the Zagat editors matched to a certain degree of popularity among Zagat reviewers. Yet, in spite of these weaknesses, Zagat reviews do reveal some trends as opinion-makers.

A second set of concerns centers on how I have counted the restaurants under various cuisines. I have excluded all numerically small categories of ethnic restaurants from the total – such as Irish and Swiss. And that is because each year Zagat lists more and more categories of ethnic restaurants – forty-nine in 1990 and sixty-seven in 2006 – and hence the percentage of every category of ethnic restaurant falls, but that figure gives an inaccurate image of the relative importance of each category over time. Hence my method of keeping the ethnic categories constant over time gives a better picture of their relative importance. One last point: when a restaurant like Vong is listed both under Thai and French, I have counted it under both categories on the assumption that such self-identified double-counting gives a better picture of the universe, rather than forcing it into one singular category according to my judgment. Now on to the data. Since 1982, when Zagat began publishing its New York City survey, Italian cuisine has sustained its popularity by remaining around a quarter of all Zagat-rated restaurants, while French restaurants (down to 14 percent in 2006 from 24 percent in 1986) and especially Continental cuisine have been losing out among the fine-dining clientele (see Table 7.1). Continental cuisine, so derided by Calvin Trillin (1994), has effectively vanished from the scene over the last two decades.

Japanese is the only ethnic cuisine with a consistently strong showing of 4–7 percent, while every other notable cuisine – Mexican, Indian, Soul, Thai and Vietnamese – hovers under 4 percent. Japanese restaurants figure in the top restaurants in almost every American city surveyed by Zagat in 2006, with the highest numbers visible in Los Angeles, New York and Miami. Part of the strength of Japanese cuisine in American restaurants is related to the rise of Japan as a major economic and cultural power, which has made its food an exotic "foreign" commodity, a designer commodity if you will, somewhat akin to the role once played by French food in the American imagination. Japanese businessmen, traveling with a strong yen after the Plaza Accord (of 1985, which halved the yen-value of the dollar) were the early

Table 7.1 Ethnicity of Zagat-rated New York City restaurants as a percentage of all ethnically identifiable restaurants (columns = percentages for selected years)

Cuisines	1986[1] (%)	1990 (%)	2000 (%)	2006 (%)
Italian	26	28	27	27
French	24	18	16	14
American	13	18	22	19
Continental	10	6	2	1
Chinese	8	7	5	4
Japanese	4	4	6	7
Pizza	4	3	4	3
Mediterranean	0	2	4	5
Mexican/Tex-Mex	3	4	2	3
Indian	2	2	2	3
Soul/Southern	2	2	2	2
Thai	1	2	2	3
Greek	1	1	2	2
Spanish	1	1	2	2
Korean	0	0	1	1
Vietnamese	0	0	1	1
Total	99[2]	98[2]	101[2]	98[2]

Note 1: 1986 is the earliest publicly available published Zagat Survey.
Note 2: Does not add up to 100 due to rounding.
Source: Printed Zagat Surveys.

patrons of expensive Japanese restaurants serving *kaiseki ryori* in restaurants such as *Nippon* and *Benihana* in New York City (Kishimoto 2006). American businessmen and professionals modeled their behavior after the newly stylish Japanese. The other part of the rising popularity of Japanese *haute cuisine* in American restaurants has to do with the end of the stream of Japanese migration into the United States, which removed the taint of the domestic underclass that every "ethnic" cuisine labors under (Ray 2006).

Interestingly, the popularity of Chinese has been falling in estimation from a high of 8 percent. Yet Chinese ingredients such as bok-choy (pak choi) and Sichuan peppers, and techniques such as stir-frying, steaming and wonton-wrapping are becoming more common in "New American" restaurants. China is both a rising economic power and a major source of migrant labor to the American restaurant industry; hence the future of Chinese *haute cuisine* in America is at a tipping point. If the Chinese economy continues to grow and out-migration recedes one can foresee the rise of Chinese *haute cuisine* in American restaurants; but if the migration stream continues I foresee a continuing struggle for Chinese cuisine to hold on to a few islands of prestige in the fine-dining arena. Revealingly, the talk about Chinese restaurants reached a peak in 1965 (if we count the number of articles on particular ethnic restaurants in the *New York Times*) and has since declined to about 20 percent from a high of 35 percent of articles. This happened precisely when the new Chinese immigration took off, which was in 1965. So I am hypothesizing an inverse relationship between the prestige of a cuisine (identifiable by price and volume of talk in the upper reaches of the media) and the number of immigrants.

Data from the annual survey of The National Restaurant Association – which unlike the previous material includes "Limited Service" establishments – shows that Italian eateries do even better as check averages fall under $25. There are hardly any French restaurants under that figure. It is interesting to note that between 2000 and 2006/7 French/Continental restaurants fell from 13 percent in the class of the most expensive restaurants (where the French have always done the best), to below 1 percent where they had to be subsumed within the "others" category. In contrast, the Italian figure has gone up dramatically, from 5 percent in 1984 to 15 percent in the most-expensive category in 2006/7; a clear sign of the upward mobility of Italian eateries.

Nevertheless French restaurants do much better in Zagat's national survey of "America's Top Restaurants" (Table 7.2), where almost 25 percent of the restaurants serve French foods of various kinds, from Bistro to Classical French, with the former increasingly replacing the latter in popularity. Consistently, over the years since Zagat began its list of "America's Top Restaurants" (1992), the number of Italian restaurants on that list has oscillated between 14 percent and 18 percent, while the French have hovered around 25 percent. The most dramatic improvement has been in the fate of "American" cuisine, especially the New American cuisine. Very clearly a self-consciously American restaurant cuisine has been born in the last two decades, and interestingly at the same time it has begun to regionalize, notably into Californian, Southwestern and Northwestern variants, especially in the leading cities of these regions, such as San Francisco, Phoenix and Seattle, respectively. (The older categories of Cajun and Creole preceded this phase of regionalization.) Looking at the ethnicity of Zagat-rated restaurants in every major American city one can conclude that the "American" trend is blowing in from the west coast, while the Italian trend has been gathering momentum on the east coast. Furthermore, the intimate relationship that was established between American elites and French cuisine at the end of the nineteenth century is beginning to disintegrate.

Immigrant Cooks

Waverly Root and Richard de Rochemont (1976: 313) opened their chapter on American restaurants with: "An incidental result of the influx of immigrants into the United States was that it provided somebody to run America's restaurants." Historical census data confirm this correlation between food-service occupations

Table 7.2 Zagat-rated restaurants among "America's Top Restaurants" (columns = percentages for selected years)

Cuisines	1992[1] (%)	2000 (%)	2006 (%)
American[2]	26	38	38
French	25	26	24
Italian	18	14	15
Continental	12	6	4
Chinese	5	2	2
Japanese	4	4	7
Asian	0	3	3
Cajun/Creole	3	2	2
Mexican	3	2	1
Thai	2	1	1
Vietnamese	1	1	1
Indian	1	0	1
Total	100	99[3]	99[3]
	(N=722)	(N=883)	(N=1010)

Note 1: Started in 1992.
Note 2: American includes American (New) + American (Traditional) + Californian + Northwestern.
Note 3: Does not add up to 100 due to rounding.
Source: Printed Zagat Surveys.

and new immigrant groups ever since jobs and birthplace have been identified in the Census, beginning in 1850. Census data show that the foreign-born numerically dominate certain occupations such as agricultural laborers, domestic servants, hotel and restaurant employees, hotelkeepers, saloon keepers and bartenders, traders and dealers in groceries, tailors and bakers. Cooks (as a subcategory of domestic servants) were first identified in the detailed published tables of the 1910 Census. Cooks were listed as a separate *public* occupation, distinct from domestic servants, in the 1940 Census. I hope to develop a detailed picture of the historical census of occupations and ethnicity over time.

For now, I can see a strong correlation between foreign birth and occupations in the food industry. For instance in 1850, in the New York City area, 70 percent of Employees of Hotels and Restaurants and 80 percent of Hotelkeepers were foreign-born, mostly of Irish and German heritage, in a context where the foreign-born constituted about a third of the labor force. Fifty years later, according to the 1900 Census, 63 percent of Employees of Hotels and Restaurants in New York City were foreign-born (mostly Irish at 22.2 percent and German at 16.2 percent) and 65 percent of Hotelkeepers were foreign-born (mostly German, followed far behind by the Irish and English-born). Restaurantkeepers, a newly significant occupation by 1900, were 67 percent foreign-born (led by Germans at 26.7 percent and followed by Austrians at 16.7 percent, Russians at 10 percent and Italians at 6.7 percent), at a time when the foreign-born in New York City were about 50 percent of the population. Even by the 1950 Census, when the immigrant wave had subsided, 64 percent of cooks in restaurants were foreign-born, Italians now replacing others at the top, constituting 8.4 percent of cooks (but only about 6 percent of the population), followed by Greeks at 8.1 percent, Chinese at 5.9 percent and Germans at 5.3 percent. In the 2000 Census 64 percent of restaurant workers in New York City (or, even more dramatically, 75 percent of cooks) continued to be foreign-born; but the leading regions of nativity were now Mexico, the various nations of Central America, the Caribbean Basin, South America, China and the old USSR. In general, from 1850 to 2000, while food industry-related occupations have been numerically dominated by the foreign-born, members of the clergy, lawyers, government officials and physicians have mostly been native- born (Ruggles *et al.* 2004; ROC-NY 2005).

Stepping back from the details of the Census data at the broadest level one can identify three immigrant waves into the United States, totaling about 65 million in all (until 2001). The dominant template for American home-cooking was provided by the first 20 million Northern European immigrants in their regionalized variants (see Gabaccia 1998), but the effect on American restaurant cuisine was minimal, because there were hardly any restaurants serving American food.

A perusal of respectable American newspapers such as the *New York Times*, the *Los Angeles Times*, the *Chicago Tribune* and the *Atlanta Constitution* shows that there were numerous reports of ethnics working ethnic restaurants. Commentary on the "dinner-saloons" and "beer-gardens" of the ethnics – often defined as German, Irish and Scandinavian up to the 1880s – were almost always embedded in racy narratives of crime, prostitution, and punishment. Public eating in ethnic restaurants was embroiled in deep-seated anxieties about race, gender and gentility. For instance, on August 6, 1871 the *New York Times* worried both about the number of immigrants allowed and that "restaurants and boarding-houses are fast multiplying, and threaten at no distant day to usurp the place of the family dinner table as well as the family mansion." Anxieties about the "domestic" in its multiple resonances – of family, home and nation – are typical in almost all commentary on "cheap restaurants," which are often referred to as "German, French, and Italian Dining-Saloons." Yet there is sometimes a hint of urban excitement, often balanced by ethnic disgust. One can see the exhilaration in an 1852 piece on Philadelphia subtitled "An Era of Saloonism," which ends with the following:

> Scores of waiters, like dumb mutes, stand ready to receive your orders, and to convey them to that concealed and invisible sanctuary whence issues so many multitudinous preparations, whose fantastic names tickle the ear, and whose superlative qualities please and exhilarate the palate. Surrounded by these exquisite means of gratification, you ... are persuaded that, lost in the mazes of the city, you have entered, by accident, into some secret avenue, which has conducted you into an elysian state of existence – some

Mahomedian paradise, adorned with marble and gold; perfumed with frankincense and myrrh; and lighted by the brilliant eyes of beautiful houris. ("Victor" 1852: 2)

In fact, this mid-nineteenth-century urban excitement with the exotic recedes by the 1880s until we get someone like Helen Bullitt Lowry in the 1920s, who has to rehabilitate and normalize the "old world" of Greeks, Jews and Italians through their foods in New York (1921). Until then, ethnic food, if referred to at all, was subject to open disgust in titles such as "Found in Garbage-Boxes stuff that is utilized for food by some people" (*New York Times* July 15, 1883) and the shrill announcement of "An Octopus Eaten by Chinamen" (*New York Times* December 6, 1880). Distaste easily marks the outer boundary of a taste community.

In contrast to ethnic places, society restaurants such as Delmonico's are welcomed with open arms. On April 7, 1862, the *New York Times* warmly embraced the new up-town location of Delmonico's with the following words:

When the best families were clustered around the Bowling-green, and gentlemen dandies who promenaded on the Battery were expected to wear white kid gloves, the name DELMONICO first became known to the lovers of good living in the City. This establishment was the resort of the fashionable, as it now is of the commercial classes of the metropolis... The establishment (which was formerly the mansion of Mr. MOSES II. GRINNELL) has been fitted up with faultless taste, and is without any exception, the handsomest place of this kind in the City. (*New York Times* 1862: 5)

Every new location of Delmonico's is received with rapture, and contained by some vague patrician referent such as "formerly the mansion of Mr. Moses." And every society ball, held in one of these venerated restaurants, is announced with much fanfare in the dailies. In general, German restaurants are unfavorably compared to Delmonico's, Sutherland and the Cable. Yet, on January 19, 1873, the *New York Times* could publish a long and relatively even-handed piece titled "German Restaurants." In it the eponymous institutions are distinguished by their cheapness and abundance. They are said to serve "the odd things that foreigners love" along with roasts, "pumpkin pies and dumplings baked." For the Frenchman there is "lentil soup, in which masses of Bologna sausage are floating, while the Irishman is vigorously to [*sic*] work on something like fish-balls smothered in red cabbage," all of which is served with an "enormous supply of coarse German bread." The unnamed author notices two customers "who are certainly Jews ... discussing Vienna sausage, with mashed potatoes and sauer-kraut." The waiters, the author suggests "are clearly German" (*New York Times* January 19, 1873: 5).

By the early twentieth century, with some regional exceptions – such as small, local traditions such as pasties in the Upper Michigan peninsula, and Pennsylvania "Dutch" food – a national text was created in the United Sates. The first step was the erasure of Native-American gustatory experience. Second, the national market, born by way of the transportation revolution, corporate consolidation, and the print media, tied together and flattened the uneven contours of regional cuisines (Gabaccia 1998). In 1935, in an article titled "Our Wide Taste in Food," Helen Morgan could write: "Strange dishes have been taken from one home to another, until, as a consequence, an American family of 1935 might reasonably concoct a meal like this: fruit cocktail, sauerkraut, spaghetti, mutton or lamb or meat balls, corn on the cob, garlic salad and apple pie." She assures us that "undoubtedly any one subject to [such] nightmares would not survive, yet such a hodge-podge is not impossible" (Morgan 1935: SM17). From our vantage point the menu hardly looks like a hodge-podge. Furthermore, such a collation was possible because the Germans, the Irish, and the Scandinavians submerged their gustatory identity in a white, Anglophone text. One consequence is that we cannot much recall their distinctive foods any more, other than as caricatures of excessive drinking – difference became drunkenness, which echoes the original anxiety about ethnic "saloonism."

This wave of 20-odd million "ethnic" immigrants – Italians, Slavs, Eastern European Jews, and Greeks – wouldn't melt away. Not because they were more virtuous than the first wave, but because of their sheer volume and concentration both in terms of space (northeastern cities) and time (1880–1924); equally because of their gravitation towards long-lasting ethnic enclaves; and to some degree because of their temporal proximity to our own times (so that we can still see them as distinct). As Donna Gabaccia notes in *We Are What We Eat* (1998), by the end of the nineteenth century, region had given way, on the one hand, to a relatively homogenized national gustatory experience, and on the other hand, to the creation of ethnic enclaves (1998: 35). Ethnic eateries flourished within the ghetto, far from the Waldorf-Astoria, Delmonico's, and the Hoffman House. It would take a long time for these folks to break into the American fine-dining scene.

From 1924 to 1965, that is for two generations, with few immigrants coming in – about 7 million over four decades compared to four times that figure before and after that period – Americans would elaborate a form of naturalized and standardized American cooking, with the help of radio and television to spread the word. It is the food of this period that most Americans today would come to identify as unambiguously American food – Germanic food, often delivered by corporations, with a few ethnic accents, which were primarily Italian, Greek, Southern and Eastern European. Cuisine, on the other hand, would be Continental, which would be a vague shorthand for the imagined food of European elites.

The next group of migrants – another 20 million or so, this time from the very places blocked by the racialized laws of the pre-Civil Rights era – would break upon our shores as a terrifying and exhilarating horde, as if the very tower of Babel had collapsed on our heads, destroying the layered sedimentations of the first and the second scores of millions. This would be the death of American food as we know it.

Since we are still in the midst of this transformation, it is not yet normalized into a paradigm. Yet the breaking of the established American mould would also allow the food of the ultimate racial other – Blacks – to be reinvented as Soul food (first mentioned by the *New York Times* on September 18, 1966). The ferment at the bottom would finally bubble up to the top to inflect American cuisine and destroy the established templates – Continental and French. Difference would be democratized. In the process we would find ourselves in the midst of a reconfiguration of the culinary canon (as was shown in the last section) and Italian-Americans – ethnic but white – would play a crucial role in our re-imaginings. In the process we would also find the courage to invent an American cuisine aided by the media, especially television this time around (see Ray 2007).

The importance of the Civil Rights Movement, which taught us both toleration and the pleasures of cultural miscegenation, cannot be underestimated in the transformation of American tastes. That movement is the single most important reason why we see so many Asian and Latino migrants in the United States today, and can taste versions of their food in fine-dining restaurants. These newer immigrant groups have become the source of substantial innovation in American cuisine, from mojitos, tacos, wraps, and salsas, to wantons, wasabi and beyond. The Civil Rights Movement provided the cultural and legal opening, while Italians and Jews provided the institutional opening in terms of restaurants and their clientele.

The demand for a new restaurant cuisine at the end of the twentieth century was met by a supply of entrepreneurs and workers from the segmented labor market that was patterned around ethnicity. For a long time, expensive American restaurants were run by French or German chefs partly because of the reputation of French and especially of "Continental" cuisine. Neither of these groups could supply enough chefs to satiate the feeding frenzy of the last quarter of the twentieth century. As the French and German economies had recovered from the Second World War, the pool of emigrants had dried up. New immigrants, old ethnics and white Americans poured into this opening, often trained in mushrooming cooking schools run by German transplants (the Culinary Institute of America) and French expatriates (The French Culinary Institute). The United States had a large supply of down-scale ethnic talent that could be quickly up-scaled.

One group of ethnics was particularly well-positioned to take advantage of this opening – Italian-Americans. Italian food was slowly rediscovered in America by way of northern Italy, which followed Milan's and Florence's style-setting standard in the world of *haute couture*, and was aided by the upward mobility of Italian-Americans and the gustemic proximity of Italy to southern France. What had been repressed by the downward mobility of southern Italian migrants was reclaimed in the name of the opulent city-states of fifteenth-century northern Italy, who after all had given Europe its first fashionable cuisine (Braudel 1981: 188). The resurgent reputation of Italian food was only one-half of the equation. There had to be a supply of chefs. And not everybody was willing to be a chef, not yet.

For instance, early in the twentieth century upwardly mobile American Jews left behind the delicatessens and hot-dog stands they had run in the nineteenth century. With higher rates of literacy than other immigrant groups, second- and third-generation American Jews quickly moved into City College and out of the delis (Steinberg 1989). They got into the retail trades of healing, teaching and litigation, which were now closed, college-certified professions. As professionals, particularly in trend-setting eastern cities such as New York, the Jewish cohort moved quickly from being suppliers of ethnic food in delis and hot-dog stands to consumers of the cuisine of others, such as the Italians and Chinese. Italians, on the other hand, burdened as they were with much lower rates of literacy, and with a rural background, continued to be the producers of some of the best American food and wine.

Gabaccia (1998), Hasia Diner (2001) and Joel Denker (2003) show quite convincingly that there would be no renaissance of American cuisine without transplanted regional Italian foods in American restaurants and Italian suppliers of California wine and local herbs and produce. Denker (2003: 62–3) demonstrates that Italian-owned pizzerias in Connecticut were replaced, after the retirement of their owners, by full service restaurants run by their children and by Greek-owned diners. In turn, he notes, the Greek owners may now be replaced by more recent immigrants from the Third World. Gabaccia (1998) provides exquisite details of ethnic entrepreneurship in the late nineteenth and early twentieth centuries. She talks about German brewers, Italian restaurateurs, Chinese immigrant cooks and Greek street-vendors, one after the other, but rarely does she thread them together over time, and theorize about who replaced whom, and why. Nevertheless, ethnic succession slips through the cracks, when she notes "Around 1900 Greeks took over the manufacture and sale of candy and sodas from German and French confectioners" (1998: 105) and how "Germans had opened the first delicatessens in New York," which subsequently came to be identified as Jewish food around the time "Lillian and Louis Zabar founded their delicatessen in Brooklyn in 1934" (1998: 108). She lets go of her historian's caution only when she talks about the Charleston market, where new immigrants challenged German and Irish dominance in the grocery and liquor trades after 1880: while the first Greek opened a restaurant in Charleston around 1900, by "1910 Greeks ran 17, and Italians 5, of Charleston's 60 restaurants" (1998: 114–15). Here we get the first clear measure of ethnic succession in her work.

For much of the twentieth century the restaurant world appeared to prefer French chefs and Italian *maîtres d'hôtel*, often working for Italian owners made invisible by the French names of their restaurants – a tradition that would slip into the twenty-first century with Sirio Maccioni's Le Cirque. Richard Duffy, in a 1909 article commenting on the New York City dining scene, had noted, "In the old days ... the restaurants cherished by gourmets were nearly all owned by Italians." But he hastened to add that "If an Italian wishes to make a fortune as a restaurateur, he gives his place a French name and models his menu after those to which Paris devotes so much talent..." (Duffy 1909: 567). That is analogous to Chinese ownership of sushi establishments today and Bangladeshi proprietorship of Indian eateries. The clientele could not figure out the difference, and the prestige of French, Japanese and Indian food was higher, mostly for non-culinary reasons. Yet it was much more expensive to hire a French, Japanese or Indian chef because of the demographic profile of immigrants from those nations. In contrast, a poorer, working-class migration from Italy, China and Bangladesh fed the supply side of the labor market equation for these establishments.

The sociology of ethnic entrepreneurship reveals the dynamic of ethnic succession. There are four parts to the theory (Granovetter 1995; Landa 1981; Light 1972; Portes 1995; Sassen 1995). First, a low capital cost makes it relatively easier for ethnic entrepreneurs to enter into the business of feeding others. Cultural capital – knowledge about unfamiliar foods – gives them a competitive edge over better-capitalized mainstream entrepreneurs in this niche market. Social capital – kin or fictive kin networks of loyalty that allow the borrowing of money on a rotating basis without collateral – enables ethnic entrepreneurs to raise the necessary cash for a small eatery without the normally required assets. Self-exploitation – long hours of work and the unpaid labor of kin and fictive kin – permits these enterprises to compete with better- capitalized businesses. Self-exploitation turns sweat and loyalty into capital. Finally and most importantly for our purposes, both migration and entrepreneurship exhibit serial patterns. That is, people who know each other, and come from the same regions, work in, and own similar enterprises, built with money and expertise borrowed from co-ethnics. They effectively develop an informal, intra-ethnic consulting and banking system. A paucity of assets to collateralize loans and unfamiliarity with the language and norms of a consumer society deepens the dependence on co-ethnic money, information and expertise.

Yet many ethnic eateries are unsuccessful in remaining in business for long because they are under-capitalized and cannot weather the inevitable fluctuations of the market, and they often run out of luck in their fragile wager on endless over-work and perpetual good health. Those who succeed send their children to college; and these on completion are unwilling to accumulate sweat capital because of their better credentials. If they stay in business it is because they have better connections, English-language capabilities, and assets to trade in, creating a more upscale business where returns are greater. A typical route is from the successful pizzeria or diner to a white-tablecloth restaurant. The Greek cohort is going through that upgrading right now.

The above of course is a broad prototype of an explanation. The theory of ethnic succession will never reveal why particular groups end up in particular niches in the first place. It can only explain why niches appear and why segmentation persists. To understand how the first Greek-Americans ended up in the diner business we need biographies and ethnographies that we do not yet have (with the exception of Manzo and Denker).

Reprise

I have argued a handful of points in this chapter. First, the recent efflorescence of fine-dining restaurants in the United States is not the first time we have seen such a surge. We need to enlarge our temporal horizon to include the First Wave between the Civil War and Prohibition. Only when we look back over the long run do we find interesting patterns. Second, I have sought to enumerate the changes in American cuisine, specifically the rise of Italian-American food, by counting what can be counted. Third, changing sources of migration have both changed the supply of cooks and transformed our palates, but in unpredictable directions. I have identified a pattern of ethnic succession in food work and in taste. I have also noted that too much or too little upward mobility is bad for leaving a mark on American fine dining. I hypothesize that large-scale migration from any source is inversely related to the number of fine-dining ethnic restaurants native to that group at the temporal peak of the group's in-migration, although the same group tends to predominate in the restaurant labor-force at the same time.

Fourth, to begin to understand the changing resonances of ethnicity and race and hence ethnic food one has to understand these classification systems – race and ethnicity – as discursive fields, where for instance the Irish did not change their color; but they did become white in the course of the Civil War (Ignatiev 1995), and hence never developed a gustatory identity distinct from the normative white culture (cf. Diner 2001; see Ray 2004: 101–14). Whereas Jews, once considered a different race because of their religious identity, are in the process of becoming white folks (Brodkin 1998) and hence are losing their capacity to retain their culinary identity as a mark of difference, and whereas Italians continue to bring a different kind of whiteness to bear on their food, which has as much to do with class as race. The demographic weight of the Italian-American community, the end of Italian migration, and the medial nature of Italian migrants, as white but not quite, plays well in the current contours of the American fine-dining market, as it undergoes gustemic slippage away from its historic Francophilia, driven by incremental distinctions in the fashion cycle.

Finally, a methodological comment. I began by pointing to a weakness in Joseph Manzo's work on Greek diners on the American landscape. To the question why there are so many Greeks in the diner business he responds that food and commensality are important to Greeks. His answer is internalist and culturalist because he only studies the Greeks in America. The study of any ethnic group over-represented in the food business leads to the same point. If we listen to the Japanese owners, Korean restaurant-keepers, Thai entrepreneurs, and Bangladeshi restaurant owners in New York they say the same thing – we are in the food business because food is important to us (Kishimoto 2006; Ongwat 2006). That is the limit of the ethnographic method in the food business at that level of generality. To get beyond that answer (and in general beyond ethnic sentimentalism) we have to study more than one ethnic group, and compare their demographic profiles over time. We need multi-ethnic studies that compare labor-force participation profiles over time to get past the internalist and culturalist dead-end. Culture is important, but only as something nested within a comparative, demographic analysis, which is often invisible to insiders.

Notes

1. Critical comments by David Beriss and David Sutton helped me sharpen the focus of this chapter. Thanks to Sierra L. Burnett for downloading the data on ethnicity and occupation from IPUMS and organizing it in a manageable format for this project.

2. This list of restaurants is based on: (a) a census of restaurants mentioned in the secondary literature – Batterberry and Batterberry (1973), Cummings (1970), Root and de Rochemont (1976), Hess and Hess (1977), Levenstein (1988, 1989, 1994, 2003a,b), Reardon (1994), Kuh (2001), Brenner (1999), Dornenburg and Page (2003), and Andrew Smith (2005); (b) verification and addition to the list through interviews with 102 chefs at *The Culinary Institute of America* in the Fall of 2004; and (c) a perusal of current newspaper and magazine articles. I am working towards validating and amending the list by a statistical analysis of the number of times these restaurants are mentioned in newspapers such as the *New York Times* (1852–2003), the *Los Angeles Times* (1891–1985) and the *Chicago Tribune* (1891–1985). The list is a work in progress, but the patterning is too dramatic to miss.

3. This claim must be taken with a pinch of salt, because Brenner is here quoting Michael Whiteman, who was the partner at *Restaurant Associates* of Joseph Baum, who owned *Four Seasons*.

–8–

From Khatchapuri to Gefilte Fish

Dining Out and Spectacle in Russian Jewish New York

Eve Jochnowitz

Everything happens in restaurants. We meet, we consume, we celebrate or commiserate, we feel utterly alive, and yet the ever-present posters instructing us on the Heimlich maneuver are a constant *memento mori*. Many of our most intense experiences occur in restaurants. In a famous scene in Rob Reiner's 1990 film "When Harry Met Sally" the Sally character played by Meg Ryan visits a Jewish restaurant and has an orgasm. Within the narrative context of the movie, Sally is faking an orgasm for reasons necessary to the plot. I have argued that in fact Sally's reaction to the multisensory and polysemic environment of a Jewish restaurant could not be more real (Jochnowitz 2000: 222). This chapter will address the performances in the restaurants of Russophonic Jewish communities of New York.

The Russian-Jewish communities of New York had little or no contact with one another in the former Soviet Union. Since settling in the United States, however, they have become united by the Russian language, Russian-language radio, television and newspapers, and their new identity as Russian-speaking immigrants. They are united as well by geographic proximity, and shared civic and political concerns. Restaurants are important places of contact and conversation within the new communities – what Shalom Staub calls "esoteric interaction," or interactions among members of one community (Staub 1989). Staub distinguishes these interactions from "exoteric" interactions between members of one community and outsiders. For the purposes of this study, I have found that a liminal category of *mesoteric* interactions between these two exists, when members of two or more Russophonic communities interact with each other. Russophonic immigrants in New York were unaware of one another's cuisines in the old country, but they have begun to sample the cuisines of other Russophonic Jews with great interest. This is one of the ways they have become, in the words of Fran Markowitz, "A community in spite of itself" (Markowitz 1993).

Jewish immigrants to the Americas from the former Soviet Union come from four distinct language and culture areas, each with its own specific cuisine. Ashkenazic Jews from Ukraine, Romania, Moldova, Lithuania, and parts of Russia itself come from a Yiddish-speaking tradition. Bukharan Jews from Uzbekistan and Tajikistan have a Judeo-Persian language they call Farsi.[1] Jews from in and around the republic of Georgia have a Judeo-Georgian language. The Kavkasi Jews from Azerbaijan call themselves "Gorski Evrei" or "Mountain Jews." Their language, an Indo-European language from the Iranian family, is called Dzhuhuri.

The interest and culinary curiosity in among the Russophonic communities is by no means symmetrical. By all accounts, all of the communities have developed an interest in Georgian cooking, which is itself widely recognized to be one of the world's great cuisines, but few outside the Ashkenazic community have expressed much interest in Ashkenazic cooking, not because it is not a great cuisine in its own right, but because the Ashkenazic community does not have as developed a tradition of restauration. The Bukharan community, which has an established restaurant tradition, attracts visitors from within and without the Russophonic Jewish community. Russian restaurants, especially the many that feature live music and dancing, have come to be favorite destinations of non-Russophone visitors. The restaurants then become sites of exoteric interactions.

At the same time, Russophonic immigrants are of course not indifferent to the many flavors of New York's culinary landscape. The younger immigrants are especially interested in the trans-ethnic grazing that characterizes the foodways of New Yorkers. One young Jewish Russophone beautifully captures the paradoxical relationships between food, restaurants, identities and the culinary landscape of New York:

> I would definitely identify myself as an American New Yorker. So within that, it's like being able to eat in every restaurant, every kind of food that is available to you and communicates so much about culture. I think that speaks for itself volumes. I can have incredible Ethiopian food for lunch and then have a wonderful Korean dinner. And *that's what being an American is.* With all the liberties to express how you feel about that, as you wish. (quoted in Kasinitz *et al.*, 2001: 51; emphasis added)

Great and Little Theaters

Ethnographers, for many years, made the distinction between "great traditions" and "little traditions" to contrast the formal literary traditions of an elite group with the more informal or oral traditions that exist within the same culture, sometimes within the same homes. Following this somewhat problematic distinction, I divide the culinary venues of any cuisine into great theaters and little theaters. Restaurants, groceries and nightclubs are what I call "great theaters" of culinary performance, to distinguish them from the "little theaters" of the home kitchen and table.

Richard Schechner understands the "single-behaved-behaviors of ordinary living" as being made into the "twice behaved behavior of art" (Schechner 1985: 52). I would add that a behavior becomes twice-behaved when it moves from the little theater of ordinary living to the great theater of art. Since producing a cuisine in the immigrant's context is twice-behaved behavior to begin with, the subsequent reproduction of this cuisine within the theatrical context of a restaurant is thrice-behaved behavior.

"Great Performances" was a public television showcase for symphonic, operatic, and balletic productions. The series could not have been more aptly named. The television producers meant to indicate that the performances transmitted were great in their size, in their quality, and in their role as part of a great tradition. A little performance, on the other hand, is one that is small in scale, not part of a tradition of "high art," but connected rather to everyday life. Watching "Great Performances" on television, for instance, is in many ways a little performance. I will focus on those twice-performed behaviors that are parts of little traditions, but that are also symbolic of something larger in people's lives. The great and little activities I will discuss are great and little in different ways. Restaurants are great theaters, but the culinary aspect of Jewish cuisine is part of a little tradition. *Kashruth*, whether honored in observance or in the breach, is a great tradition. Examining an individual egg for minuscule blood spots is a small performance, but part of a great tradition.

Great theaters in general and restaurants in particular have been fertile fields of enterprise for new Jewish immigrants from the former Soviet Union, as they have proved for many New York immigrant groups in the past. Many new restaurateurs had other professions in their native countries. For immigrants facing a language and cultural barrier, opening a small business is easier and more practical than negotiating the labyrinthine bureaucracy needed to practice their own professions (Hong 1999: 298–9). Raising the necessary capital and running a restaurant are by no means easy, but being independent offers fewer obstacles than attempting to become licensed in one's own field.

Restaurants are the theaters in which a community performs all the values it cherishes most. Whether they are choosing to honor or flout *kashruth*, to display awesome skill and virtuosity, or simply a scrupulous attention to wholesomeness and cleanliness, a skillful staff and proprietor can design the patrons' experience so that from the moment they walk in the door all their senses receive signals that reinforce the message. As Barbara Kirshenblatt-Gimblett has noted, restaurants are prime sites of designed experiences, collaboratively produced (Kirshenblatt-Gimblett 2004: xii).

Great Theaters: Jewish Dietary Laws

Great theaters in the Jewish context differ from little theaters as well in the public performance of the observance of or indifference to *kashruth*, the Jewish dietary laws. In the context of a private home where the cook observes *kashruth*, her (or his, but usually her) level of observance is not subject to outside inspection. Her family, including her husband, who might well exceed her in halakhic expertise, relies on her practical expertise in keeping the kitchen kosher. Within traditional societies, a

Jewish cook bases her decisions in keeping her home kosher on a mimetic tradition, one that she is most likely to have learned from her mother or other senior female relatives or affines (Soloveitchik 1994). No rabbi or *mashgiakh* certifies her work. Within her private domain, she is the *posek akharon*, the court of the last resort. Complications arise because privately prepared food enters the public realm as a matter of course. Friends and relatives visit one another for meals or bring along gifts of food. They are able to accept privately prepared food because they know that the people who prepared it hold to standards of *kashruth* compatible with their own. Privately prepared food crosses over into commerce as well. Beatrice Weinreich quotes a Jew who recalls that his mother prepared at home the rendered goose fat that the entire municipality used for Passover because all knew that her level of observance was unimpeachable (Weinreich 1960). The same kind of understanding could certainly extend to restaurants as well. In fact, in the non-Ashkenazic Russophonic communities, many restaurants are traditionally kosher by consensus. In such a situation, the clientele knows the proprietor and knows that he or she (almost always he) adheres to a strict standard of *kashruth*, and they do not need independent rabbinical supervision to confirm this. One member of the Bukharan community helpfully explains: "You know the difference between kosher and *glatt kosher*? With *glatt kosher*, Rabbi is always *sitting* there." The distinction he is describing is the one that the non-Russian community would call the difference between kosher by consensus and kosher by supervision. His stress on the word "sitting" shows that the added value of rabbinic supervision is not as crucial in the context of a small community. The system that works for this kind of small community, or the town recalled by Weinreich's informant, is not considered acceptable within the Rabbinate-driven universe that is American kosher supervision, where a restaurant which has no rabbinic supervision is simply not kosher. In fact many Russophone restaurateurs in America whose restaurants are kosher have chosen to work with rabbinic supervision both for the sake of exoteric interaction with non-Russophone guests and because they desire to be a part of the larger American Jewish community.

Other Jewish restaurateurs choose not to present themselves as kosher, either because they want the freedom to serve non-kosher foods, or to serve diary products as well as meat, or because of disdain and distrust for the infrastructure of American kosher enterprise. As one such restaurateur explained, "Believe me, if I gave a rabbi two thousand dollars, this place would be kosher so fast you wouldn't believe it." His point is that he views rabbinic approval as having more to do with a restaurateur's willingness to participate in and support the system than with the actual condition in the kitchen. He is also referring to the conflict of interest, troubling to many, caused by a system in which the certifiers are paid by the certified. It is for this reason that new rabbinic organizations have begun in the last fifteen years to seek independent funding so that they may inspect restaurants without accepting payment from them, or for greatly reduced fees.

Ambivalence about the American *kashruth* practices is a hurdle in exoteric interactions with non-Russophone Jews. This comes as a painful surprise to many who were identified as Jewish in the Former Soviet Union because of their foodways. They can be said to have come from a place where they weren't considered Russian enough because they were too Jewish to a place where they aren't considered Jewish enough because they are too Russian.[2]

Culinary Tourism: Introduction

Exploratory eating is the folklorist Lucy Long's term for the intentional consumption of foodways that may be separated from the consumer by time, space, religion and class. "We may not like the food at all," Long notes, "but we can have fun trying it" (Long 1998: 218). Culinary tourism is an exploratory relationship with the edible world (Kirshenblatt-Gimblett 2004: xi). Foods, music and venues familiar to one group are exotic to visitors. Culinary tourists "discover" the exotic world of a new cuisine, whether they do so by traveling to new culinary landscapes or by bringing the exotic into their own kitchens in new ingredients and recipes. The varied cuisines of the former Soviet Union are a magnet to both local and out-of-town tourists as well as to Russophones who have begun to sample one another's cuisines with varying degrees of interest.

Culinary Tourism: Travel through Space and Time

Most frequently, when we think of tourism, we are thinking of travel through space, or in the case of immigrant and ethnic cuisine, foodways coming to us from another place. In the Jewish context, culinary tourism is frequently about travel through time. The rabbi leading a tour of a present-day matzo bakery in Crown Heights, Brooklyn, invites visitors to "step into the eighteenth century" as he guides them into the building, and then leads the visitors even further back in time as he says "Inside these doors we make the matzoh exactly as it has been made for thousands of years. This is the real thing" (Rosa 1997: 11). The message could not be more explicit: what is old is real. We will see below that Hasidim in particular are asked to represent the past even when they do not explicitly choose to do so themselves. Jewish eating establishments along Szeroka Street in the Kazimierz neighborhood of Krakow provide food and entertainment, but they also seek to provide tourists with a taste of Poland's Jewish past (Jochnowitz 2004). The restaurant *Pod Golema* ("The Golem's Place") in Prague reminds visitors of the legend of the Maharal of Prague, Rabbi Judah Loew (1520–1609), although there is nothing in the rabbi's legend to indicate that the Golem would have operated a restaurant. It is the Golem's association with Prague's Jewish history and popular imagination that add value to a restaurant as a tourist attraction. Similarly, Jewish eating establishments in the New World trade on real or imagined oldness for the amusement or interest of their customers. Katz's delicatessen in New York deliberately maintains its original décor and fills its front window with dusty and yellowed press clippings about the restaurant and letters from satisfied customers, including one dated 1967 from Vietnam (Jochnowitz 2000).

Nor is culinary time-travel tourism exclusively tourism to the past. The New York World's Fair of 1939–40 employed food-related exhibits to invite fairgoers to view "The World of Tomorrow," a clean, safe future where foods would be better because they would be purer, safer, and untouched by human hands. Industrial exhibitors offered a look "behind the scenes" at their on-site factories, where fairgoers could see the speed and efficiency that technology would bring to food production. The Jewish Palestine Pavilion featured "Café Tel-Aviv," a restaurant that offered a glimpse of a Jewish future in a national homeland (Jochnowitz 1999).

Culinary Tourism: Exoticism and Palatability

To function properly as a tourist attraction, food needs to fall sufficiently outside of the familiar to be exotic, but sufficiently inside the circle of what is palatable (Jochnowitz 2004: 104). Eating unfamiliar foods can be both recreational (an adventure) and an assertion of one's own sophistication as well (Hong 1999: 41). Paul Fussell attacks as a "tourist of the grossest kind" a traveler who wrote a letter to the editor of the *New York Times* travel section asking for advice on how to avoid Chinese food while visiting Hong Kong (Fussell 1988: 151). Fussell privileges the most elastic palate. His point was that the traveler should have taken an interest in trying the food of the place he would visit. The traveler's fear of trying new foods stands here as well for a reluctance in a larger sense to open one's mind as well as one's mouth to new ideas and experiences.

The play between what is unfamiliar enough to be titillating and familiar enough to be palatable is analogous to the play noted by Barbara Kirshenblatt-Gimblett between what is worthy of viewing (and therefore worthy of display) and what has visual interest (Kirshenblatt-Gimblett 1998: 17). Kirshenblatt-Gimblett makes the point that certain items are displayable even while they are of little visual interest, implying that there is a scale of increasing visual interest. Kirshenblatt-Gimblett begins with a discussion of the display of dried meat at the Minnesota Historical Society. The reason that the dried meat is displayable is that it was preserved before 1918 by Hidatsa women in Minnesota. The meat's value lies in its authenticity, not in its visual interest.[3] Following Kirshenblatt-Gimblett, I can imagine a division of all displayable objects into categories that could be laid out in a four-quadrant graph, where one axis runs from least visually interesting to most visually interesting, and the other runs from least compelling in content to most (Table 8.1).

Table 8.1 Attributes of Displayed Foods

Authentic but not visually interesting			Authentic and visually interesting
Increasing authenticity ↑	Dried meat, dust from Jerusalem, etc.	Works of art	
	Perhaps a reproduction of a piece of dried meat or some dust?	Copies of works of art	
Authenticity ↑ **Interest** →	*Increasing visual interest* →		**Visually interesting but not authentic**

Lucy Long similarly offers a four-quadrant system for understanding culinary tourism that divides foods along the lines of familiar to exotic and palatable to unpalatable (Table 8.2).

A third axis, extending out of the page, could represent the authenticity of familiar or exotic food.

Both culinary tourists seeking to mitigate the challenges of unfamiliar foodways and immigrants seeking to recreate the familiar in a new environment will frequently hybridize, using familiar cooking techniques on new ingredients, or introducing their own ingredients to newly adopted recipes.

Hybridization is crucial, but it is also crucial to note that a hybrid does not necessarily fall somewhere between the two parent cuisines (Lockwood and Lockwood 2000: 515). I cannot draw a straight line with Russian or Jewish or

Table 8.2 Attributes of Displayed Foods

Exotic and unpalatable			Exotic and palatable
Increasing exoticism ↑	Depending on the visitor, possibly: meat of dogs, reptiles, insects; spoiled or unsanitary foods	Depending on the visitor, interestingly spiced and decorated dishes, unfamiliar flavors	
	"fast food," "junk food," processed foods, badly prepared or spoiled foods	"home cooking," "comfort food," brownies, pasta, apple pie	
Exoticism ↑ **Palatability** →	*Increasing palatability* →		**Familiar and palatable**

Russian Jewish foodways at one end and American foodways on the other and then point to some spot in the middle and say that Russian Jewish food practices in New York can be predicted or anticipated to fall there. Timothy Lloyd studied a case hybridization in immigrant cuisines in which a traditional Greek meat sauce with some resemblance to Southwestern chili con carne has become a component of a dish associated not with Greece or Texas, but Cincinnati, Ohio (Lloyd 1981). Similarly, Russian sushi, such as smoked salmon sushi with cream cheese, is a delicacy equally unknown in Russia and Japan. Krishnendu Ray shows ways in which cuisines of the Old World and the New converge in the course of a day (Ray 1998). Ray has observed that among Bengali Americans, breakfasts are frequently more Western, while the evening meal is more likely to be traditional. I have found that in Russian restaurants in New York, frequently the main course is Russian, but dessert is Western.

Cuisines begin as systems of classification, which necessarily involves classifying some items as not-food. Stephen Mennel notes that no human social group is believed to have eaten everything of potential nutritional value available to it (Mennell 1996: 3). To speak of these classifications, which include historic, symbolic and cultural content, as food "avoidances" does not address the question, or does so only partly, because in order to be "avoided" a food must first be classified as a food within one's culinary system.

Culinary Tourism: Problems of Region

In exoteric interactions, eating establishments emphasize pan-Russian or Russophonic identity rather than regional identity. Arbat is the name of a major street in Moscow; Rasputin, a figure from Russian history. The National could be named for this nation or the one left behind, but all of one or the other. Best Pearl Café and many others have generic names. Restaurant Rafael, Gan Eden, and The Kosher Restaurant refer to Jewish identity in their names, but not to their geographic origins. Mels Palace Glatt Kosher Restaurant is not a restaurant that belongs to a man named Mel, as an non-Russophone might assume, but takes its name rather from the initial letters of the names of Marx, Engels, Lenin, and Stalin. The acronym, familiar in the former Soviet Union, was a name sometimes given to boys born in the 1950s, and is used ironically in the new world. Shalom Staub observes that Yemeni restaurateurs give their New York restaurants generic Middle Eastern or pan-Arab names, or frequently use "Morocco" or "Moroccan," a name that does refer to a specific region, but not one that has anything to do with the restaurant (Staub 1989: 157).

Just as travelers will find New York iconography is thicker on the ground in eating establishments the farther from New York one travels (Jochnowitz 2000: 218), culinary tourists will observe that ethnic restaurateurs signify place differently for different audiences. Different national groups often make the same culinary accommodations (Lockwood and Lockwood 2000). A Georgian restaurateur explains patiently that the Georgians were creating civilization while the Russians were still living in trees. His restaurant has a generic name, and he presents himself and his cuisine to tourists as Russian. For the purposes of exoteric interactions, employers and workers in ethnic restaurants produce and reproduce selected images and stereotypes of their own ethnicity (Hong 1999: 104).

Restaurant patrons are seeking a nourishing meal and to participate in an exotic experience. They are concerned with the quality of the food and the price. Musical elements and décor, and the presentation of one's own culture as exotic are elements that satisfy customers as consumers and travelers.

It is worthwhile to examine a number of case studies of New York venues of Russian-Jewish restauration. I have selected the restaurants in this study to represent Russophonic New York's geographic diversity by profiling eating establishments from the city's far-flung Russophonic enclaves and business districts, and to represent the culinary diversity of the Jewish communities of the former Soviet Union by including establishments that prepare Ashkenazic, Georgian, Bukharan, Mountain Jewish and Great Russian cuisines. I have also selected establishments to show a range of types of restauration, including inexpensive and informal lunch spots as well as grander venues.

The Past is a Foreign Country: Performing Russia's History as a Restaurant

A notable number of New York's Russophonic eating establishments provide a fantasy of Russia's history along with the main course.

"The Fulfillment of a Collective Dream": Primorski

The most famous restaurant on Brighton Beach Avenue is Primorski. By day one can take advantage of the $3.99 lunch special. In the evening a night of food, dancing and vodka can easily exceed one hundred dollars per person. Primorski is an omnibus restaurant. While the highlights of the menu are the Georgian specialties such as *Khatchapuri*, flaky pastry filled with cheese, spinach and cheese, or red beans scented with cloves, *Loubia*, a soup made of red beans, garlic and walnuts, *khinkali* (dumplings), and Georgian mineral water, Primorski is a venue for other cuisines as well. Gestures are made on the one hand toward a kind of pan-Jewish cuisine with the inclusion of gefilte fish, pickled herring, and Israeli salad, and on the other to an imperial pan-Russian cuisine with caviar and blini.

Buba Khotoveli opened Primorski in 1981. It is now one of the city's oldest Russian restaurants, and has come to be recognized as one of the best. Primorski is a privileged site in the mythology of Russian Jewish New York. The novelist and gonzo-journalist Gary Shteyngart's comments in *Gourmet* magazine this year are typical of the newest and youngest Russian immigrants' views of their seniors in age and residence:

> Gluttony on this scale disturbs the American mind, but suffice it to say that many of the patrons, indeed most Russian immigrants, have led difficult, anxious lives from which they seek a maximalist form of relief. For some, only a 20-course meal followed by a dozen bottles of vodka and a Barry Manilow classic played at an earth-shattering pitch on a keyboard synthesizer will do. We Russians came from a land where good food and indulgent service were scarce, where public activities were staged and contrived. The Primorski, with its swell grub and easy gaiety, is in many ways the fulfillment of a collective dream. (Shteyngart 2004: 170)

Empire of Color: Firebird Café

The Firebird Cafe in the theater district offers Royal Russian cuisine and a fantasy of pre-revolutionary Russian aristocracy in the style of the late Russian Tea Room. The restaurant is large, but maintains a feeling of intimacy and devoted individual attention by serving food in several small dining-rooms, each of them lavishly decorated with Russian antiques in a different color and style. Diners frequently choose to take a "tour" of the restaurant's museum-like rooms and, if the restaurant is not fully booked, to choose the room that most appeals to them. The restaurant's specialties are richly elaborated versions of Russian dishes somewhat toned down to suit Western tastes, such as *Utka s-Fruktami* (roast duck). Caviar, blini, sturgeon, and vodkas dominate the menu, which does not make any explicit reference to Jewish cuisine. Extravagant desserts can be accompanied by a glass of Russian tea in a silver *zarf* sweetened with cherry jam. Visitors report that they are impressed with the "awesome décor," but alarmed by the prices.

The salons of the Tsarist Empire on which the designers of Firebird base the fantasy were entirely closed to Jews. Jews were not permitted to travel within Russia itself, which was beyond the Pale of Settlement during the era of the Russian Empire. While this law was regularly bent in many Russian cities, the city of St Petersburg itself, the jewel in Russia's crown, was strictly forbidden to Jewish travelers. Why then, would Jewish restaurateurs choose to celebrate the foods and images of this regime? In a way, Jewish fascination with St Petersburg goes back to the Tsarist era. In the stories of Sholem-Aleichem, Petersburg, or "Ehupets" as it is nicknamed, is an eponym for everything that is distant and unattainable.[4] In the post-Soviet era, Jews have co-opted the imagery of Imperial Russia to such an extent that it has become a Jewish signifier in itself.

Concealed and Revealed: The Jewish Restaurants of West 47th Street

The Kosher Restaurant

> Gratification from contact with the wider world is not usually derived only through interaction with its representatives, but more often by simple co-presence and people-watching. (Duneier 1992: 103)

Manhattan's diamond district covers West 47th Street between Fifth and Seventh Avenues. No signage marks the exterior of an office building on West 47th street to indicate that one of the city's best restaurants of any kind is upstairs. No sign displays the restaurant's name, and indeed, the restaurant does not seem to have a name. People who know about it call it "The Kosher Restaurant."[5] An otherwise unmarked door at the top of the third flight of stairs bears a small sign with the words "Kosher Restaurant." The small but sunny space has eight tables. A hand-washing station and laminated copies of the grace after meals indicate that the restaurant accommodates strictly observant clients; but many of the men (and the clientele here is overwhelmingly male) are sitting with uncovered heads, indicating that the guests follow a diverse range of practices. Almost all the clients are diamond merchants taking their lunch breaks, and sometimes a large group will reserve a table for a big meeting. Sometimes non-Russophonic, non-Bukharan and even non-Jewish colleagues attend; but the spot is not visited by tourists, and does not engage in tourist productions, such as having an exotic-sounding name for instance, or any name at all.

The space is pleasant, but it is discernible that one is in an office building. The white lace tablecloths are covered with plastic. The dishware is colorfully painted china. The short menu is in English and Russian, and it features salads, soups and meat dishes. Freshly baked hot flatbread, also called "Turkish bread," appears on the table. The menu is overwhelmingly dominated by meat, but also offers assorted salads, including *babaganoush* made with mayonnaise instead of sesame, fish kebabs, and *shorba*, a broth with vegetables, chickpeas, and *cilantro*, which can be ordered with or without lamb.

In the course of this study, the Kosher Restaurant has changed somewhat to become more tourist-friendly as word about the restaurant has spread. An all-English menu provides pictures of the dishes offered to guide guests unfamiliar with the cuisine, and the chef has added *kasha* and Israeli salad to the menu, but in essence the restaurant is unchanged. Guests linger over generous dishes of *plov* and kebabs and enjoy the parade of a myriad of types of visitors. Almost all say it is the quality of the food that draws them back.

Diamond Dairy

Many Russophones who work in the diamond district will occasionally choose to dine at Diamond Dairy, a few hundred feet down 47th Street from the Kosher Restaurant at 6 West 47th Street. The Diamond Dairy's proprietors are not Russophone, but the 400 or so square feet that make up this tiny diner-style coffee shop may be the most densely multilingual real estate in the city. In addition to Russian and English diners will hear Hungarian, Yiddish, Hebrew and Spanish ("*There* you are! I was looking for you in Hong Kong," shouts a Hebrew speaker to a Russian speaker, in English). The restaurant is a time machine. The faded pink linoleum floor and pink and blue wall tiles, the typeface on the menu, and most notably, the menu itself all speak to the era of the restaurant's beginnings nearly sixty years ago. The menu offers noodles and cheese, cabbage with *varnishkes* (bow-tie noodles), and *shlishkelekh* (gnocchi-like dough lumps served with butter and toasted breadcrumbs), dishes that have fallen out of the kosher *milkhik* canon, even as blintzes and *pierogi* remain relatively well known in Jewish and eastern European restaurants. The menu also offers a section of "Chinese specialties" such as Chow Mein, a vestige of an earlier era of kosher restauration.

Even more remarkable than the menu is the venue. To find the restaurant, one must enter the Jewelry Exchange, walk through several rows of retailers' booths, and climb one flight of stairs. The mezzanine is not accessible by elevator. The proprietor, seated at the register at the top of the stairs, apologizes and says he has been trying to buy the building and bring it up to code. In the Kosher Restaurant, the warm and homey décor partly disguises the fact that the restaurant is in an office building. The Diamond Dairy makes no such attempt. On the contrary, the restaurant is a fishbowl right in the Jewelry Exchange itself. Diners may observe the hustle and bustle of the floor below as they sip their soup or slurp their *shlishkelekh*, or, they may choose to sit at the counter, turning their backs on this concourse.

Like the Kosher Restaurant, the Diamond Dairy is invisible from the street and makes no attempt to attract walk-in traffic. It is an old place that looks old, but *de facto* rather than by design. Unlike Katz's, where a patina of age is part of the carefully produced image, the Diamond Dairy has not achieved shabbiness, but has had shabbiness thrust upon it. I have occasionally had difficulty explaining my enthusiasm for Diamond Dairy; as one correspondent protested: "That place has absolutely no class!"

For the Kosher Restaurant and Diamond Dairy, and a third restaurant on West 47th Street that closed during the course of this study, the entrances are not visible simply because they do not need to be seen in order to function. Their clientele knows where to go. It is only because of a peculiar quirk of twenty-first century restauration that the very same invisibility has become a point of pride among the city's most sought-after venues, especially in the East Village, in Williamsburg, and on the

Lower East Side. For the clients of these invisible restaurants, simply being able to find the venue is a mark of being part of an informed inside group. The people who work in New York's diamond district *are* in fact an especially informed inside group, but not one that any outsider especially wants to join. They are a stigmatized group, doubly stigmatized by their religious observance and by their profession. Oddly, restaurants that serve one of the most stigmatized groups in the city employ exactly the same practice as the restaurants that serve the most glamorous and sought-after. This practice has evolved for one group as a tactic for coping, and has been invented by the other as a strategy.

It is possible that the history of prohibition in the United States has influenced the social meaning of secrecy in dining establishments.[6] Restaurants that operated as speakeasies in the years when alcoholic beverages were prohibited (1919–32), concealed their function out of necessity; but necessity became a virtue, and dining establishments with concealed entrances became fashionable and desirable. Secrecy, in such situations, is a means of communication which is, in the words of Barbara Kirshenblatt-Gimblett, itself inherently performative (Kirshenblatt-Gimblett 1998: 256).

The Comforts of Home: Registan

Named for a province of Uzbekistan, the Registan restaurant in Rego Park, Queens, like the Kosher Restaurant in Manhattan, specializes in Bukharan cuisine. The clientele is almost entirely local and almost entirely Bukharan. The restaurant occupies two non-contiguous storefronts on 99th Street in Rego Park. Each storefront is a small, sparely decorated dining-room furnished with long folding tables. The walls and tablecloths are pale green. During the day, when there is lighter demand for tables, only the westernmost location is open. Russian-language television usually plays at high volume, giving the small storefront the feel of a neighborhood bar. In the daytime, the site is most likely to be filled with middle-aged and older men, sometimes eating, but most often sipping tea, conversing, or simply enjoying one another's company in silence. Registan serves its community by providing beloved regional foods of the old country, and also by providing a safe space for just this kind of congregation.

The menu features such *zakuski* as *Achik shchok*, a tomato onion salad, *lobia*, a dish of red beans with walnuts, pickled cabbage, tomatoes, mushrooms and cucumber, *satee*, an eggplant salad, and *morkovcha*, a garlicky salad of marinated julienne carrots. Meals are accompanied by *lepeshka*, (pronounced "lepyoshka") or nan, the crusty *bialy*-shaped white bread. Traditional mutton and beef kebab, as well as fish kebabs made with salmon or bass, and lamb testicle kebabs are popular offerings. Many of the restaurant's special main courses, including *plov*, are only served to groups of ten or more.

Many seeming contradictions pervade the atmosphere at Registan. The restaurant has kosher supervision and provides a handwashing station for observant guests, but the two television sets frequently play videos of scantily clad lovelies gyrating in the background. The china is elegantly painted and the fragrant black and green teas arrive in tea sets which are particularly beautiful examples of Bukharan pottery, but the food is served on folding tables, only partly disguised by glass tops and large tablecloths.

Performing Excess: Rasputin

The largest and best-known of the Russian nightclubs in Brooklyn is Rasputin at Avenue X and Coney Island Avenue in Sheepshead Bay, adjacent to and slightly inland from Brighton Beach, away from the bustle of Brighton Beach Avenue. "A true supper club on the grand scale," Rasputin has advertising and some narration in English, but the clientele is overwhelmingly Russophonic.

"The exterior of Rasputin conforms to the industrial sprawl along Avenue X. Only the sight of the doormen in bright red uniforms trimmed with gold braid hints at what lies within a hulking grey monolith" (Field report, November 24, 2000). The venue is enormous, with a circular dining room surrounding a spacious round dance floor. Lights are low, but not so low that it is too dark to see. Most guests have come in large parties, but there are a few tables for two as well.

The dance floor displays two elaborately decorated birthday cakes. One, "Happy Sweet sixteen, Julia," is decorated with a white Cinderella-style slipper, dark and white chocolate, and red roses. Julia's table is also decorated with orange roses and African daisies. The other, "Happy 50th, Piter," is all chocolate and has a chocolate champagne bottle and red and white roses. I cannot think of any venue outside the Russophone community where a girl of sixteen and a man of fifty would both choose to celebrate their birthdays.

Our table is already laid with a rich array of *zakuski*, or appetizers: zucchini in tomato sauce, beet salad, boiled potatoes with dill, cucumber, tomato and radish salad, assorted pickles (cucumber, cabbage, carrot, pepper, tomato), grapes, pickled mushrooms, white cheese, chicken breasts in sauce, five kinds of cold cuts, and *babaganoush à la Russe*. An ice bucket holds our bottle of Vodka Kremlyovskaya. As soon as we are seated and begin eating, the procession of hot dishes starts to arrive. Flaky cheese pastries and blini with sour cream and salmon caviar join the cold appetizers.

At 9:30, after most of the guests have been appeased with abundant appetizers and vodka, a bilingual message welcomes us to Rasputin and an electric band begins playing on a raised platform behind a scrim. A female singer dressed in a sparkly metallic dress sings in Russian and a few couples drift to the dance floor. The next singer, also a woman, sings in heavily accented English and wears a black leather camisole. The waiters bring rice and stuffed chicken breasts with dill, and a male singer in a black leather blazer and sunglasses takes the stage. A trio of women wearing camouflage-patterned uniforms sing an Andrews Sisters' song of the 1940s. A constantly changing parade of costumed singers perform songs in Russian and English, and a few in French and Spanish. Towards the end of the evening, after the floor show, a woman in a skin-tight shimmering black leotard sings Tum Balalayke in Yiddish, provoking the most enthusiastic response from the crowd all night.

At 10:30, a PA announcement warns us that we have four minutes to return to our seats for the floor show. The restaurant is plunged into total darkness. Steam fills the room as colored laser lights play across the space. The steam clears and the lights lift to reveal sixteen young women in clown-face and clown costumes dancing to a Hip-Hop number played on an accordion. The next dance is a techno piece performed by women dressed as robots in cellophane costumes. A tango number with dancers in fedoras follows, and then during a brief intermission, we see a speeded-up film of the dancers changing their costumes backstage.

In the second half, girls dressed in yellow and black matador costumes dance to a Spanish song, and a French song is danced by girls in red cobwebby suits reminiscent of the costumes of Jewish silent film vamp Alla Nazimova. The next act is danced by men in cowboy suits to a bluegrass tune with Russian words. A trio of women in costumes made of glow-in-the-dark string dance to Aretha Franklin's "You make me feel" and the show closes with another Hip-Hop number danced by women wearing neon bungee cords. After the show, credits for the singers, dancers, designers and lighting roll on an enormous video screen. These credits are in English only.

At 11:30, the main courses arrive at our table: chicken Kiev and chicken and beef kebabs on French fries. The dance floor is packed as the band continues to play and the singers continue their costume changes. At 12:30, they bring us nested coffee cups, carafes of coffee and tea, melon, berries and apple strudel with chocolate sauce. At 1:00 a.m., a voluptuous woman brings down the house with a rendering of *Tum Balalayke*. The singing and dancing continue late into the night.

The evening at Rasputin is designed to produce sensory saturation. The lavish overabundance of food and liquor is overwhelming. The broadcast flow is jarring, including as it does an anomalous mix of styles such as Bluegrass music, Hip-Hop, theater, popular and folk songs in the context of one show and in some cases within one number, as when an accordion plays lead on a Hip-Hop piece or when a gorgeous young woman sings Tum Balalayke in a provocative sexy costume.

Other than the performance of Tum Balalayke, nothing in the program explicitly signifies Jewishness, and the menu is exuberantly *treyf*, but the very weirdness of the combination of styles and genres implicitly signifies Jewishness. The privileged position that the Yiddish song occupies at the peak of the evening and the appreciative response of the audience indicate that it is more than just another element in the multilingual mix of the program.

Conclusion

The great theaters of restauration are prime sites at which Jews present themselves and their performance of Jewishness to other Jews and to non-Jews. In some cases, as in contemporary Poland, Jewish restaurants serve as stages for the performance of Jewishness by restaurateurs, many of whom are non-Jews, to an audience that may even include Jews (Jochnowitz 2004).

> The following story exemplifies this aspect of modern post-Soviet Jewish identity. In August, 2000, I visited a Jewish restaurant that had recently opened in St Petersburg. The decor included paintings of Jews wearing black hats and long dark coats; there were old Yiddish newspapers on the wall. Musicians played popular Yiddish and Israeli music. The menu was first class, full of delectable dishes composed of gourmet ingredients, but in combinations that would be considered highly unusual for a Jewish restaurant. For example, one chicken dish was called 'A la Jewish grandmother' [and] included a cream sauce (according to the Jewish tradition, dairy and meat products can not be consumed together). … The oddities did not stop there. The manager of the restaurant then told me that their 'best day' was on Yom Kippur, as floods of customers arrived late in the evening after hearing *Kol Nidrey*[7] in synagogue (when traditionally, Jews are expected to be fasting). 'Because they come here to eat on Yom Kippur', complained the manager, 'rabbis won't give us official sanction as a Kosher restaurant. We can not afford to be closed on Yom Kippur.' Therefore, fasting, one of the essential parts of the traditional observance of Yom Kippur, is omitted by many St. Petersburg Jews. They celebrate Yom Kippur because they think this is an important Jewish holiday. They know that during holidays, people normally eat a special festive meal. Consequently, because they see Yom Kippur as a Jewish holiday, they go to a Jewish restaurant. (Shternshis 2001)

Shternshis's rich description reveals the many roles a Jewish restaurant is made to fill. The restaurant she visited in Petersburg presents a fantasy of a Jewish past. Actual Jewish dishes share menu space with fantasy dishes such as "chicken à la Jewish grandmother," a dish which neither exists in any form of Jewish cuisine nor conforms to the Jewish dietary laws. The restaurant, alongside the synagogue, functions as a great theater in which Jews in St Petersburg perform their Jewishness, even as they depart radically from Jewish tradition. In this restaurant, the clientele performs twice-behaved behavior that was never once-behaved to begin with.

Culinary tourism brings visitors to unfamiliar foodways, or brings the foodways to the virtual visitor. For Russophone immigrants in New York, the dining experience offered is that of another place. In the case of Rasputin and Firebird, which evoke the Tsarist era, or Primorski and Mels, which evoke the Soviet era, the performance of otherness includes the otherness of time. Rasputin and Firebird, as well as the late Russian Tea Room, choose the iconography of the Tsarist era to symbolize romance, plenitude and indulgence of all kinds. Of course in the real Tsarist era, close to 85 percent of the population, including serfs and all Jews, were entirely excluded from the lavish performances and foodways recreated, or imagined to be recreated, in these venues. Primorski and Mels co-opt names and iconography of the Soviet era, but certainly do not by any means claim to reproduce the scarcity and rationing of that time. For Primorski and Mels, the reference to the Soviet era is winking and ironic. It is also half-hidden, since few non-Russophones will recognize the Soviet references. Diners ordering identical dishes and sitting at identical tables will perceive their experience very differently based on the extent to which they understand the joke. The Tsarist era and the Soviet era were both periods of abjection, want, and terrible persecution for Jews in Russian-speaking lands. Nevertheless, the co-option of the language and iconography of these empires has become a peculiarly Jewish enterprise, both in the former Soviet Union and in the Russophonic Diaspora in Israel, Germany, and the United States. In this context, Russophones recognize Tsarist or Soviet signifiers as Jewish signifiers.

Restaurants are anomalous in that they bring the private activities of eating and cooking into the public, while at the same time offering many a welcoming shelter within the public world. As Allen Weiss has noted "while inaugurating the most intimate pleasure, cuisine simultaneously offers an incontrovertible aspect of social façade" (Weiss 2002: 85). For immigrants navigating a foreign language and culture, a restaurant that provides familiar flavors is a city of refuge (Kirschenbaum 1939). For tourists wishing to broaden their horizons of language and culture, as well as flavor, by visiting the foodways of an other, a restaurant itself can be the most patient and helpful tour guide. Sometimes, the culinary other is not just the other in space or time, but, as Craig Rosa has noted, the other within (Rosa 1997: 13).

Notes

1. Not to be confused with the Indo-European language from the Iranian family commonly called Farsi.
2. Winnifred Tovey, personal communication, May 2003.
3. As difficult as it might be to imagine going to an exhibition of authentic dried meat, it requires quite an imaginative leap to think that it might be worthwhile to display fake dried meat. And yet, such an item, along with some fake dust from Jerusalem, might well be on display in a museum of the visually uninteresting. Kirshenblatt-Gimblett creates such a museum, a virtual one, in the opening paragraph of the essay.
4. Today "*Ehupets*" is an ingeniously named scholarly journal of Russian Jewish studies.
5. The restaurant does have an official name for business purposes and telephone listings: the geographically and ethnically ambiguous *Taam Tov* (Modern Hebrew

for "good taste"); but I have never heard staff or diners refer to this name in conversation.

6. Thanks to Yael Raviv for this observation.

7. *Kol Nidrey* is the prayer recited at the start of Yom Kippur.

–9–

Daughters, Duty and Deference in the Franco-Chinese Restaurant
Winnie Lem

As I walked through the doorway of Le Salon Impérial after an absence of six months, I noticed that the counter that displayed trays of prepared stir-fried vegetable and meat dishes, stews, steamed pork buns, dumplings and other delicacies had disappeared. In its place was an area with tables and chairs that extended the seating of the restaurant considerably. Lorie, the sister of the owner greeted me, invited me to sit down and immediately set about making tea. As she filled the pot with hot water, she said that Christian (the owner of the restaurant-caterer) would be back soon, assuming, in her unassuming manner, that it was he I wanted to see. She set down a pot of steaming tea and two teacups. I remarked that Le Salon is no longer a restaurant-*traiteur*, but has become a real restaurant, to which Lorie replied that they were a business in transition. The family did not want to turn away their faithful take-out customers from their business, so it was a bit of both at the moment. At the precise moment I asked what prompted the change, Lorie's brother Christian burst through the front door carrying a big box of greens and other supplies for the restaurant. Lorie sprang up immediately, relieved her brother of his burden and receded to the kitchen, explaining that she had to help with preparations for the evening. "You noticed the changes," he said after exchanging greetings with me. "What you see," he said proudly, "is the result of my family's hard work. We were doing very well, particularly at lunchtime, and almost every day we had to turn people away, so we decided to renovate and expand to add more seating." I congratulated him on his success. Christian joked in response "There are two things that the Chinese know and know very well. Food is one thing. The other is how to succeed in business. This particularly is the case" he said with a wink "if you are a Chinese immigrant from Wenzhou."

Introduction[1]

France has been one of the major European destinations for migrants from Wenzhou prefecture in Zhejiang province. Located on China's coast, Zhejiang province has had a long history of migration, with flows of Wenzhou people moving to

Europe and more recently to North America. While Wenzhou itself is an important destination for migrants from other parts of China, having been one of the first areas to achieve the "miracle" of economic growth through market reforms and privatization, migration has continued to flow outward from that area.[2] Transnational relocation beyond Zhejiang's and indeed China's borders has both resulted in and been a product of the class polarization and regional disparities in income and wealth that have accompanied the opening up of China to market forces. Members of Wenzhou households across different socio-economic classes migrate not only as a strategy for survival, to improve absolute incomes, but also to improve their relative incomes under circumstances where average real incomes in Wenzhou have increased since the 1980s (Massey *et al.* 1993). These forces inform the compulsion to migrate, and this compulsion is often reported by migrants as motivated by a desire to "get rich quickly in Europe." One of the ideas that circulate among the Wenzhouese in Zhejiang is that wages earned as servers in restaurants in Europe far surpass any wage that might be made in the most lucrative of forms of waged work in China, so that one can actually become quite wealthy as a server in a restaurant (M. Li 1999). The result of these forces is that there has been an increase in the numbers of Chinese migrants to Europe and a growth in the economic activities pursued by migrants in Europe.[3] The Chinese restaurant is a case in point. In Paris, the number of restaurant-caterers operated by the Chinese and Asians has grown from roughly under 200 in 1960 to well over 850 in 1992, and accounts for over 50 percent of Chinese economic activity (Pairault 1990; Live 1998). A number of factors have fostered the heightened mobility of global migrants in recent times.[4] Political crises in such Southeast Asian nations as Laos, Cambodia and Vietnam prompted the departure of large numbers of Chinese residing in those countries. The efforts made by the Chinese government to reform and restructure its economy and society to create a socialist market economy have meant increasing flows of Chinese seeking to make a living inside France's borders. For migrant men and women alike, this often involves the work trajectory of making a living initially as workers in restaurants, and then later as owner-operators of restaurants serving Chinese and other Asian cuisines.

In this chapter, I wish to address the question of the reasons behind the dynamics of growth in Chinese restaurants as an example of immigrant entrepreneurship. By examining the organizational practices of the restaurant-caterer (*restaurant-traiteur*) operated by Chinese migrants in Paris, I address problem of what I call the "thesis of Chinese culture" that has been advanced in contemporary scholarship to examine the nature of Chinese enterprise and reasons for the success of businesses run by Chinese entrepreneurs. This thesis proffers the idea that particular features of Chinese culture and its value system are responsible for the growth and expansion of businesses and firms run by the Chinese. Using examples from fieldwork conducted in restaurants run by Chinese migrants, I will argue that while certain values are brought forth, by both analysts and subjects alike, to explain and to also justify certain management strategies and organizational practices in the restaurant-caterer, their growth and expansion cannot be reduced to the presence of those values. Rather, the inclination toward growth can be more attributed to the structural logic of the family-run restaurants and the ways in which they operated as family-based petty enterprises. This logic, I further argue, transcends the specificities of any given cultural group.

The Franco-Chinese Restaurant-Caterer

The restaurant-caterers operated by the Chinese are often family owned and operated with a labor force that is composed both of kin and non-kin employees. There is some degree of variation in the form that such restaurants take. While Chinese restaurants proper in Paris resemble Chinese restaurants in Toronto and New York, having kitchens and a serviced dining area, the restaurant-caterer is a hybrid of a restaurant and a delicatessen, called a *traiteur* in France, which has pre-prepared dishes displayed in a refrigerated glass case for the purposes of take-out – *pour emporter*. *Restaurant-traiteurs* will often have a few tables and a kitchen where orders from a menu are prepared for customers who wish to eat on the premises. Other establishments are *traiteurs* only, with pre-prepared foods mainly for take-out. Many *traiteurs* tend to have no tables. Some are able to accommodate the rapid consumption of meals that have been reheated in a microwave by providing a counter space. Restaurant-caterers and caterers only tend to be small operations, while restaurants proper tend to vary in size from small establishments that seat twenty or so around five or six tables to very large establishments that seat hundreds of diners. While Chinese restaurant-caterers are scattered throughout Paris, most are concentrated in the three Chinatowns of Paris. In many establishments identified as a Chinese restaurant (*un restaurant chinois*), and Chinese caterer (*un traiteur chinois*), menus are not restricted to specifically Chinese items, and pan-Asian dishes are served. The presence of Thai, Vietnamese, Laotian, and Cambodian as well as Malaysian dishes on Chinese restaurant menus (see Figure 9.1) reflects the provenance of the migrants who make up the population of Asians in Paris, all of whom are frequently glossed by insiders and outsiders alike as "Chinese."

The growth and expansion of the Chinese restaurant sector as well other commercial sectors of Chinese business in France in the past few decades is often seen as evidence of the kinds of miracles that have taken place in the global economy, in which the Chinese have participated as entrepreneurs since the early 1980s. In the context of the 1980s, scholars began to try to track down the roots of the economic success of Chinese entrepreneurs in Asia and elsewhere, and, within the context of Asian "miracles," the "thesis of Chinese culture" emerged.[5] I present the thesis in some detail in the next section and then, in the body of the chapter, I discuss its limitations through an ethnographic exploration of restaurants owned and operated by Chinese émigrés in Paris.

Figure 9.1 Le Prestige. Photo credit: Corin Sworn.

The Thesis of Chinese Culture

The thesis of Chinese culture is a variant of Weber's idea that culture drives the economy (Weber 1970) and recently journalists, social scientists and management specialists alike have maintained that certain sets of values were distinctive to the Chinese firm and responsible for making it the major engine for economic growth in Asia. Redding (1990) in particular claimed to have discovered the driving force behind eastern capitalism, and claimed that it lay in Chinese culture, and particularly in the values associated with Confucianism. The Confucian Ethic, so he asserted along with Kahn (1979), was the eastern counterpart of the Protestant Ethic, which Weber claimed around the turn of the twentieth century as the driving force behind Western capitalism. The Confucian Ethic produced a specific form of capitalism, i.e. "Confucian capitalism."

The central tenets of Confucianism have been given different emphases by different authors who have written about the role of the Chinese values in economic life. But, in general, authors emphasize the significance of collectivism, familism, hierarchy and authoritarianism, paternalism and patriarchy as principles that are key in the organization of the Chinese firm.[6] The primacy of the family requires the subordination of the desires and wishes of the individual member to the wishes of the collective. Further, the values of male authority and filial piety require the submission of the wife to the husband, children to parent, and sisters to brothers. In particular, filial piety, the respect and obedience of children to their parents, is emphasized. From this, it is claimed, stable, harmonious hierarchical relationships can be formed. Stability and harmony are needed for firms to thrive and expand. Redding and other proponents of the thesis of Chinese culture, such as Hamilton (1996) and Wong (1996), argued that the high value placed on family, kinship and hierarchy is thus the key defining feature of businesses run by the Chinese and is responsible for the success of Chinese businesses. Indeed, the premises of family, values, culture and the particularities of certain ethnicities have been applied to many other groups to explain the establishment, operation, stability and success of different forms of ethnic enterprise. In confining the discussion to food services, it has been applied for example to Greeks in the pizza business in the United States (Lovell-Troy 1990).[7]

While these values governed the relationships within the family and the firm, they were also extended outside it. The ethic of communality and the primacy of the collective were expressed generally in terms of a cultural affinity and personalism. For immigrants in particular, who must live and work in the alien environment of host societies, cultural affinity and personalism are considered to be a response to the problem of establishing reliable ties between people in social interactions where trust cannot be assumed. In this way, the thesis of Chinese culture is tied to what I call the "thesis of marginality" to explain the economic success of the Chinese as a minority group in different national settings.[8] The thesis of marginality focuses on the fact that, owing to discrimination, migrant and minority groups were marginal to the societies where migrants have relocated. So, in discussions of Chinese who have migrated to other countries, it is argued that the opportunity structures in the new host societies are blocked. Chinese migrants, and also other ethnic minority groups, are therefore compelled to seek alternative avenues inside an ethnic enclave to make a livelihood (see Lovell-Troy 1990).[9] Living inside an ethnic enclave allows immigrants, so it is assumed, to remain attached to the traditional values of their home country. Fostering an ethnic business sector allows Chinese migrants to avoid competition and in some cases hostility from the dominant group, relying instead on maintaining relations with those who are known. Thus, personal relations become very important in the workings between people, and members of the Chinese community rely on dense networks and ties in their dealings. Social bonds are economic bonds.

These bonds of trust and social networks amongst the Chinese are generally referred to by analysts and subjects alike as *guanxi* (M. Yang 1994; Gold *et al.* 2002). Chinese migrants are thought to import these cultural assets to their host societies, and so, for example, familism enables the overseas Chinese to use family ties and clan ties to support the establishment of restaurants and other businesses by providing financial support through rotating credit societies and providing labor to work in businesses (Light 1972; Light and Gold 2000). These bonds also transcend national boundaries, and represent the avenues along which flows of information, goods, labor and other resources travel between migrants and other Chinese in different global locations. They are also the means by which Chinese culture and its values are sustained. In sum, this is a contemporary iteration of Weber's idea that culture drives the economy (Weber 1970). It is contemporary in that it applies his premise to the economic developments that have taken place in an age that has been variously called the "age of globalization" and "the age of migration" (Castles and Miller 2003). What follows is an ethnographic examination of the workings of several Chinese restaurant-caterers in Paris as a way of criticizing the "thesis of Chinese culture" described above.

Work and Women in the Franco-Chinese Restaurant-Caterer

I turn now to my research on restaurant-caterers run by Chinese immigrants in Paris, and will explore some factors that contribute to the growth of the restaurant sector in France as well as of the individual enterprises that make up that sector.[10] I first present the case of management strategies in a restaurant-caterer owned and operated by a Laotian-Chinese family in the smallest of the Chinatowns located in central Paris. In particular, I will focus on the role that Lorie, the sister of the owner, plays within that enterprise. By focusing on Lorie, I wish to make the point that the growth of enterprises rests less on the mobilization of a value system that is distinctively Chinese than on the structural logic of family-owned and operated restaurants. Through this example, I also illustrate the ways in which the social marginalization of Chinese immigrant women is reproduced through their work in small family-run restaurants. The second example I present also illustrates the ways in which women who have been socialized within the milieu of the Chinese migrant community become disposed toward taking up certain forms of livelihood activity that, in effect, sustain their marginality and confinement to an economic, though not necessarily an ethnic, enclave. In other words, in the second example, I explore what might be called the "habitus" of Jenny, in this case the daughter of the owners, to understand the ways in which she, like many other informants who are the children of immigrant parents, becomes inserted into local and national societies and economies.[11] I do this by outlining the forces at work that generate a disposition toward certain forms of livelihood in the global economy.

Le Salon Impérial[12]

Le Salon Impérial restaurant-caterer is owned and operated by Christian, a Laotian Chinese refugee, and his wife Annie, an immigrant from Wenzhou. Shortly after they married in 1989, Annie and Christian secured funds for its purchase through an informal rotating credit association of friends, compatriots, relatives and friends of friends. The Chinese in Paris refer to this as a *tontine*.[13] Annie mentioned that she managed to locate the restaurant and organize the *tontine* through *guanxi*. They cultivated a network of social ties and family connections to secure the loan. Since they took over the restaurant, the family has managed to expand it from an establishment that seats twenty to one that now seats forty. I suggest that this expansion has taken place because of a structural logic that requires that increasing amounts of surplus value be extracted from those who are employed in the firm.

As a restaurant business that is run using family labor, Christian and Annie employ Christian's two younger sisters, Ginette and Lorie. Ginette is employed as the cook and Lorie, the youngest in the family, works as a server and general odd-job person in the restaurant, doing a little bit of every thing, from working behind the counter, to cooking in the kitchen when it is busy, and managing the restaurant when her brother and sister-in-law are absent. Sam, an illegal immigrant from the province of Fujian, is the only non-family employee, and works as a *sous-chef* and dishwasher in the kitchen. One of the ways in which Annie and Christian have been able to expand their small business is by employing family labor. They also employ illegal or undocumented labor who are paid less than the minimum wage. Ginette receives the minimum wage, while Lorie is paid less than the minimum. Ginette receives a higher relative wage to reflect the value of her specialized work as a cook in the restaurant. Sam is paid the lowest wage.

Some details of Lorie's life and work particularly encapsulate the mechanisms at work in the organization and management of this small restaurant-caterer. Lorie left Laos at the age of fourteen in 1984 to join other members of her family who had arrived earlier in Paris. She is thirty-five years of age, single and childless. Having immigrated at quite a young age and having had some familiarity with the French language, Lorie entered into the education system in Paris and struggled through it to graduate with a degree in accounting. After working for a few years in an accounting firm, Lorie was asked by the family to quit in order to work in the restaurant that her brother and sister in law had bought. Lorie claims that although she was reluctant to leave her employment, she said that her duty was to help her family establish themselves in Paris. So she dutifully left her accounting job and began to work in the family restaurant. After having worked in the family business for quite a few years, Lorie confesses:

> I regret that I was not able to make use of my training as an accountant and that I was not able to make a living from it. To be honest I prefer to work for my other employers. They were not members of my family. I prefer that to working for my brother and his wife because I had just one set of rules to live by. One set at home and another set at work. To work for my brother means I have to live by his rules both in the home and also at work.

Lorie continued by contrasting her work routines in a business run by what she called "French," i.e. Franco-Europeans and Asians:

> When I worked for a French boss, I had regular work hours. I worked from 9:00 to 7:00. I had a two-hour lunch and I worked a five-day week. I also had all the holidays off, and, as you know, in France there are a lot of holidays, especially in May. When I left the office my job was finished. In the restaurant-catering businesses run by the Chinese everybody has to work longer hours and at least six days a week, often without any holidays.

Lorie describes her routine at work:

> My day begins at 10:30 and I finish around midnight and often later if there are customers who linger after closing time. Because I work such long hours and six days a week I am not able to see many of the friends I made while in school. These friends are not Chinese, and so they do not understand why I am never able to socialize with them. My friends ask me why I don't get an apartment of my own because that living on my own would give to have more freedom to come and go.

But Lorie asserted that the Chinese had a different way of living, and drew on the value of the family as well as family values to explain why she did not take her friends' advice:

> The Chinese live with their families until they are married. The family is very important for the Chinese and family ties are very strong in Chinese culture. Because of this I have to go along with the decisions and plans that are made by the family because everybody has to contribute to the well-being of the family.

Lorie's contribution to the well-being of the family has resulted in sacrificing her own career in order to work in the family restaurant. It also involved a material sacrifice, as she receives less pay working for her brother than for her work in an accounting firm. But she feels that such sacrifices were necessary for the sake of ensuring the success of the family restaurant.

Her sacrifices were not unrecognized by her family, as Christian notes: "Without Lorie's help, we would not have been able to keep the restaurant going." He adds that: "As long as Lorie lives with us she does not need to be paid as much as an employee who is not a family member, because she does not need to pay rent or to pay for groceries. We share everything."

Both Lorie and Sam are paid less than the minimum wage and also "under the counter." Paying Lorie a living wage, then, is seen by her family as unnecessary so long as she lives with and is partially dependent upon the family for her own subsistence. In this way, the family business has been able to exploit the labor of Lorie precisely because she is a member of the family and indeed of the household.

By this method of payment and by relying on Lorie to work such extreme hours the family business is able to sustain its profits and realize its potential for capital accumulation (cf. Bubinas 2003).

Maintaining Marginality

This accumulation orientation is also realized as a result of the hierarchical structure of the business. As a hierarchy based on gender and age that must be maintained through concrete practices as well as supported by a set of values, many have argued that Chinese family businesses tend to be largely a male preserve in which men tend to monopolize the high-paying positions and positions of authority (Greenhalgh 1994). They become established as the managers and bosses. In Le Salon Impérial, Christian is referred to as *le patron* and Annie is *la patronne*. But Christian is the absolute *patron*, and his directions overrule any that Annie might issue, if they are in conflict. But as the senior members of the family and the firm, they are the bosses, and together they manage, serve and oversee the day-to-day running of the business. Positions of authority and power are occupied by the seniors in the family, particularly the senior males. The least favorable jobs with the lowest responsibility are allocated to daughters or sisters. This hierarchy is seen a "natural" by workers and Chinese customers alike, all of whom automatically refer to Christian as *le patron*, or *laoban*. And the fact that Lorie receives lowest pay (next to Sam) makes it increasingly difficult for her to disengage herself from the value system and work context in which she is embedded.

The family firm is also a male preserve in another sense. Like many migrant entrepreneurs, Lorie's brother had to face the problem of how to stop the lowest-paid, lowest-ranking members of the family firm – the junior women – from demanding more independence from the family. He also had to face the problem of how to prevent demands for more pay, as well securing stable labor for the family firm. This was done in two ways. First, Lorie's independence was curtailed by a strategy that ensured her sustained 'marginal status' in French society. The only way that Lorie is able to live on her low wages is by living with her brother and sister-in-law. Lorie does not have the financial means to live independently in her own apartment, as she says, "like French people." She is financially dependent on the common family budget, and is thus by necessity securely embedded in the family and the enclave of Chinese migrants. Second, the dependence and docility of junior women is assured through other management practices. As Greenhalgh (1994) points out in her study of Taiwanese enterprises, entrepreneurs in many retail and restaurant businesses do this by arranging job and incentives within the family firm so that women's jobs are the most uninteresting and as well as the lowest paying. They run the cash register; they stock the shelves and clean up. Women are discouraged from thinking of their jobs as careers, and because their roles in the firm are undervalued and of low status, they often aspire to "traditional" roles. Married women talk of returning to their roles as wives and mothers, which they find more rewarding and more highly valued.

Annie underscores this desire:

> If I were able to stay at home to care of my three young children, instead of working in the restaurant, I would do this. I feel that this work takes me away from my kids. They have a baby-sitter; but having a baby-sitter look after your children is not the best way to raise them. A babysitter is not a substitute for a mother.

But, as in the case of many wives who run family restaurants with their husbands, Annie's labor is indispensable in the day-to-day operation of the business.

In the case of women who are unmarried, many seek to become wives and mothers to escape from the drudgery of their position in the firm. Lorie outlines her intentions: "I will work for my brother until I get married and start having a family. When I start having babies, I will quit to raise my children. But for the moment I will continue to work in the family firm as long as I am needed."

Lorie sees her job as a temporary phase in her life, something to which she is not committed and certainly not a part of her career. As she sees herself as just working temporarily, she does as her brother tells her and seldom raises a fuss when he claims to not be able to pay her or to pay her more. Through these practices Christian and Annie have been able to enjoy the compliance of their employees and stability in the workplace, where the authority of men and senior men and women goes unchallenged and obedience is the norm. Owners, then, are well positioned to exploit wage employees so as to permit increased levels of accumulation. This contributes toward the success and also the expansion of restaurants and other petty enterprises. Owners are able to benefit from and exploit the dependent status of relatives, particularly women, and also the illegal status of employees like Sam, who is unable to find work as a regular registered member of France's labor force.

Lorie's case also demonstrates the fairly rational calculating strategies exercised by the family to ensure a steady supply of labor to the firm and therefore harmony within the firm and the stability of the firm. This harmony and stability *is not a simple extension of the values of familism and collectivism.* Consensus, when achieved, is reinforced by material constraints and determinants, where the interests of certain categories of people, junior women in particular, are subordinated to the interests of other categories of people, particularly senior men, within the family firm. In other words, it involves processes of disciplining individuals and creating the political and economic conditions that will lead them to conform to the needs of institutions and enterprises. In the context of the Chinese family firm, the "values" of Chinese culture are the ideological means through which individuals are disciplined to assimilate the priorities of the family. This is done through a process of "self-orientalization." This process supports the material requirements of the family firm. Moreover, the example of Lorie belies the assumption that there is a common good that prevails and that everyone in the family benefits. The "common good" is in fact based on sustaining power differentials between junior women and senior men, and therefore differentials in the ability to exercise control over material resources. Finally, the example of Le Salon Impérial shows that harmony and obedience are not the natural outcome or manifestation of some essential quality of Chinese culture. The harmony and stability that are so highly valued for the purposes of capital accumulation are produced by a structural logic that requires that the management practices of an enterprise run using family labor are embedded in a hierarchy based on gender and age. In this way, the orientation toward accumulation is thus built into the structure of petty enterprise. As a logic that is built into the structure of family-based enterprises, it transcends the specificities of any cultural group and any particular work activity.

This structural logic and orientation toward accumulation can be found amongst family-owned and operated enterprises in China and elsewhere (see, for example Lem 1997; Murphy 2002; Smart and Smart 2005). It can be found in family operations in contemporary contexts[14] as well as in the past (Roseberry 1986; Cohen 1991).

By participating in and being subjected to such organization and management practices, women often acquire the knowledge and "cultural capital" required to participate in host societies as entrepreneurs. Lorie claimed that she still hoped to be married one day, but confesses in a rather frank manner that this is not likely, as she is already 35, with no prospect of a husband in sight. Having worked for such a long time in the restaurant business, Lorie says that it is unlikely that she will ever work as an accountant again; but she could see working opening a restaurant of her own:

> I have the experience and the knowledge required to take over my brother's restaurant when he retires. I don't know if I will inherit his business because he might give it to his children. But I doubt that they will want to work in a restaurant because they were born in France, unlike me, and will have a French education and will want to do other things with their lives. Let's face it, working in a restaurant is not for the well educated. But at least for my part working in my brother's restaurant has given me the knowledge and work experience to be able to start a restaurant of my own. This isn't a bad thing altogether, because it is always better to be the employer than an employee and a restaurant owner than a worker.

Thus, the effect of the organizational practices on those who are subject to them is double-edged. The cultural capital of entrepreneurship is transmitted between individuals to enable the participation of immigrant women and men in host economies; but it also sustains the social marginality of immigrant women who are socialized to work within the confines of the restaurant sector within an ethnic enclave which is also often an economic enclave or sector, even when that sector is part of what has been referred to as a "global network" or "worldwide web" of Chinese business (Kao 1993). While some, like Lorie, have received training for other forms of work, they still succumb to the social and cultural forces that have drawn them into this sector. The prevailing forces at work drawing women into the "worldwide web" of Chinese business are illustrated in the example of Jenny, who, unlike Lorie, was born in Paris and thus able to enjoy some of the benefits of being able to be more easily integrated into the French education system. She completed university, which resulted in more options for higher-status work, as is illustrated below. Jenny is the daughter of Peter, who owns and operates Lotus Gardens, a restaurant-karaoke in another of Paris's Chinatowns.

Lotus Gardens

Peter was born in the prefecture of Wenzhou and arrived in Paris in 1965, after having first emigrated to Hong Kong with his family. Like many other migrants, Peter worked in restaurants as a dishwasher and cook when he first arrived in France. He was finally able to establish his own small restaurant in 1975, after marrying his wife Marie. Together they were able to secure funds to help set it up through a *tontine*, consisting of friends, relatives and friends of friends. After five years, they moved to a larger location, having expanded the family restaurant from an establishment that sat 30 to one that now seats 130. They also added a karaoke room. Peter, *le patron*, runs this restaurant with Marie, and employs his sister Lily. Most of the servers are immigrants, both women and men, who have arrived from Wenzhou. Lily and Marie run the cash, work serving tables and clean. Marie manages the front of the restaurant. Peter cooks and manages the kitchen where there are five employees, consisting of cooks and *sous-chefs*. At various times, Peter admitted he hired illegal immigrants – *sans papiers* – to work in the kitchen and basement of the restaurant to clean and prepare vegetables and meat.

Their daughter Jenny was born in 1980, and, until Jenny entered university, she was sent to spend at least one month each summer with cousins in Beijing to immerse her in the Chinese language and Chinese culture. Peter describes the transnational network of reciprocal exchanges that allowed him to maintain an "education in Chinese" for Jenny:

> I paid for the plane fare and once she was in China, everything was taken care of. She stayed with relatives who put her up because I sent money to help my relatives set up a couple of businesses in China. They set up a restaurant in Wenzhou and a small grocery shop in Beijing with my help. So this was a way of paying me back.

Once Jenny entered university, she stopped going to China and spent her summers in Paris, working in the family restaurant. She was paid only a token sum for this work. Her labor was needed because some of the restaurant staff wanted to take holidays, and summers are slow, and August – the traditional month of holidays in France – is a time of particularly low revenues. Peter said that Jenny hated working in the restaurant when her friends were all traveling around Europe, or going to their houses in the south of France. But Peter added, "She is a good daughter, and good daughters obey their parents."

In Chinese, when children are being assessed as good or bad, the term for obedient – *ting huà* – is often used as a synonym for good (*hao*). Peter recounted a story of a girl who was a "bad daughter" because she was not obedient (*bu ting huà*). She was the daughter of one of his friends who defied her parents on everything, from learning Chinese as a child, to allowing her parents to select her friends, to working in the restaurant and studying hard: "My friend cut her off completely, once she was 16. They did not support her when she wanted to go to university. They said she was on her own, and we think this young woman now works in a very bad job, maybe in a club in Paris, somewhere."

Peter implied in our conversation that this was one amongst many other stories often related to Jenny as a cautionary tale while she was growing up.

But Jenny went on to university, financially supported by her parents. As a "good girl" until she started university, Jenny was also required to study Mandarin in Paris as an extracurricular activity. She resented this, as it meant that the available time for socializing with friends was limited. But as an "obedient daughter," she respected her father's wishes. Jenny eventually obtained a post-secondary degree in business. Obtaining a degree in business was also Peter's idea. Peter reports that he anticipated that China would one day be an economic success story and wanted to prepare his children to be a part of it, "to be able to live and be a success in two worlds," so he reports. He proudly points out that because he was so prescient, his daughter now holds a management position in Air France and helps to direct their operations in Beijing. While working in a restaurant was genuinely a temporary phase in Jenny's life, her habitus, her part in the family firm as an organization, the work relations and family relations in which she was embedded and the expectation that she would submit to her parent's will all inclined her toward working within a Chinese milieu, if not necessarily a Chinese enclave.

Now Jenny travels frequently between Beijing and Paris, and on one of her visits I managed to interview her. Jenny comments:

I lived up to my father's expectations. I listened to him and so did not really have the kind of childhood that many of my friends had. I had to work hard not only in school but to learn Chinese, and I had to work in the restaurant for the family, when all my friends were living a very French way of life – enjoying their summer holidays and traveling or making money in jobs for which they were paid. I felt excluded from them and from their way of life. They had money at the end of the summer, and could spend their money in any way they liked on clothes and parties. I did not. For any pocket money I needed I had to ask my parents. They usually gave it to me; but I always had to tell them what it was for. My French friends were free to spend money. Sometimes I used to think that we learned in school that the French Declaration of the Rights of Man guaranteed liberty, fraternity and equality for all citizens of the Republic. But when I was a kid and saw the lives that my friends lived, I rather believed that the constitution only applied to French people. I did not feel all that free, and certainly not equal.

But Peter announces that Jenny benefited immensely from her upbringing.

Jenny does not work in a Chinese restaurant because, let's face it, running a restaurant is really something for people who do not have much education or can't speak French. But because of her training and my insistence on keeping up her language and her knowledge about how Chinese business works, she is still working among the Chinese; and look at China now!

Peter plans to return to China eventually. He plans to sell his restaurant in Paris "when the time is right" and set up a business, perhaps a restaurant which serves French food, in Beijing or Wenzhou. Peter elaborates enthusiastically:

With China's economy growing and business people moving back and forth, tastes will be changing, and I think there is an opportunity here to fill a niche in China's restaurant sector. My daughter reports that there are very few Western restaurants in Beijing. She says that she would help me set it up with her knowledge of international business and how business is conducted in the new China. I already have family members there who would be able to help me and work in the restaurant – many nieces and nephews from Wenzhou who now live in Beijing, and more of my family members are leaving Wenzhou to look for work in the city.[15]

When I asked Jenny about her future plans, she replied:

I would like to have my own business. I don't want to be an employee working for a big company forever. While my job is a good one, there is only so much room for advancement and promotion, especially for women. It makes no difference that I am a Chinese woman working in a Chinese market. I work with many men, both Chinese and French, who started after me and who earn larger salaries and are promoted more quickly. Air France is a French company after all. So, I'd like to run my own business with my family. My father made sure I was raised with the right values and with what I know of the restaurant business and how to conduct business in China, it seems natural for me to be able to start up something one day. It also seems logical since my father made sure I had all the Chinese qualities needed for success, so I think that whatever business we start up will grow in no time. Look at my father's restaurant. He started with very little and made it grow quite big. The Chinese seem to have a talent for business.

Conclusion

While many analysts have produced cogent critiques of the cultural thesis and Confucian capitalism (Greenhalgh 1994; P. Li 1993; Yao 2003), the idea that Chinese cultural values drive the economy remains one of the most popular explanations for the growth and expansion of local and national economies in Asian and non-Asian countries. It is popular among scholars, analysts and policy-makers, as well as officials in immigration bureaus. It is also popular amongst many Chinese subjects themselves. Apart from the fact that it resonates with some of the oldest stereotypes held in the West about the Chinese, there are also historical and political reasons why the cultural thesis remains so powerful. Many critics have noted that the whole idea that there is a Confucian form of capitalism was widely promoted in the press in the North America and Europe, particularly in the 1980s. At that time, the industrialized nations of the West were suffering through a period of economic decline and recession. In this context, the thesis of Chinese culture became part of the mythology surrounding the east about how these poor underdeveloped nations have managed to achieve extraordinary levels of growth through an emphasis on the traditional values of hard work, cooperation and the importance of the family. In the 1980s, such mythologies led Western commentators to raise nationalist fears that they would be overtaken by Asian "tigers" and "dragons." More recently, there has been much made in the media about the coming of the "Pacific Century" and about the twenty-first century's becoming the "Chinese century."[16] Fears are focused on the growing political and economic ascendancy or influence of China and the Chinese in the world as growth rates in the East continue to surpass those of Western economies. However, a second emotional reaction has been added to the fears of being overtaken in the age of globalization. The spirit of global entrepreneurialism was being stirred, as individuals and companies in the West are being challenged to capture their share of the Chinese market and to take advantage of the very successful form of capitalism that many Western analysts suggest is based on Confucian values.

Yet, as I have pointed out, it is not only Westerners that subscribe to the stereotype. Many Asians themselves – scholars, journalists and immigrants alike – accept the force of such values as well. Thus many informants speak of the virtues of Chinese values in a fashion similar to Jenny, and hold that Chinese business practices will enable their participation in the "Chinese Century." Many owner-operators such as Peter, as well as other workers in Chinese restaurants and retail shops in Paris, cite the values of kin solidarity, a familistic morality combined with a competitive entrepreneurial ethic as the motive for providing resources to relatives and friends in China to start up businesses in rural villages, towns and cities. "We are helping to make the miracle in China," so Peter claims.[17] Like Peter too, they also commonly talk of their own plans to return to China with their earnings to invest in businesses and infrastructure, and are busily ensuring that their children learn Chinese so as eventually to be able to work in China. Many informants speak of Chinese business practices and values as being well suited to the age of globalization. Many Asian informants speak also of how they as Chinese immigrants are model citizens[18] in host countries, because they run their businesses with the help of their families with loans from their friends, without bothering or depending on anyone. This is often cited as the reason such businesses are able to thrive. The informants I interviewed often stated that because there was such an extensive network of friends and associations in the Chinese community, Chinese immigrants are able to help each other, and they do not need to get involved in politics. Nor, in fact, could they, as their work routines are filled with long working hours, which leave little time for politics and leisure.

In drawing on these examples of restaurant entrepreneurship as examples of small enterprises run by Chinese migrants, I have stressed that the organization principles and work routines have meant the marginalization of migrant men and particularly migrant women in different sectors of the French economy. I have also stressed that within the sector of family-owned and operated businesses, such as restaurants, the principles of organization actually rely on the maintenance of disparities of power and material resources between men and women, as well as elders and juniors. These disparities are mirrored beyond the family firm, in other areas of the economy. This is illustrated by the example of Jenny, who was bypassed for promotion in Air France. Beyond discrimination in the world of corporate and transnational capitalism and exploitation in small-scale firms in local economies, these disparities are reflected in society at large in the political, economic and cultural limits that such practices impose on the participation of immigrant women and men in their host societies and on the ability of such "model citizens" to exercise the full rights of citizenship.

Notes

1. I wish to thank David Beriss, David Sutton, and Gavin Smith for comments on earlier drafts of this chapter. The research upon which this chapter is based was generously funded with grants from the Social Sciences and Humanities Research Council of Canada, the Wenner Gren Foundation for Anthropological Research and Trent University.
2. For discussion of the "Wenzhou Model of Development" see Liu (1992), Parris (1993) and Nolan and Dong (1991).
3. See Benton and Pieke (1998) for details of the history of Chinese migration to different countries in Europe as well as the social, political and economic activities in which they are engaged.
4. See the discussion in Castles and Miller (2003); Glick-Schiller (1999); Glick-Schiller *et al.* (1992) and Ong and Nonini (1997).
5. For a discussion of the different ways in which the thesis of Chinese culture emerged to explain entrepreneurial success in different countries, see P. Li (1993; 2001), Moore (1997) and Yao (2003).
6. See, for example Koh (1993), Wong (1988, 1996) and Hamilton (1996).

7. See also Caplan (1997).

8. This is also referred to as the "blocked mobility thesis" or the thesis of "disadvantage" (see P. Li 1993).

9. See, for example, Light (1972), Moore (1997) and Bonacich and Modell (1980).

10. Paris has three main Chinatowns located in the 3rd, 13th and 18th *arrondissements* or districts. The smallest and the oldest is in the 3rd *arrondissement*.

11. Bourdieu's idea of habitus is generally understood as a structure of dispositions that reflect a 'field of objective possibilities' open to agents at a particular historical moment (Bourdieu 1977: 82–3). For further discussion see Lane (2000: 25) and Brubaker (1985: 758).

12. Names of restaurants and research subjects are pseudonyms.

13. A *tontine* in this context resembles a rotating credit society, in which investors each advance small loans to the borrower, who repays each investor with interest according to a pre-determined schedule. For a detailed discussion see Pairault (1990).

14. See Smart and Smart (2005).

15. For a discussion of internal migration in China see Murphy (2002); L. Zhang (2001); M. Zhang (2003).

16. See for example the series of articles under the title "China Rising – Are We Missing the Boat?" in *Globe and Mail* October 23, 2004 and in *Le Monde diplomatique*, October 2004 edition on "China, Past Present and Future" (Lew 2004).

17. On the issue of remittances, M. Li (1999) points out that while some funds are used for the purposes of investment in businesses, much of the money that is sent back to China is often spent on conspicuous consumption. She reports that it is expected for migrants who return and for those who receive remittances from migrants abroad to display their relative wealth.

18. See Lem (forthcoming) for a discussion of immigration and the ideals of citizenship under neo-liberal governance.

–10–

Authentic Creole
Tourism, Style and Calamity in New Orleans Restaurants
David Beriss

To many tastes Galatoire's serves the best food in New Orleans. In its specialties it is unexcelled. But one tends to overlook that Galatoire's is basically a family restaurant and like Antoine's is not primarily a commercial enterprise. New Orleanians seem to exist for food, and it would be looked upon as a calamity if anything ever changed at Galatoire's. (Collin 1970: 52)

On April 27, 2002 the management of Galatoire's restaurant in New Orleans fired Gilberto Eyzaguirre, a waiter who had worked there for over twenty years. His

Figure 10.1 Galatoire's. Photo credit: David Beriss.

dismissal was based on complaints of sexual harassment from other staff members. In most other cities – indeed, in most other restaurants in New Orleans – the firing of a waiter would hardly be worthy of comment. However, as Richard Collin pointed out over thirty years ago, any changes at Galatoire's would be regarded as a calamity, and the firing of Gilberto (he is referred to by his first name even by those who have never met him) rapidly escalated into the scandal of the summer – perhaps of the year – in New Orleans. A group of over 150 regular patrons of the restaurant, many of them among the city's elite, assembled a bound collection of letters denouncing Gilberto's dismissal and presented it to the restaurant's board of directors. The scandal escalated over the next few months, with rumors flying in gossipy food notes in local newspapers, radio talk shows and online discussion groups (Gilberto's supporters also created a website, http://www.welovegilberto.com/, where many of the letters presented to management can be read). In July, the New Orleans *Times-Picayune*, the city's main daily newspaper, published a 3,500-word article (nearly three full pages of the paper) devoted to the scandal (Anderson 2002). The newspaper's letters column was soon full of comments and, according to one of the regular columnists, the *Times-Picayune* received more letters to the editor on the subject of Gilberto's firing than on any other subject since the terrorist attacks of September 11, 2001 (Rose 2002). By late July, Chris Rose, a witty *Times-Picayune* columnist whose pre-Katrina beat focused mostly on celebrity gossip, organized a satirical reading of letters written in protest at Gilberto's firing at a local cabaret, with the proceeds from ticket sales going to a food bank. Entitled the "Galatoire's Monologues," the theme of the satirical fundraiser was "feeding the hungry on the indignation of the overfed." All performances were sold out.

Like other social dramas, the Galatoire's affair illustrates many of the social fractures that run through New Orleans society. The incident raises, for instance, questions about shifts in the gendered division of labor in fine-dining establishments, long dominated by men (cf. Prewitt 2000). As the theme of the satirical fundraiser noted above indicates, the affair also points to conflicts over the privileges of the social elite in New Orleans. Perhaps only race – a topic that infuses virtually all aspects of life in New Orleans – was explicitly missing from debates about Gilberto's fate. Yet even that absence implied, as the discussion below will show, the hidden place of African-Americans in the world of Creole restaurants, where they are rarely seen in the front of the house, but are among the key workers in the kitchen. All of these contributed to the controversy that followed Gilberto's dismissal. However, gender, class and race were not central to the debate. Culture, indeed, the very identity of the city, was.

Gilberto's firing did not become a scandal because of sexual harassment, nor was the debate that followed primarily focused on over-privileged elites or on racial injustice in restaurant kitchens. Instead, the public debate reflected deeper concerns with the representation of New Orleans culture in a society where representations have become commodities themselves. My argument here builds on recent scholarship that focuses on struggles over the authenticity and ownership of "culture," as manifested in festivals, monuments, food or other objects and practices (Dávila 1997; Leitch 2003; Regis 2001; Scher 2002). Much of this literature points to the ways in which claims about the authenticity of particular objects and practices are often based on contested (or, at least, contestable) historical narratives and reflect the interests of some groups over others. Food and food culture are central to ideas about what is specific about New Orleans. Restaurants have long played a fundamental role in defining that cultural specificity. Gilberto's firing, along with other changes at Galatoire's and other old-line New Orleans restaurants, triggered a debate over the proper representation of New Orleans culture and about who should be able to define that representation.

Such representations are more than markers of identity or tools that legitimize particular groups. Like other cities, New Orleans has, in recent years, been increasingly defined as a space of consumption where, as Sharon Zukin (1998) has argued, particular kinds of lifestyles are one of the main objects of consumption (cf. Bell and Valentine 1997; Florida 2002). Representations of the city's culture are thus consumed by locals, seeking out authenticity in their lifestyle choices. But they are also produced for and consumed by tourists. Tourism, as a number of recent analyses have indicated, carries a great deal of ambiguity, contributing to economic life and validating cultural distinctiveness while, at the same time, threatening to reduce that distinctiveness to a kind of "Disneyfied" homogeneity (Castañeda 1996; Howe 2001; Long 2004). With the increased significance of tourism in New Orleans' economy in recent decades, many locals consider that the city's cultural authenticity is under assault. Tourists may make restaurants profitable; however, many city residents would argue that without significant local clientele, chefs, managers and owners will lose sight of their putative responsibility to reproduce the local culinary culture. Demanding that Galatoire's recognize its responsibility to represent that culture correctly was central to the affair. Tourists might be the motor behind the economy, but their tastes would not be allowed to define New Orleans culture.

In what follows, I argue that the Galatoire's affair was fundamentally about the correct way to represent New Orleans' cultural identity. The debate resonated with locals precisely because they have long been told that the city's cultural distinctiveness is under assault by the homogenizing forces of America and by the tourist masses. I begin, then, by describing the unfolding of the Galatoire's affair in more detail. In the next section, I examine the role of chefs and restaurants in the production and reproduction of New Orleans culture. Their place in the city's cultural landscape – its foodscape (Ferrero 2002) – is, I argue, different from that of chefs in other American cities. One of the sources of this difference is that New Orleans has a long-standing food culture, a cuisine, built from local products, that is regularly produced in homes and restaurants and frequently discussed around local tables and in the local media. This context, as I show in this chapter's final section, is what made the debate about Gilberto's firing possible, and what made it take the form it eventually took. In what may be a purely postmodern twist, the affair itself came to be seen as a significant representation of the ongoing health of New Orleans culinary culture. In the end, cultural, if not culinary, authenticity was demonstrated and reasserted through the public debate. Gilberto's fate was entirely peripheral.

Tourists as the Demise of Culture

Established in 1905, Galatoire's has been called the "cornerstone of fine Creole dining" by a local food critic (Fitzmorris 1996: 134). Located on Bourbon Street, in New Orleans' French Quarter, the restaurant is certainly distinct from the surrounding businesses, which include the usual range of Bourbon Street commerce, such as daiquiri shops, strip clubs, and purveyors of exotic undergarments and other New Orleans souvenirs. Galatoire's main dining-room reflects a sense of elegance that dates back to the early twentieth century, with long walls of mirrors and tiled floors and ceiling fans, along with tuxedoed waiters who, until the mid-1990s, were all male. Until recently, the main dining-room was the only dining-room, and Galatoire's did not take reservations. Customers would line up on the Bourbon Street sidewalk, dressed in their finery, often sweltering in the New Orleans heat as they waited for their table. Local legend claims that a host of dignitaries have been made to wait in the line, from US Senators to French President Charles de Gaulle (Burton and Holditch 2004: 135). It is one of the few restaurants left in New Orleans that still requires men to wear a jacket and tie. Galatoire's menu also reflects a sense of tradition, with little apparent change in decades.

Galatoire's has also long been a cornerstone of New Orleans high society. The restaurant's regulars include a significant portion of the city's business, political and arts elites, many of whom eat there weekly. During Friday and Sunday lunches regulars usually turn the main dining-room into an elegant party, often extending into the evening and dinner. Regulars rarely consult the menu, depending on their waiters to tell them if they should order the crabmeat *maison* or if fresh pompano is available. They can depend on the waiters, because regulars *have* waiters, whom they request when they enter the restaurant. I have heard New Orleanians refer to their waiter as a kind of family inheritance, bequeathed by their parents after years of dining together, or as a trusted family servant. Until recently, Galatoire's waiters prepared drinks for customers themselves, often generously. Those who dine regularly at Galatoire's are made to feel that they are members of an exclusive club. But since Galatoire's is open to the public, the club holds its meetings in public. That, of course, is part of the attraction. One is not merely a member of the club, one can be seen to be a member.

This club, however, may be under assault. This is because the restaurant under-took a major renovation in 1999, and in the wake of that renovation several changes occurred. First, the Galatoire's family hired a general manager, Melvin Rodrigue, who was the first non-family member to run the restaurant. The renovation led to the reopening of dining-rooms on the second floor – closed since the Second World War – and the restaurant began taking reservations, although for the second-floor dining-rooms only. They installed a bar, where customers can wait for tables, rather than standing outside in line. With the bar, they hired bartenders, who now mix the drinks. In a major concession to the late twentieth century, they purchased an ice machine, so that waiters no longer have to hand-chip ice for drinks. The dress code for men was relaxed at lunch. Each of these changes was noted with concern by the regulars. That concern erupted into open revolt with the firing of Gilberto.

Gilberto's dismissal served to crystallize the fears of Galatoire's regulars. His firing, many believed, was linked to an effort to rid the restaurant of its long-time patrons, with their tendency to linger for hours, and replace them with ill-dressed, but faster-eating, tourists. For instance, Mickey Easterling, a prominent New Orleans socialite, wrote to the restaurant's board of directors:

> It is past time for you to return Galatoire's to what it is famous for and to start re-membering the needs and desires of those who have supported you over the years. The price increases do not bother me and I'm glad your quality of food is returning.
>
> But … what … does … bother … me is:
>
> Your overt effort to get rid of all (one by one) the long term dedicated wait staff by assigning them to upstairs duty hoping you will get the 'old regulars' to go there … you can forget it…. The upstairs dining room should and was … to be for those poorly dressed tourists, and others. (Easterling 2002: 1)

Dr Brobson Lutz, former director of the city health department, noted ominously that Antoine's, another temple of high Creole cuisine, was a "prime example of a multigenerational New Orleans institution gone to hell in a handbag" because "they ran off all their good waiters, skimped on quality, price gouged, and went after the tourists years ago" (2002: 1).

Writing in support of Gilberto provided many with an opportunity to complain about other changes in the restaurant. The new manager was, some suggested, trying to rid the restaurant of old waiters because they challenged his authority. Machine-made ice melted too rapidly, watering down the drinks, which had gotten too small anyhow. Other waiters had left too, some voluntarily, and management had done too little to keep them. The relaxed dress code had opened the door to all manner of riff-raff. Ken Holditch, a retired English professor, wrote that "I still have trouble with the fact that the dress code has, for the most part, been abandoned, and that people who seem to be arrayed to go to the beach or Disneyland, wearing blue jeans and sweatshirts or worse, are ushered in to be seated next to a table where some well dressed elderly couple, long-time patrons, sit, mourning the passing of a more gracious era" (2002: 1). He goes on to suggest that the renovations were an attack on the very soul of the restaurant, asking, "Do you want the traditions of your historic establishment to be swept out by a new wave of clueless youth" (2002: 2)?

Many of the letter-writers suggested that meals at Galatoire's had been central to their lives since childhood. Their letters provide short life histories around the theme of repeated visits to the restaurant. Holditch, for instance, attributed his entire career to a visit to New Orleans with his parents in 1949 during which he ate at Galatoire's. The memory of that meal led him, he adds, to accept a position with the University of New Orleans 15 years later (Holditch 2002: 1). Gilberto and other waiters are prominent in these life stories as faithful friends, who remember what their clients like to eat and drink and who are always available when needed.

Letter writers also invoked the link between Galatoire's and prominent figures in New Orleans history. Dakin Williams, brother of Tennessee Williams, wrote about the role played by Gilberto and Galatoire's in New Orleans' annual Tennessee Williams Festival (Holditch 2002: 1). Others wrote of visits by William Faulkner, Walker Percy, Ernest Hemingway and the Duke and Duchess of Windsor, hinting that any fundamental change at Galatoire's would imply the denial of that illustrious past. New Orleans, these letters seemed to suggest, is at the center of an intellectual and artistic world, and Galatoire's is the place where that world meets.

For many of Galatoire's regulars, Gilberto's dismissal, when placed in the context of other changes at the restaurant, signaled the end of an era. The regulars feared that they might no longer be recognized at Galatoire's. Their letters linked the preservation of their club, the world of Galatoire's diners, to a particular culture, centered on a way of dining in New Orleans. In this view, firing Gilberto was a sign of the end of those traditions and of the culture they defined. Galatoire's represents the soul of New Orleans and Gilberto the soul of the restaurant.

Restaurants and the Representation of New Orleans Culture

Food figures centrally in the idea of New Orleans cultural specificity. Food critics consistently rank New Orleans with much larger and more cosmopolitan cities such as New York and San Francisco as a major American restaurant town. However, unlike the culinary eclecticism that characterizes contemporary American restaurant cooking, New Orleans' reputation is built on the reproduction and re-invention of a particular indigenous cuisine, defined by seafood and crafted out of the local *mirepoix* – what local cooks call the "holy trinity" – of onions, green peppers and celery (garlic, in an extension of the Catholic metaphor, is referred to as the "pope"). It is the task of local restaurants and chefs to situate themselves creatively *vis-à-vis* this cuisine and its proponents. Their success requires them to cook the mythology of New Orleans cuisine, representing their food as both interestingly creative and still part of the culture of high Creole cooking. Gilberto's firing can best be understood when placed in the broader context of the relationship between restaurants, chefs and the representation of New Orleans culinary and cultural specificity. This relationship has been especially evident in the careers of chefs.

I first began thinking about the role of chefs in representing New Orleans culture because of a somewhat startling newspaper article. On June 6, 1998, the *Times-Picayune* carried a front-page article headlined "The Palace Guard" (Mullener 1998: A1). The "palace" was Commander's Palace, one of the city's better-known restaurants and the flagship for a branch of the Brennan family, a local restaurant dynasty. The article advanced the claim that, since the mid-1970s, Commander's Palace has served as a sort of culinary academy, training and then launching the careers of more than two dozen of the dominant chefs in New Orleans. A "culinary family tree" is included with the article (Mullener 1998: A10), showing three lineages that have emerged from Commander's executive chefs since 1975, Paul Prudhomme (1975–80), Emeril Lagasse (1982–9) and Jamie Shannon (1989–2001).[1] The article claimed that these chefs and their culinary offspring have:

> enlivened the scene in a city where a chef can be a celebrity, the food arts are an abiding part of the culture and good eating is a part of every good day. They have taken the grand traditions of Creole and Cajun cooking and made them grander. And now they are spinning off chefs themselves, out of their own restaurants, creating a second generation with the genetic code of Commander's Palace in their gumbos and remoulades and étouffées. (Mullener 1998: A10)

In short, the Brennans and their famous executive chefs have produced an entire generation of New Orleans chefs and have been at the center of the reproduction of New Orleans culinary culture.

This article raises several interesting questions about the reproduction of New Orleans culinary culture. It is not unusual to note that chefs form networks, that they train each other or that some kitchens turn out many well-trained chefs likely to start their own restaurants.[2] New Orleans chefs, the article suggests, go beyond this. They are linked by a particular culinary heritage. "If the alumni of Commander's Palace have anything in common, it is their celebration of the traditions of Cajun and Creole cooking" (Mullener 1998: A12). Rather than producing the individualist artists that are celebrated in contemporary American food writing, Commander's-trained chefs seem to be reproducing New Orleans food culture. Certainly, given the importance of tourism to New Orleans' economy, it is hardly surprising that developments in the restaurant business are of great local interest. But this article is not primarily about the tourism business. It is about the way the Brennan family and the executive chefs at Commander's transmit the culture to the chefs who work there. The prominence of this article suggests that chefs play an interesting role in New Orleans culture.

The idea that a kind of "chefly lineage" is important in defining New Orleans restaurants and, by extension, the city's culture was reinforced at a seminar I attended in May 2002. Entitled "Paul's Protégés," the seminar was part of an annual five-day event, the "New Orleans Wine and Food Experience," that brought together wine-makers, wine-sellers, chefs and assorted gastronomes. While similar to events held in New York, San Francisco and other cities to promote wine, the New Orleans version places more emphasis on food than the others. While many of the seminars at the event focused on wine, several were designed to celebrate New Orleans food, including one on how certain old-line restaurants have managed to survive and renew themselves, and another on the particular success of the Palace Café, one of the restaurants in the Brennans empire. "Paul's Protégés" was organized around the life of Paul Prudhomme and the careers of some of the chefs he trained at Commander's Palace and at K-Paul's. Hosted by Margaret Orr, a local television personality, the panel included Prudhomme himself, Randy Barlow, former chef-owner of Kelsey's, Greg Sonnier, co-owner and chef of Gabrielle, Frank Brigsten, chef-owner of Brigsten's and Paul Miller, the executive chef of K-Paul's. All are or have been among the most prominent chefs in New Orleans and, in addition, each has won national recognition for their food.

Each chef, including Prudhomme, was given an opportunity to discuss the main elements of his career. Several of the themes that I have encountered in interviews with New Orleans chefs and restaurateurs, linking local chefs to the region and to each other, emerged in these descriptions. A great deal of discussion centered on the kinds of local ingredients, from Creole tomatoes to shrimp, crabs and various kinds of fish, that they began to appreciate while working for Prudhomme. This appreciation included the pleasure involved in seeking out the elements of this cooking, with particular attention to fishing, which appears to be the favored leisure time activity of New Orleans chefs. More importantly, they learned to establish ties with local purveyors, from farmers to fishermen. In Prudhomme's kitchens, they not only discovered new ingredients, but learned how to transform them properly. This apprenticeship was connected to the tradition at Commander's, started by Prudhomme, of preparing as much as possible from scratch, from butchering meat, to making cheeses and sausages. At Commander's and at K-Paul's these chefs were trained in the work ethic of professional cooking, with a particular emphasis on the use of local and seasonal products.

But there was more than work. Prudhomme, they said, provided an education in what might be called the philosophy of Louisiana and New Orleans cooking. Long conversations about food, about what dishes mean and about their "emotional weight" were apparently a regular part of their apprenticeship. As Brigsten put it, rather than going to the Culinary Institute of America, his cooking school was K-Paul's, where he learned to give meaning and emotion to food. The idea that food can carry an emotional charge is central to Prudhomme's view on cooking. This, he argued, is precisely what distinguishes south Louisiana food from food elsewhere in the United States; the food here, he said, has an "emotional taste." This emotional taste comes first from an attention to technique and ingredients, which Prudhomme illustrated with a long description of how to butcher a hog properly and then prepare pork roast with dirty rice and candied yams. Emotional flavor also comes from proper spicing, which, contrary to popular belief, should not be overpowering. Rather, as Barlow described it, flavors should be layered, "from the bottom up."

At Commander's Palace and at K-Paul's, the men on the panel were initiated into a culture, given a body of knowledge and the means to reproduce it. For some, this was understood as a logical step after learning cooking with their fathers, uncles and grandfathers in fishing and hunting camps. For others, it was the step that awakened them to the possibilities of a creative new career and lifestyle. In addition to knowledge, the apprenticeship with Prudhomme linked the chefs to each other and to many others, forming an extremely ramified set of cooking lineages in the restaurants of New Orleans. In fact, all the panelists met their spouses while working at K-Paul's (Miller noted that he met *both* his wives there), linking the bonds of fictive and real kinship. Working at Commander's and K-Paul's, they became New Orleans chefs.

It would be hard to overestimate the influence of Commander's Palace on the culture of New Orleans chefs and on the menus of New Orleans restaurants. In fact, it would be easy to extend the kinship chart from the "Palace Guard" article into another and perhaps even a larger third generation. In addition, the Brennan dynasty is not the only significant network (or lineage) of chefs in New Orleans. Chefs and restaurants figure largely in New Orleans culture. Gossip about chefs' careers and personal lives appears in the local papers on a regular basis. Charity events are organized around featured chefs and restaurants almost weekly. Cooking demonstrations are a central part of the farmer's markets in New Orleans, and local chefs hold demonstrations and seminars at the annual New Orleans Jazz and Heritage Festival. Tom Fitzmorris, a prominent local food critic, hosts a three-hour daily radio show on a commercial radio station that focuses on food and restaurants; and, of course, chefs are the subject of (and participants in) many of the discussions. New Orleans chefs are also regular guests on local and national television shows – some even have their own (cable television's Food Network has sometimes been referred to as the "Emeril Network," in a reference to the seeming ubiquity of New Orleans chef Emeril Lagasse on its programs). Chefs also represent themselves, through biographies on their menus, through cookbooks and on their restaurant websites.

In recent decades, the careers of elite American chefs have been followed with an interest similar to that of movie stars and athletes. This was not always the case. Before the 1970s, restaurants serving *haute cuisine* were more likely to be known for the owner, who was rarely a chef (Kuh 2001). Priscilla Parkhurst Ferguson and Sharon Zukin (1998: 93) link the rise of chefs as stars to the growing importance of consumption in the way Americans think about society. In the case of restaurants, however, it is a particular kind of consumption. Since the 1970s, American fine-dining restaurants have shifted their focus away from French cuisine and toward the use of seasonal and local ingredients, creating what is often referred to as a new American cuisine. For American elites, there has been a parallel "gentrification of taste" (Bestor 1999: 222), in which the consumption of local foodstuffs as part of "rediscovered" regional cuisines have become signs of social distinction. In the newer fine-dining establishments, chefs can, to paraphrase Zukin (1991: 204), juxtapose the traditional and the "authentic," in the form of dishes and ingredients (the aptly named "heirloom tomatoes," for instance) with the latest techniques and technology, giving their customers, members of the economic and cultural elite, the sense that they are consuming art and tradition, real things in an economy of representations.

Chefs and their restaurants often seem to stand for the city where they work, so that one comes to think of some kind of necessary link between Los Angeles and the cooking of Wolfgang Puck, between Chicago and Charlie Trotter and, of course, between New Orleans and Emeril Lagasse or Paul Prudhomme. Eating their food links diners to the spirit of their cities. It is probably not surprising that some analysts see similarities between the rise of new American restaurants of this sort and neighborhood gentrification (Zukin 1991, 1995; Bestor 1999; cf. Bell and Valentine 1997: 136). There are, however, some important differences between these processes. People who gentrify neighborhoods often seek urban "authenticity," but their very presence drives up housing prices and drives out the people who gave the area its putative authenticity in the first place. In the case of new American cuisines, chefs draw on local ingredients, French techniques and their own imagination to create a kind of post-industrial, non-standardized cuisine (cf. Bestor 1999: 222). In other words, these new chefs create authenticity where before there was only industrialized food (cf. Goody 1982; Appadurai 1986). Chefs are viewed as artists, which lends cachet to the dining experience, but also as artisans, whose craft and knowledge allow them to stand as legitimate interpreters of local ingredients and as expert guides in the creation of local taste. In creating new regional American cuisines, chefs link diners to nature, so that in some ways, when you eat in their restaurants, you are eating more than food, you are eating the region itself.

While much of this applies to restaurants and chefs in New Orleans, there is an important difference there in what local chefs are mediating for diners. New Orleans chefs are as likely as other American chefs to emphasize the use of fresh local ingredients, but unlike others, they are also working within a well-established regional culinary canon. In the rest of the country, chefs work to link diners to nature and, in so doing, attempt to create new regional cuisines. In New Orleans, chefs do more: they link diners to culture. When you eat in New Orleans, you eat the region's "natural" bounty, but you must also digest the city's history and culture.

What We Eat and Where: New Orleans Cuisine and Restaurants

The distinctiveness of New Orleans food and restaurants is certainly something that is often asserted. Trucks from Leidenheimer's Bakery have, for instance, been painted with a cartoon featuring Vic and Nat'ly, two working-class Yat characters created by the local cartoonist Bunny Matthews, who suggests that we "Take a Bite of New Orleans Cultcha" by eating a Leidenheimer's Po-Boy.[3] The *Times-Picayune* writer Lolis Eric Elie has quite seriously suggested that only people specially licensed and trained in Louisiana be allowed to cook Louisiana food (Elie 1997). Local cooking luminaries can also be quite fierce about the need to be well-grounded in Louisiana culture to cook the food. When I had the temerity to ask Paul Prudhomme why the rice in my jambalaya was often soggy, given that my recipe came from a cookbook written by a well-known, but not native, food writer, he growled that that was only to be expected given the source of the recipe. The idea that local chefs are distinct grows out of the claim that they know where the food comes from. This really means two things. First, knowing the natural sources of the ingredients – that Creole tomatoes can only be grown in the soil of Plaquemines and St Bernard parishes, for instance – is clearly essential. But it also means knowing the history of the food and the place of various dishes in New Orleans' cultural canon.

As it is usually told, the story of the modern American restaurant and the heroically creative American chef focuses on two elements. One is the gradual supplanting of French owners and chefs by American owners and chefs, with their own distinctly commercial understanding of how to run a business. The other is the formation of American tastes through the distribution of books by Julia Child and other writers and cooks. This narrative points to a distinct Americanization of restaurants and tastes. Alice Water's restaurant, Chez Panisse, established in Berkeley in 1971, is often cited as critical to both of these narratives. Chez Panisse broke with the traditional menus of classic French restaurants, in favor of more rustic French cuisine. More importantly, Waters and the successive chefs there promoted the use of fresh, seasonal and local ingredients. Food writers usually portray these choices as a significant break with the then-dominant ideas about what *haute cuisine* should be (see Kuh 2001 for an example of this very widespread narrative).

Those familiar with New Orleans can guess what comes next: the story of New Orleans cuisine is different from the broader American pattern. Most chefs, food critics and assorted gastronomes will begin any description of the native New Orleans cuisine by asserting that, by contrast with the case in other parts of the country, there is in fact such a thing. Its origins are usually attributed to the mixture of the cooking styles and ingredients of the immigrants that settled there. French explorers, unable to recreate their own cuisine without the proper ingredients, turned to Native Americans, who contributed local substitutes (rice for wheat, for example), as well as herbs. The Spanish added their own flavorings, followed by the Africans, who contributed both ingredients and cooking skills. Later arrivals, Germans, Irish and especially Italians, each added their own styles to the development of Creole cuisine. Virtually every New Orleans guidebook and cookbook I have run across includes some form of this story (see Collin 1970; Galatoire 1994; Lagasse 1996; and McCaffety 2002 for a few examples).

The narratives that describe the Americanization of *haute cuisine* are usually linked to the transformation of the 1960s counterculture into a kind of "back-to-the-land" movement and, at least in the versions in which Alice Waters is one of the leaders, are often seen as a form of anti-elitist form of political engagement. The New Orleans narrative is also political; but it makes sense in the context of local politics and history. Thus, it parallels other stories about the origin of New Orleans' culture, contrasting the explicit mixing of groups in New Orleans with efforts in the rest of North America to maintain sharp ethnic and racial boundaries. Even the metaphors used to describe this mix differ from those in the rest of the US, so that the melting-pot becomes, in New Orleans, a gumbo, with flavors carefully layered and combined until they become something new. Of course, by itself this story does not explain why the different cuisines came to form one cuisine, rather than a hodge-podge of separate ethnic cuisines. But as a foundational myth, it is not required to explain everything. In addition, the story usually glosses over any question of domination of one group by another. Thus, while some writers recognize the central importance of African-Americans to the famous kitchens of New Orleans (see Collin 1970: 13, for instance), most tend to erase their presence in favor of more famous white chefs and owners (but see Burton and Lombard 1978 for a rare exception).

Before Alice Waters thought of the idea, New Orleans restaurants were building their menus around local ingredients, even when they sought to present themselves as representatives of high French style. Richard Collin argued that New Orleans food could not be reproduced elsewhere precisely because of its dependence on local ingredients (Collin 1970: 13). He described the food in fine-dining establishments as an extension of what people ate at home, so that while the service style might be French, the food reflected the region's environment and the city's culture. Contemporary New Orleans chefs often describe the local origins of their ingredients, but many go further, describing the cultural context where they learned how to prepare those ingredients. In their cookbooks and at cooking demonstrations New Orleans chefs will tell stories about the neighborhood joint, small-town restaurant or home where they first learned about an ingredient or technique (e.g. Lagasse 1996).

Local ingredients and history are also reflected in a kind of geography of restaurants that defines the cultural frame within which all others operate. Antoine's, Arnaud's, Brennan's, Galatoire's, Pascal's Manale and others have invented many of the dishes that define the canon of New Orleans Creole cooking. Unlike residents of other parts of the United States, New Orleans diners have palates trained for *haute cuisine*. They may be presumed to be familiar with dishes such as Oysters Rockefeller, Oysters Bienville, Shrimp Clemenceau, Barbecue Shrimp and Bananas Foster. More importantly, they can be expected to have strong opinions about how these and other dishes should be prepared. Finally, the core old-line restaurants of New Orleans continue to shape palates and continue to play a fundamental role in the city's ritual cycle, especially for New Orleans elite families.

Sidney Mintz has argued that a genuine cuisine is the food of a community, more than a series of recipes, "a cuisine requires a population that eats that cuisine with sufficient frequency to consider themselves experts on it" (1996: 96). This is certainly the case in New Orleans, where locals take pride in their obsession with food of all sorts. Although the organization of restaurant kitchens and the style of food preparation owes much to the French *haute cuisine* model (cf. Trubek 2000), New Orleans cuisine has been formed by its relationship to local ingredients and local food culture.

Restaurants are and have long been central to the idea of New Orleans culture. Although the controversy surrounding Gilberto's firing could be attributed to the decline of elite privilege, the place of restaurant culture in the city provided some legitimacy for the complaints of the restaurant's regulars. They were not merely defending their own membership in an exclusive club. They were standing up for the very core of a culture shared by all New Orleanians. This, it turns out, was a plausible excuse. But it had to be filtered through a kind of postmodern lens before anyone would believe it.

The Galatoire's Monologues

For the first few months of the controversy, it was clear that the broader public did not think highly of the Galatoire's regulars' rush to defend Gilberto. With few exceptions, the letters to the editor published in the *Times-Picayune* supported the firing, given the context of sexual harassment. Writers to the paper felt that there was a double standard at work, since the charges of harassment ran against the interests of the elite. This point of view was supported by the presence, among Gilberto's supporters, of many lawyers, including a former US Attorney. The paper's editorial writers and other columnists took every opportunity to write amusing comments about the affair at the expense of Gilberto's well-fed supporters. Finally, in July, the *Times-Picayune* columnist Chris Rose organized the "Galatoire's Monologues," a satirical reading of the letters at a local cabaret.

Several local celebrities participated in the readings, adding music and inter-pretative dance to the performances. A young woman, dressed in a white shirt, waiter's apron, and little else danced around the stage while several of the letters were read. The effect of all of this was quite hilarious, and the readings were immediately sold out. Given the apparently devastating critique of the self-absorption displayed by Gilberto's supporters, I was surprised to learn that many of them attended and apparently enjoyed the readings. Gilberto himself was said to have attended the event several times. The website devoted to saving his job posted a link to the cabaret's website.

In addition to these readings, the national media had, over the summer, taken an interest in the controversy. National Public Radio's Weekend Edition and *USA*

Today, among others, ran stories (Simon 2002; Shriver 2002). These stories focused on the controversy as a sign of the uniqueness of New Orleans culture. *USA Today*, for instance, quoted the former *Times-Picayune* food critic Gene Bourg as saying that New Orleans has different priorities from those of other cities (Shriver 2002: 1D). Here, he said, people take restaurants seriously.

In February 2003, the Galatoire's Monologues were performed as part of a conference at Copia, the museum of the American Center for Wine, Food and the Arts, in Napa, California (Anderson 2003). On their website, Copia is said to be "dedicated to exploring the distinctively American contribution to the character of wine and food in close association with the arts and humanities, and to celebrating these as a unique expression of the vitality of American life, culture and heritage" (http://www.copia.org/). With this, the firing of Gilberto left the realm of class conflict and was fully integrated into the postmodern machine of representations. The whole thing was about culture, after all.

Conclusion

The philosophy driving New Orleans restaurants and chefs seems in some ways to reflect broader trends in American restaurants in the last four decades. The Americanization of management of *haute cuisine* restaurants, the education of American palates and the turn toward seasonal and local ingredients all seem to parallel trends in New Orleans. In addition, the growing celebrity status of chefs seems to mirror the rest of the United States, as the idea of the "Emeril network" so aptly illustrates. Yet, as I have shown here, these trends do not entirely explain the place of restaurants and chefs in New Orleans culinary culture. Chefs outside New Orleans can be linked to the processes of the "gentrification of taste" (Bestor 1999: 222) and to post-industrial (or postmodern) searches for the authentic. New American chefs work to create authentic food culture by linking their customers to a particular vision of nature. While New Orleans chefs do this as well, they also must link diners to the culture of the city.

This obligation to recreate, or at least work within, the New Orleans culinary canon does not mean that local restaurant owners and chefs cannot be creative. On the contrary, like chefs in other cities, they must be creative, but they must work within stricter rules, with a heavier responsibility. Because New Orleans is a city defined, in part, by its food, restaurant owners and chefs are in a position to reproduce the city's identity, which they must accomplish while still carving out their own culinary identity. *Haute cuisine* restaurants in New Orleans are more than sites where the social elite can confirm its existence, they are also seen as an extension of the broader culture that ties the entire city together, across class and ethnic lines. It is a cliché, in New Orleans, to claim that New Orleanians do not eat to live but, rather, live to eat. This is because, of course, what is served in New Orleans is not food. It is the city itself.

The conflict over Gilberto's firing started out with accusations of sexual harassment, escalated into class conflict, but ended in a peculiar consensus over the representation of New Orleans cultural distinctiveness. It was this last that was at stake all along. The call for a restoration of traditions perceived by Galatoire's regulars to be dying – hand-chipped ice, drinks mixed by familiar waiters, elegantly dressed diners – was at first met with satire and derision. It soon became apparent, however, that if there was a cultural distinction to be preserved, it was less likely to be found in the experience of actually dining at Galatoire's, than in the experience of talking and writing about dining in New Orleans in general (cf. Ory 1996: 448). The general sense, in the end, was that there might be something distinct about a city in which the firing of a waiter could spark a major conflict, but that there was definitely something special about a place that could unite the participants in that conflict around self-conscious satire of themselves. This meant, above all, that even if the tourist hordes had entered the city, the residents were still in control of the ways in which that city would be represented.

Postface

This chapter was initially written before Hurricane Katrina and the floods it triggered devastated New Orleans. The issues I discuss are now more relevant than ever. However, the deaths of over 1,500 Louisianans in the storm, including many involved in the restaurant industry, have made the discussion of these issues much less light-hearted than in the past. For more information on the state of the New Orleans restaurant industry after the storm and on some of the debates that have developed in that context, see the introduction to this volume, as well as Beriss 2006a and 2006b. As a sort of homage to the spirit of the city before Katrina, I have left the article mostly as it was originally written. Galatoire's survived the storm and floods, publishing a cookbook in late 2005 (Rodrigue 2005) and reopening for business on January 1, 2006. Like Galatoire's, the culture of New Orleans will survive.

Notes

1. The dates are the years when each was executive chef at Commander's Palace. The *Times-Picayune* article was written when Jamie Shannon was still chef. Shannon died in 2001 and was replaced by Tory McPhail, who had trained under Shannon.

2. I have found similar accounts of chef's lineages in Boston (Jenkins 1994), New York (T. Hall 1993) and San Francisco (Burros 1984, *San Francisco Chronicle* 1991).

3. Yat is the term used for a native working class New Orleanian. The term derives from the phrase "where y'at," spoken with an accent very similar to Brooklyn, New York. A Po-Boy is a local sandwich, built on New Orleans French bread, often filled with fried seafood or roast beef.

–11–

Food, Family and Tradition in Northern Italy
The Rise and Fall of a Michelin-starred Family Restaurant
Gerald Mars

Introducing the Family, the Restaurant and the Region

When my wife and I mentioned to friends that we planned to visit Emilia-Romagna, they advised us to visit a Michelin-starred family restaurant run by friends of theirs. This is, after all, the region providing much of the food now exported worldwide as iconic Italian. To name Parmesan cheese, the "traditional Balsamic vinegar of Modena" and Parma ham is to single out but three of the region's famous products. Here "slow food" thrives, in opposition to mass-produced "fast food."

Emilia-Romagna's reputation is not new. Pepys was so concerned to safeguard his two Parmesans during the Great Fire of London that he buried them (Latham and Matthews 1970–83). Paeans for balsamic vinegar date from the mid-eleventh century (Johns 1999).

Our friends enthused not only about this restaurant's food but how the family worked together, describing this as "balletic": "There's no need for a word to be spoken: they have perfect coordination – they always work in harmony."

I was intrigued. As an anthropologist who had worked in, studied and written about restaurants (Mars *et al.* 1979; Mars and Mitchell 1976; Mars and Nicod 1984), none that I knew could remotely be described as "balletic" (but see Erickson, this volume, Chapter 1). They more often expressed *ad hoc* crisis management, territoriality, turbulence, discord and blame.

We were told the restaurant served the region's traditional cuisine, had an organic kitchen garden, and was run by a three-generation family based around three brothers. Their reputation was becoming established; but only later did I appreciate the historical bases of their cuisine and the singular nature of their organization. At that time I was primarily interested in sampling the food and the organization producing it.

They had a long history to draw on. The family published an abridged version of a manuscript in Trinity College Library in Cambridge, England, written in Italian in 1611 by Giacomo Castelvetro of Modena (Castelvetro 1989). Castelvetro, a Protestant refugee sheltering in England, missed the food of his homeland, and rightly thought the English might benefit from knowing about it. He showed how the Modenasi grew their produce and how they cooked and served it. There was to be no English version for over 350 years – until an excellently illustrated and annotated translation appeared in 1989. I was told the family used Castelvetro's book and followed many of his techniques.

I explored the region's history and cuisine, and then went to sample the food. It was delicious, and the family proved extremely welcoming. Questions, some too simple, arose. How and why were this family so successful in producing their food? How typical was it, and the family producing it? What made their organization "balletic," if indeed it was? Finally, would the Belmondis[1] agree to cooperate? They did – though they reasonably and frustratingly limited access to their busy kitchen.

I was awarded a small research grant[2] funding just one month's fieldwork. My plan was to treat the restaurant as a unit where labor processed raw materials (ingredients) using a form of organization and following a design accommodating its market. Underpinning its organization are values determining how resources should be obtained and allocated. The best way to unravel these threads – the food, ingredients, organization, values and market – was, in my experience, through ethnographic fieldwork – participant observation – complemented by structured interviewing.

The most appropriate theory to guide collection of material is, in my view, Dynamic Cultural Theory (DCT), linking forms of social organization and behavior to the tenets of a justifying world-view.[3]

Fieldwork with the Family

On arrival, I found the family's promised cooperation had a price! The Belmondis' *quid pro quo* required a study and write-up of their family's history and farming background. This was not what I'd planned. Conscious of time constraints, I agreed only with reluctance. It was fortunate I did. I couldn't have understood why their food was so good or how they were organized to produce it, without understanding their past. And only by exploring the history of the local community did I come to understand their place and that of their cuisine within it. What began as the study of a restaurant and its food now, therefore, involved two tasks: teasing out the culture and social organization of the restaurant and, retrospectively, that of peasant farming. Later I saw how the two were related.

On a chill October morning I was introduced to the village of Castelfiore, in the flatness of Emilia-Romagna's Po valley. Walking against a wind that blew the damp mists for which this area is renowned, I wondered aloud to Paolo, the eldest son, if there didn't seem a suspicion of urine in the air? Paolo confirmed it. He explained, with anger, how agribusiness and massively intensive pig rearing affected the region's water table. Agribusiness, it emerged, was a focus for this family's scorn not just of non-traditional food but also of big business and big organization in man's affairs. Later Eduardo, the father, nodding at a nearby factory producing balsamic vinegar, asked:

"Do you know how long they take to mature their *balsamico*?"
"No. How long?"
"Twenty minutes. Do you know how long it takes us to mature ours?"
"No. How long?"
"At least twelve years!"

In the Second World War this region had been a centre of partisan, anti-Nazi opposition. It suffered badly, and then more from the later Allied invasion. Post-war development has replaced many old stone buildings with concrete houses and apartment blocks, though there are still some large three-story farmhouses that had housed the extended agnatic, sharecropping families of the past. Later emphasis on nuclear families has, however, led to a plethora of small apartments. Stefano the middle son, pointing to their steel-fenced gardens, invariably patrolled by snarling guard dogs, noted a sad contrast to the friendly openness of the past – a commonly reiterated family theme.

As their story unfolded, I learned how much of the restaurant's organization and their attitude to food appeared based on practices adapted from sharecropping, the form of peasant farming indigenous to the region. Asked why they did things as they did, the family frequently referred to sharecropping values and practice. In justifying aspects of their organization, their style of cooking and their selection of traditional ingredients, they acknowledge their debt to the past. Paolo the chef: "When I cook, the memories and smells of my grandmother's cooking always come back to me: her wonderful cooking still inspires me."

Researching both ethnographies, farming in the past and the restaurant in the present, revealed two shared pre-eminent aims. First, the importance of maintaining family unity and autonomy. Second, the desire to produce highest-quality food from the freshest ingredients – irrespective, it seemed, of time, effort or cost. In both, there were similar divisions and expensive foods gifted to significant contacts. In both farm and restaurant, food had symbolic importance beyond the gustatory.

Food, forms of organization and the past were inextricably mixed. The questions I started with were beginning to require answers more complex than anticipated.

The Restaurant and the Family

That family orbits round food.

A family associate

Descended from generations of sharecroppers and, latterly, part-owners of their farm, Eduardo and Margherita Belmondi with their three sons left the land in 1960 to open a workingmen's *trattoria*. It took twelve years' hard saving to start the restaurant. They refused to borrow.

Close to the village center, Restaurant Belmondi occupies the ground floor of an anonymous concrete block. There is residential accommodation for both the unmarried sons, their parents, and an aged uncle, and a small *pensione,* run as a sideline. Paolo and his wife, son and daughter live nearby, in a house on family land adjacent to the vegetable garden.

The restaurant is approached through a reception area leading to a rectangular dining-room. There is little "décor": a few dried flowers, a small number of pictures and a couple of shelves displaying traditional pots, pans and cooking equipment. The interior appears stark, though seating is comfortable and tables well spaced and of a decent size. Opposite the reception are two longer tables for groups – in all offering thirty-six covers. Their kitchen is larger than might be expected.

Numerous well-wishers have suggested the family lighten the overall impression with fancier lighting, fresh flowers, perhaps more pictures. The family, however, see the restaurant's unadorned simplicity as defining its function – it is a place for serious gastronomy, even if its décor suggests asceticism. This too reflects values from their sharecropping past.

The family work long hours, fifteen-hour days being standard. They cover all the restaurant's labor needs, those of their one-hectare, strictly organic vegetable and salad garden, and all emergency mechanical, plumbing and electrical needs. In this, they follow the self-sufficiency ideal of sharecroppers.

Signore Eduardo (68). Meat chef, particularly roasts and *bollito* (mixed boiled meats); he purchases craft-produced salami, hams, and *culatello* (haunch of ham slow-cured in a pig's intestine, a specialty of the area between Parma and Piacenza) and processes his own tripe. All-purpose handyman.

Signora Margherita (66). Daily prepares the fresh pasta, a skilled and onerous task taking several hours. She is occasionally helped by two, and sometimes three, part-time skilled, elderly ladies; and always by her daughter-in-law Carla. General kitchen work.

First Son, Paolo (46). Principal Chef, gardener and mechanic; married to Carla.

Second Son, Stefano (38). Maitre d' and accountant. Maintains contact with outsiders – journalists, food scholars, tax and municipal authorities. A self-taught scholar of historical gastronomy, he has supplementary expertise as a *sommelier.*

Third Son, Toni (32). Sommelier, waiter, deputy *Maitre d',* maker of "traditional" balsamic vinegar.

Carla (43). Married to Paolo. Helps make the daily pasta and assists variously in the kitchen. A *patissière,* she has introduced some Czech dishes. Paolo says: "Carla is key. She's like the person in the football team who can play every position."

Matilde (19). Paolo and Carla's daughter. Waitress and general kitchen work. Her commitment to the restaurant is uncertain. She is affianced to a computer programmer. Her brother, Leonardo, studies engineering.

Living with them, but inactive, is Eduardo's unmarried elder brother, Bruno.

Part I: The Past in the Present: Sharecropping – An Inheritance Emphasizing Quality Food

Sharecropping in Emilia-Romagna involved groups of brothers living and working together, on tenanted farms with wives, parents and dependants. Sharecroppers gave up a proportion of their produce in return for the tenancy of their land, a house, and (usually) use of the landlord's livestock. This system operated as late as the 1960s (Sereni 1997). Their households collectively acted as both production and consumption units.

Sharecroppers lived insecure lives. Contracts were renewed annually, while sickness, blight, war, disastrously adverse weather and the periodic collapse of markets had all been within the experience of the current family members. Near-starvation was not uncommon, and most people lived close to subsistence despite working long hours in the fields. In the worst winters it was common for children of the poorest households, the landless *braccianti*, to have to beg for food.

How then, in the midst of such poverty, did Emilia-Romagna develop such a renowned cuisine?

They achieved it in part because, as Castelvetro showed, they benefited from superb, locally sourced ingredients, a refined knowledge of husbandry and the cultural inheritance of skilled techniques refined over time. These were aligned with a variety of social mechanisms that valued high-quality food to an iconic level.

In this turbulent milieu, effective survival required cooperation – both within and between households. Following the "honor and shame" ethic, household members had to cooperate – and be seen to cooperate – to gain the respect and support of other households. Women and men were expected to work flexibly together – to do jobs skillfully, assiduously and in harmony – as shifting needs determined. If a household cooperated well in one sphere this was taken to show that they did so in others. The quality of their food indicated whether they were an effective family.

Bonds linking all farms in the community were consolidated through a myriad institutions. There were ongoing exchanges of cows between farms – cows bore a personal name and the surname of their household of origin. Bonds were also consolidated through the Church, its festivals and feasts; by mutual arrangements for welfare; through interactive leisure, at convivial gatherings of neighbors in the byres on winter evenings; and by participation in *consortia* (cooperatives) producing cheese and wine.

Cooperation was vital too at communal harvesting during *vendemmia* "the mad time" – and through the shared labor of three or four neighboring households (*Zorla* groups) who were expected to be fed by recipient households. Paying for labor, other than with food, and except in emergencies, was considered irresponsible.

The food households shared on these occasions was discussed, carefully assessed and rated as to taste and quality.

Because households "imported" wives and "exported" daughters, this too made for cooperative bonds between them. As Eduardo explained: "The women are like cows, the cows are like women." He meant that both women and cows served the same function – they both bonded living links between farms.[4]

Food, Honor and Social Mobility

Sharecropping in Emilia-Romagna was unusual in two ways: first, households were permitted a form of social mobility; second, there was the emphasis they gave to appreciate, discuss and comparatively rate their food. The two were linked; producing good food and its contribution to family honor was necessary to gain social mobility.

Sharecropping households were ranked into three main grades who, as they climbed, retained increasing portions of their output, depending on whether they managed to acquire first, their own cows and eventually their own land, and whether these were mortgaged.

Transition between grades needed credit. Since sharecroppers were largely outside the money economy, credit-worthiness was determined in part by perceptions of how well a household's members cooperated, which was taken to demonstrate their effectiveness as a farming unit. Not surprisingly, sharecroppers gifted their most valuable products – salamis and hams – to their assessors, even when they themselves were reduced to survival on polenta.

Each transition needed positive assessments from three constituencies. First, the landlord, whose role was central. His capital financed the transition, and he was the lender of last resort – since banks were eschewed even in crises. Landlords, by the terms of the contract, were entitled to specific food offerings as well as being recipients of food gifts. Second, other households, as peer equals, assessed the food given on the occasions it was shared. Third came the priest, who assessed moral worth and was given food gifts on his pastoral visits. Food accordingly was imbued with material, communal and, not least, moral valuations.

Households (and thus the wider community) were linked to the town through "brokers" – urban providers of specialist emergency services, such as veterinarians, medics, bankers and lawyers – who, as a form of insurance premium, were also given regular food gifts.

Since the cost of a single transition was high, it was rare for a household to achieve more than one in a generation. Its honor therefore had to be perpetually sustained – and the quality of its food likewise.

Gender Differences and the Prestige of Different Foods

Though many jobs on the farm were carried out by both sexes, food preparation was gender-based, and this influenced the prestige ratings of different foods. Grain-based dishes such as polenta and mixed grain/egg-based products such as pasta, made by the *Resdora* (see below), had lower status than dishes derived from the rearing and killing of pigs or cows, which were under the control of men. This distinction conforms to the more general ranking of animal protein as superior to the grain products associated with women. And chicken was rated lower than pork or beef, since rearing chickens was women's responsibility.

Food, Authority and the Transmission of Cooking Skills

Both sexes on the farm shared in collective decision-making, and women's voices were often significant in the collective gatherings called to discuss issues arising. Nevertheless, there were two prestigious authority positions: the *Resdor* (farm manager and "Head of the Family"), usually but not always the father or eldest son (Eduardo, a younger son, the last *Resdor* on his family's farm, was chosen "out of order," the family say, for his pre-eminent talents), and the *Resdora*, the cook/housekeeper, the senior woman [*resdor/resdora* (pl. *resdorae*) are dialectal]. In addition to her skill as a cook, her authority was buttressed by her allocation to co-wives and their children of the small resources she earned from egg and chicken sales. She also arbitrated their disputes. By these means she asserted control over consumption of such items as ribbons, apparently a common feminine indulgence: conspicuous consumption had no place in sharecropping, as we saw in the operation of the restaurant.

In addition to preserved meats prepared by the household's men and gifted to outsiders, the basis of a household's community assessment owed much to its *Resdora*. Her cooking skills were honed through continuous, critical discussion. And since being the daughter of a celebrated cook was an asset in the marriage market, there was an ongoing and strongly motivated transmission of cooking skills from mothers to daughters.

Though *Resdorae* were competitive, they did not produce new dishes, but variations within the established culinary tradition. A household might express pride in their *Resdora*'s cooking, but it was still recognizable as traditional cooking. So Paolo spoke of his *Resdora* grandmother:

"Anything she needed she had to earn from the farmyard. So with a very small amount of meat, she made wonderful casseroles. One rabbit would feed ten people. Its good sauce made up for the lack of meat."

Resdorae were concerned with freshness as well as flavor, since stale food was blamed for illnesses thought likely to hazard their households' economic bases and thus their honor ratings. Not surprisingly, fresh ingredients are still integral to this area's cuisine. A good cook is still highly rated, and stale food still pronouncedly associated with illness.

Resdorae, through their cooking skills, emerge as the guardians, not only of their households' honor, economic viability and prospective mobility – but also, indeed, of this region's traditional cuisine.

Part II: So, What Makes This Restaurant's Food So Good?

To find answers to this question we need to see whether we can detect sharecropping structures, values and behaviors in this restaurant and see how they influence its operation.

The Restaurant's Organization: How the Family Pursues its Twin Aims

> This family is like a solar system – with each member having their own orbit.
>
> Stefano

To maintain its autonomy and produce top-quality food, the family employs four organizing strategies. First, it fosters collective capital accumulation by employing only family labor, shunning outside finance and limiting personal expenditure and display. Second, it adopts an unusual division of labor, expecting all family members to demonstrate a range of skills. And third, it disperses power, risk and blame by collectivizing decision-making. All have their roots in sharecropping.

I examine these strategies in the restaurant, and then in the kitchen garden, before describing how together they produce a menu adaptive to the seasons, recognizably "traditional" but effectively adjusting to the changing demands of modernity. A fourth strategy – regulating the family's outside relationships – will be discussed separately.

Fostering Capital Accumulation: Counters to Orthodox Economic Practice The family see autonomy and producing top-quality food as symbiotic. Both would diminish, they say, if they took on employees. They would lack the motivation to ensure the same quality as family members have or, lacking ties of family loyalty, would leave after expensive training. Employees, they pointed out, would also involve the high social security payments that are required by Italian law.

By rejecting outside labor, refusing borrowed finance and working extremely long hours, the family, in effect, convert their labor into capital. Long hours limit spending on leisure and socializing, and this permits further capital accumulation.

The family retain their accumulated fund in corporate ownership rather than distributing it. As a result they now collectively own the restaurant's premises, its *pensione*, the house where Paolo and his family live, and the hectare of ancestral land that is their garden. They also own various properties in and around the village. Whenever I raised questions about credit and borrowing, there were references to a dissolute great-grandfather who had plunged the family into debt. This took the collective efforts of several generations to clear.

Self-financing means deferring plans that outside finance could have made immediately effective. It involves long-term strategies, with extensions to the planning stage that rarely apply in restaurants. As in sharecropping, it reflects the caution typically found in groupings with long-term views of their collective future.[5]

As the décor of the restaurant shows, this family eschews conspicuous consumption. Paolo, a competent mechanic, delights in his small, aged and battered Fiat with over 290,000 km on its clock. He proudly told me: "I'm aiming to double that."

Their financial strategy involves the family in apparently uneconomic practices. They could, for example, readily buy in top-quality *tradizionale* balsamic vinegar, but instead produce their own. They have set up a *batteria* – the equipment to produce it; paid for tuition and are committed to the labor it requires. They have planted their own balsamic vines, which take five years to become established, while the product requires between twelve and twenty years to mature – another indication of their essentially long-term planning.

Though they can physically accommodate more covers, the mounting strain on the parents as they age precludes any increase, and has even made them think of stopping lunches. With outside labor they could achieve more covers *and* secure their lunchtime trade. Instead, they work longer hours.

Paolo put the case against maximizing profits at the expense of changing organization: "…[If we were to hire] two more waiters, two more chefs and double the covers we'd quadruple the profits. We've thought all this through – but there's an optimal size to keep the quality. We'll never be as rich as the Agnellis[6] – but we have gastronomy: it's job satisfaction."

Producing high-quality food means seeking out ingredients primarily on taste – with cost a relatively negligible priority – a questionable strategy by orthodox business criteria. It is also extremely labor-intensive – as Eduardo's unremitting search for craft producers of quality foods reveals. As he put it:

> The EC [European Union] and Big Business together are squeezing out small producers with regulations no one can follow – not if we're to keep traditional quality. To keep up quality you have continually to search. I go around tasting and buying. Always on the lookout – always tasting – not looking for competitive prices. If that was it we could get the commercial rubbish. It's the small producers we go to.
>
> It's under cover – we keep it secret. A small producer of salami is excellent. He produces a thousand and they're wonderful. But if he extends it to ten thousand – the quality crashes.

These labor-intensive endeavors that prioritize quality above cost are possible only because the family's labor is essentially underpaid, its earnings are undistributed and the hours worked, by any usual standards, are excessive. A "normal" restaurant supplying above-average food with the same number of covers would expect to have one senior and one junior chef, a kitchen helper, and two waiters (perhaps one half-time). Total staff-hours, assuming normal outsourcing, would approximate to 40 a day, equating to about 240 hours a week. Restaurant Belmondi's seven staff work on average over 100 hours a day or *c.*600 hours a week, often extending through Sundays – though this figure excludes work in the kitchen garden. The difference means that more than half the Belmondis' efforts are available to ensure quality.

Divisions of Labor   Labor is organized in three ways; the first two involve "multi-skilling."

- The "one and one-third" rule

Working such long hours means that staff can spend at least a quarter of their working days on a secondary task. Everyone shares their expertise and everyone does at least one and one-third jobs, so that each job-holder is assured a deputizing shadow. But this does mean that the family's investments in training have had to be considerable.

Though Paolo is entirely self-taught, the family sent Stefano and Toni to the region's excellent Trades College to train respectively as *Maitre d'* and *sommelier*. Stefano required a year's lodging in Modena, followed by the need to subsidize his poorly paid apprenticeship at a top Florentine restaurant. He then trained other family members, especially Toni. The family later paid a retired expert from Modena to tutor Toni in balsamic vinegar-making, a skill he is passing on to Stefano.

Paolo is a partial exception to "the one and one-third rule." Being chef and gardener takes all his time. Stefano, *Maitre d'* and accountant, though not regularly shadowing anyone, fills in as deputy *sommelier* when needed. Toni the *sommelier* acts as deputy *Maitre d'*. And all periodically help in the garden and, if necessary, in the kitchen.

In short-term crises through illness or incapacity, the family has always coped and never (except for part-time pasta-making and occasional stillroom help) hired outside labor. Instead they reduce output – produce fewer meals – or/and work even longer hours.

With its "one and one-third" rule the family is independent of "outside" labor, always has spare trained capacity to meet normal, shifting surges in demand so typical of restaurants, and can cope with staff shortages in emergencies – a common bane of restaurants (Whyte 1948; Mars and Mitchell 1976, Ch. 4). Eduardo explains: "Two years ago we were all ill with flu at the same time. There was an epidemic and we had to close the restaurant – but in over twenty years that was the only time."

- The "purity of mission" rule

A second way the restaurant's labor is organized is a requirement that everyone can cook to an advanced level. This ensures that the restaurant's primary task remains the focal point of everyone's experience, contributing to what can be called its "purity of mission."

Together, the two rules ensure the achievement of the benefits both of specialization and of generalization – as on the farm. No one becomes detached from the restaurant's basic function – preparing quality food – and no one lacks a specialized expertise.

- Food and prestige rating: divisions of labor by gender

In the restaurant and, as we saw, on the farm most jobs are carried out by both sexes; but making fresh pasta was always done by women. Accordingly, pasta had – and still has – a lower prestige rating than meat products prepared by men. Made as it is from flour and eggs, the making of pasta involves standing and rolling thin sheets by hand for several hours until they are translucent. It is the Senora, Margherita, backed by Carla and two or three older village ladies, who makes the restaurant's fresh pasta each morning. It takes longer than it used to, and is more onerous for Carla. There is a shortage of skilled older ladies – and Margherita too is getting older.

Time also influences the prestige of food, long preparation cycles invariably attracting higher prestige than short. Fresh pasta, prepared daily, has lower prestige than preserved meats processed over several months. Preparing food over long time-cycles also involves an inherent capital appreciation that accrues over time (MacClancey, in press). On the farm, preserved meats were the exclusive concern of men – which again raised their prestige – and were traditionally given as gifts by men to other men – just as in the restaurant it is men who obtain and cook the meat.

Food also has an internal/external dimension. On the farm, preserved meats were gifted for consumption outside the household – the realm of men - whereas pasta was consumed mainly within the household – the realm of women, though women were by no means limited to the home; to summarize:

- Men (higher prestige) – Dealings with "superior" animal protein – pork and beef (not "inferior" chicken and eggs); less repetitive, longer production cycles. Externally oriented.
- Women (lower prestige) – Dealings with chicken and eggs (not "superior" pork and beef); dealings with grain/egg products (pasta); highly repetitive, shorter production cycles. Internally oriented.

Pasta-making is the only task subject to neither the "one and one- third" nor the "purity of mission" rules, which further entrenches it as "woman's work."

Dispersing Power, Risk and Blame   When a person is the only one in a workplace able to do their job, they have a degree of monopolist control that affords them considerable power. In the restaurant, operation of the two rules reduces such power: everyone has wide experience and everyone is qualified to discuss wider issues. Power to make unilateral decisions (Douglas 1992) is thus dispersed. This, the family argue, encourages decision-making by consensus. As Eduardo put it: "No one ever makes alterations or innovations by themselves. Everything is discussed."

The family insist that discussions never produce stalemate. With consensus, they say, responsibility is shared. But if things go wrong blame cannot be focused. It follows that responsibility remains unallocated – no one can be blamed. Difficult decisions are therefore likely to be avoided to maintain family solidarity.

Policy and planning strategies are discussed at about fifteen meetings a year. Though I attended none, I was told that at these meetings one's age, main job, family position or gender granted no overriding authority. I was assured there had been no succession crises. As parents age and the going becomes harder, the fluidity of roles, the family say, permits them gradually to reduce what they do. Such "gradualism" again defers the need for decisive decision-making. It may be satisfying to the parents to give up some demands on them, but is it as acceptable to those who take on their work – given their already long hours? When I raised these questions, however, the family denied there was an issue.

The organic garden.   The Belmondis' one-hectare organic garden, like the restaurant, nicely demonstrates how the family's organizing strategies work to achieve autonomy and top-quality food.

Their labor-intensive garden is Paolo's pride. Providing superbly fresh produce, it nevertheless appears irrational on economic grounds. With his role as chef, it involves Paolo working fifteen- to eighteen-hour days. Even this is sometimes inadequate, and has to be supplemented by his father and brothers. While I was there a microstorm, common in this region, caused devastating damage to the garden. All the men worked long hours to repair the damage. Paolo regrets that his long hours involve some neglect of his (nuclear) family; but employing outside labor has never been considered.

Paolo harvests each day's produce – before lunch and dinner – to ensure freshness: "If we were to run a restaurant in Milan I wouldn't be able to do it with herbs I haven't grown. These freshly grown herbs [he gestures] have to be used immediately – or their essential oils diminish."

Besides vegetables, Paolo grows forty or so edible aromatic flowers and herbs for salads. These appear throughout the year as an emblematic part of the menu. Numbers vary with the seasons and as he learns of new varieties or tracks down old ones. Many serve dual or triple functions – nasturtium, served in salads, also deters aphids – though he even cultivates aphids at certain seasons to encourage their predators.

Their garden links this family to their culinary past, though salads with aromatic herbs are not indigenous to the area and derive from remembered meals of Paolo's maternal grandmother. She had "a passion for gardening," and introduced them from her native Mantua.

Paolo's quest for new and better varieties parallels Eduardo's for small craft producers. He is helped by Stefano. Stefano, for example, sought an old variety of parsnip, unavailable locally but referred to in Castelvetro. He finally obtained it from the UK via Gillian Riley, Castelvetro's translator. When he obtained seeds of an old and rare breed of potato, *purimo*, normally unavailable from commercial sources, Paolo test-grew them, made them into a purée, and now serves them with braised beef, *brasato*, originating from Piedmont. *Purimo*, Paolo told me, takes a lot of space, has a low yield and a short growing season, and is prone to disease. "So why grow it?" I asked. "Well," he admitted, "it does need a lot of care – but it's worth it for the taste." So it is. It tastes better than any potato I've ever tasted: an intense essence of potato that perfectly complements the beef.

When a new variety of vegetable or aromatic flower has been located and successfully grown, Paolo presents it to the family for tasting and assessment, since whatever appears on the menu has to be collectively approved (see the section on "Sunday Lunches" below).

At slack times Paolo will escort visitors round the garden. His knowledge is extensive and generously offered. He explains that it is not a tidy garden (nor is it) but enthusiastically demonstrates how its various natural systems ensure an integrated, organic totality. Paolo is pleased to show his species-specific nesting-poles, artificial nests and bird-tables that cultivate great tits, blackbirds and robins, which all eat different insect pests. ("Robins like orange pieces, and they have to be fed in winter.")

Their garden, economic rationality aside, has considerable symbolic value for the Belmondis. They frequently refer to it as "family land." Paolo, in the garden: "We have this big advantage – this family land – our land – we've worked it for generations." Their garden not only roots the family in the practices and values of their past, but offers them control, autonomy and the possibility of creativity in a present seen as increasingly threatening. Threats are evident at all levels – not just from hunters and dogs but from mass food, multinational Big Business with its associated pollution, and official bureaucracies – particularly the European Union, with its food regulations. They are seen together as restricting the traditional production of craft foods and together as calculatedly destroying memories of traditional taste.[7]

This organic garden offers the Belmondis their way to fight commercial and governmental influences. Through it they demonstrate a heroic micro-environmentalism, while the hedge emphasizes and symbolizes the family's insulation, independence and rejection of aspects of "the outside." It demonstrates the family's holistic and alternative world-view – a continually reaffirmed ideology that successfully produces high-quality food through autonomous family organization that is rooted in sharecropping.

Regulating Outside Relationships   This family's fourth strategy is to regulate and limit outside relationships. In this they differ from their sharecropping past.

While the farm family was enmeshed in a web of external social links, the Belmondis have few. Working long hours precludes social involvements; avoiding external finance not only averts contact with potential funders or partners but excludes exposure to alternative economic rationalities; excluding non-family labor avoids interacting with employees. Nor are the family churchgoers. They avoid political affiliations. There are few links to other families through kinship and none through marriage. Of the family's three sons, two are bachelors, well into marriageable age, who show little sign of potential marriage. Paolo's marriage to Carla, a Czech lady he met on holiday abroad, provides no local kin. Surprisingly, for a North Italian family they are socially relatively isolated.

The family, however, does have three business-driven links with "the outside": to suppliers of produce, food writers, and "brokers." All are functional to the restaurant's operation or reputation; but all are arranged to preclude close involvements.

● Suppliers

Eduardo's cultivation of a diminishing number of traditional craft producers is kept contractual and uncolored by sentiment. He frequently changes suppliers, and settles each transaction as it arises. "Once you get involved in credit with a supplier it's never easy to change him – and the quality is likely to go down." Eduardo justifies his stance by referring to sharecropping practice. Forty farmers would set up a Parmesan *consortia*, a cooperative cheese-making venture, and collectively hire a cheese-maker whose continued employment was entirely dependent on the quality of his cheese. "If he produced poor cheese for two years running then he'd have to go – there was no sentiment."

Lack of sentiment on the farm is directly comparable to how Eduardo buys specialized meats for the restaurant, and it determines how Toni, the *sommelier*, manages his relationships with wine merchants. "I put wine down to ensure continuity, but I shift suppliers to ensure quality." Stefano, as the restaurant's accountant, insists that his father's lessons from the farm (when he was *Resdor*) govern his own unsentimental dealings with representatives of firms and bureaucracies.

● Sunday lunches for food-writers, journalists and food scholars

Sunday lunches with food specialists provide useful contacts and publicity. All the family attend, together with six or eight significant guests. Here, after prior testing by the family, Paolo's adaptations of traditional dishes are offered, and genuine comments on quality and taste are expected. These lunches contribute to the menu's continuous adaptation.

Though extremely sociable, Sunday lunches are nonetheless "working lunches," usually lasting all day and well into the evening, to include dinner. Guests from outside the local community are given overnight accommodation. They leave after lavish hospitality, excellent food and fine Lambrusco wine, either with a bottle of home-brewed *tradizionale* balsamic vinegar or home-brewed *nochino* – a traditional local liquor the family make from husks of unripe green walnuts.

- Brokers and their secondary contacts

Brokers are vital to the restaurant in linking and extending family contacts to products, knowledge and sources of influence – in the same way that sharecropping households were linked to the town. Some brokers with a specific and useful knowledge of food may be invited to Sunday lunches. As with its other outside involvements, the restaurant family limits its commitment to its brokers. My own relationship to them was via the broker/food scholar who had arranged my introduction. Though welcomed and entertained by the family, it was made clear that I was this broker's contact and her responsibility. Having made the introduction, she controlled its development. When she independently decided that contact should cease, I queried with the Belmondis whether this decision had come from them: they assured me it hadn't, it was entirely the broker's decision. "It's up to her – entirely up to her."

Links to "the outside" are seen as a threat to family solidarity. Dealing with brokers as they do, however, allows the family access to useful contacts while limiting obligation, involvement and emotional investment. Stefano wrote to both "my" broker and to me: "When writing to the family, please do not write to one member of the family but to 'Famiglia Belmondi' [to the whole family]."

- The adaptive menu

I have shown how the family's four organizing strategies, particularly their long hours and capital retention, operate to create surplus but undistributed resources that sustain the high standard of their menu and allow its continual adaptation. They permit top-quality ingredients to be sourced irrespective of time and largely of price; they allow the chef to practice and experiment with labor-intensive preparation. They make resources available for research, for nurturing significant brokers, for maintaining their labor-intensive organic garden, and for extensive staff training – all of which contribute to a menu that continuously adapts.

"Traditional" food is, of course, at the core of the menu. But the menu comprises more than a mere rehash of the "festival foods" of yesteryear. Though it represents an idealized past, it is firmly set in the present – a present that continually shifts. As an example, while the menu includes and transcends festival foods, it serves and adapts everyday peasant staples of the past, polenta and, to a degree, pasta. These now appear as subsidiary parts of meals, so that their contemporary proportions are reversed: staples diminish, while first-class protein increases (Szathmary 1983). And when they do appear, staples are subject to modification.

Fifty years ago lard was basic to many local dishes. Now customers from a wider cosmopolitan base prefer a lighter cooking medium, so that in many traditional dishes lard has been replaced by grape-seed oil. Lard does, however, reappear as *lardo aromatizzato alle erbe aromatiche*, thin shavings of lard flavored with the garden's aromatic herbs, and served on the *antipasti* menu with home-baked wholemeal bread.

Gift foods and cash products – salami, balsamic vinegar and Parmesan – make an appearance much as before; but their role, too, is amended. With other traditional constituents they can be added to a dish, omitted, shifted to different parts of the menu or replaced over time. The technologies and processes applied to them vary similarly, while historical research frequently reinstates forgotten practices and ingredients of a previous age. Stefano and Paolo's search for and adaptation of especial varieties of parsnip and potato, as discussed, are good examples – as the use of Castelvetro's seventeenth-century work illustrates.

Tomatoes served as a salad (*pomodori in insalata*), in their historical turn, also represent innovation: Eduardo recounted his grandfather's surprise at his first sight of them when, as a young man, he traveled outside the region. As the restaurant's geographic base widens, so innovations from farther away reflect newer tastes. Carla has introduced dishes from her native Czechoslovakia – rabbit with cream, duck with cherries and tripe soup are now favorites. Vegetarians too are accommodated – with charcoal-grilled vegetables appearing as a main course instead of meat.

The gender-based divisions of the past, however, are still dominant in determining the "shape" of the restaurant's menu. The core of each main dish (with the exception of vegetarian options) is always high-grade protein (associated with men); there is no place for chicken or egg dishes (which historically have always been associated with women).

Underlying innovation is sensitivity to changes in customer tastes. But though adaptation is extensive, it occurs within limits set by historical inheritance. Working within these limits is here more important than radical innovation.

● The past in the present

Parallels between the farm and restaurant are now evident. Major differences between the two lie in the farm family's extensive outside links compared to the restaurant family's minimal ones and the lack of any arbitrational/authority role in the restaurant on a par with those of the *Resdor* and *Resdora*.

Conclusion to Parts I and II

The question I started with – "Why is the food so good?" – has involved explorations of space and particularly time. Searching for answers involved uncovering the historical role of food in the sharecropping culture of Emilia-Romagna. It has shown how a cuisine inherited from the past has been adapted to the present. To do so it has demonstrated the family's success in orchestrating, bonding, and motivating holders of a range of different but complementary skills and interests. To prepare their exceptional food has therefore involved the creation of a complex and sophisticated form of social organization. This, like the cuisine it has effectively adapted, is also firmly set in sharecropping history. It has allowed the family to harness imaginative intelligence, high levels of skill, scholarship and unremitting effort. But to produce food at this level obviously demands something more: it requires dedication, sacrifice and not a little fanaticism.

Drawing general rules, or attempting to provide formulae applicable to other restaurants, should be approached with caution. Certainly, aspects of their divisions of labor might well be transferable; but Restaurant Belmondi is unique – as is the past from which it has emerged.

Part III: A Family Schism: The Restaurant Falls

While writing up after fieldwork, I learned there had been a long period of disagreement, after which Carla, amidst strong recriminations, had left Restaurant Belmondi to work in another restaurant. Paolo then left too, and the couple decided to start their own restaurant. The rest of the family had to acknowledge they couldn't continue. As a result, the superbly successful Restaurant Belmondi, with its ingenious and enterprising innovations, its networks of contacts, its uniquely varied and coordinated skills, folded amid bitter accusations. A brief visit in 2004 revealed a family schism that seems irreconcilable.

A Trouble Case

"A trouble case" (Hoebel 1954) is an event involving a breakdown in norms. It "highlights" and thus aids examination of aspects of social organization normally hidden. It makes it possible to understand how what had contributed to this restaurant's outstanding success also accounted for its sad collapse.

The Immediate Cause of Schism   Discussions with Paolo and Carla, admittedly only one side of the dispute, pointed to a shortfall in the labor available to make the daily pasta as the trigger to the schism. The steadily increasing work over the past year fell largely on Carla as Margherita found it more and more difficult to cope. And the supply of part-time skilled village ladies was diminishing, as they too were aging.

Paolo, as chef and gardener, was also carrying what the couple saw as an unduly heavy burden. Compounding their problem was the family's unwillingness to bring in outside labor or reschedule Margherita's work or – as Carla and Paolo asserted – to discuss the problem or take it seriously. Underpinning Carla's difficulties was the gender distinction by which pasta preparation was allocated as women's work. In the absence of available women, she was left as the principal pasta-maker, since the "one and one-third" rule couldn't be applied. The problem was made worse because Stefano and Toni remained unmarried, and so failed to bring in wives. Carla and Paolo said they tried to raise their mounting workload in and out of formal meetings, but to no effect. With no visible solution, they finally saw their problem as resolvable only by a complete rupture.

Underlying Bases for Schism: Nuclear Loyalties vs Loyalty to the Extended Family
A shrewd resident of the village who has known the family well over the years, while full of admiration for their achievements, described them as "a throwback." He meant they lived and worked as an extended sharecropping family of the past, not as a nuclear family in the present – the societal shift to which is so graphically revealed in the region's domestic architecture.

Transfer of a family structure appropriate to sharecropping was bound to be problematic in the new Emilia-Romagna. Paolo's nuclear family offered a powerful and rival focus of loyalty to the extended family. These significant differences between the two contexts defined a "fault line" primed for fission. But there were other contributing factors.

Money: Its Visibility, Retention and Distribution   When occasional money entered the sharecropping household it was channeled through the *Resdor* and, to a lesser extent, the *Resdora*. Their authority and distributions went largely unquestioned, since precedents were well established and amounts relatively small. After settling commitments, balances were readily allocated to corporate resources.

When money more fully permeates an economy, one individual's contributions can readily be assessed and compared with another. Similarly, rewards can be measured against inputs, and comparisons drawn between them: the very presence of money makes for visibility.

The visibility of money made it evident that resources controlled centrally within the restaurant family would bypass the nuclear sub-unit. Carla and Paolo's children, having no ambition to join the family enterprise, would face disinheritance – despite their parents' years of effort and involvement.

The Role of Women Farm women had little say in their choice of work.[8] This was not so in the restaurant. Carla readily found work outside. Stefano, in blaming her for the schism, remarked when she moved out: "She was never a *contadina* wife – she was a townswoman." One recognizes here echoes of established precedents by which "imported" wives in patrilocal societies are readily slotted into the role of scapegoat/witch (Gluckman 1955, p. 98).

Decision-Making and Conflict Resolution Though farm family members had a say in decision-making, there was a firm hierarchic core focused through the *Resdor* and *Resdora*. They had the authority to settle disputes and allocate responsibilities and blame, and they controlled resources buttressing their authority. In the restaurant's more egalitarian "enclavic" regime, there was no ultimate arbitrator; conflicts remained unresolved until the situation became untenable.

Relations within and between Households – and the Connections While the farming family was enmeshed in a web of communal interactions, these were not available to the later Belmondis.

Participation by farming families in the activities of the Church and its festivals and feasts, through *Zorla* groups and collective harvesting at *Vendemia*, by involvement in the various *Consortia* and, not least, through movements of cows and women on marriage, all enhanced the bonds of community and opportunities for collaboration. In addition, informal dances, the deferential fostering of the old (in exchange for expertise), and drinking and chatting in neighbors' barns, as well as courtship and the seeking out of spouses, together extended and strengthened links between households, and in doing so reduced the intensity of emotions within them. In effect, they "pulled members out" of their households (Gluckman 1955, Ch. 3).

The restaurant family limited their outside emotional involvements and focused their psychic resources inward: they were not churchgoers and eschewed local politics. External suppliers were frequently changed, and involvements with specialists and experts were truncated by mediation through brokers – a position very different from practices on the farm.

Outside labor was avoided in both contexts but significantly, where pasta-making was so important, no additional female labor, except for Carla, had been gained through marriages or links gained from in-laws. More important, there seemed no prospect of change. The restaurant family's lack of external interactive links meant that, for them, their emotions remained undispersed and, in effect, undiffused.

Summary of Part III: Reasons for the Schism

By closing the boundary between family and external environment, the family had to solve its problems internally, and could not call on the supportive external exchanges that made the sharecropping system work. Given an increasing demographic disequilibrium between work demands and labor supply, the family had little alternative but to "ratchet up" demands for greater effort from its own labour. Its "one and one- third" and "purity of mission" rules could only go so far. Eventually, given the hours they were already working, ratcheting-up couldn't be extended.

In this interplay between social structural forces and cultural values, their increasing divergence and the absence of any legitimated arbitrational role ensured that schism became inevitable.

Postscript

Two years later the schism remains unresolved, with no contact between the family's two segments. Paolo, Carla and Leonardo (who has given up engineering) flourish in their new restaurant and seem very happy. Their daughter, Matilde, sides with the family's other segment.

Paolo now runs a 100-meter garden rather than his previous hectare, and has twenty-four covers rather than thirty-six. The balance between covers and staff hours is thus more in line with average levels. He buys in most vegetables and *balsamico tradizionale*; the couple employ outside part-time labor and there has been a reining-in of the historical research and adaptations to it that had defined the Belmondi Restaurant.

There are less time and resources to search for specialist craft producers or entertain significant outsiders. Paolo has no aspirations to regain his Michelin star. More Czechoslovak adaptations appear; but they carry many of the same dishes as before, and the quality is very good. Paolo has replaced his Fiat with a new and smarter Peugeot.

Notes

The author exerts his moral rights to be regarded as the author of this material. Copyright is claimed by him under the relevant legislation. © Gerald Mars 2007.

1. To preserve privacy, I have changed family and personal names and the name of the village.
2. Fieldwork was supported by a "small grant" from the Nuffield Foundation.
3. DCT posits two dimensions of social organization by which *all* social entities can be measured: the degree of constraints facing members (deriving from rankings

and rules, for instance – Grid) and degrees of incorporation in face-to-face groups (Group). Used as two continua, these produce four archetypal fields – low grid/low group; low grid/high group; high grid/low group and high grid/high group in a two-by-two matrix. Each field has been found to correlate with clusters of appropriate behaviors, and with four distinct and justifying sets of values and attitudes.

This model underlies the exploration of the correlations in this restaurant. It conforms to expectations of what DCT terms an "enclave culture" (high group/low grid), marked by sharp inside/outside distinctions, a strong group identity, and a lack of internal constraints from ranks and rules. Boundaries are maintained as "a wall of virtue," and "the outside" is seen as morally inferior, indeed dangerous.

Enclaves, essentially egalitarian, minimize authority, and therefore arbitrational roles. Grievances therefore tend to fester, leading to eventual sudden, and often disruptive, schism.

4. Eduardo wasn't referring to women as "cowlike" in any other sense.
5. A theme elaborated throughout Dynamic Cultural Theory (Thompson *et al.* 1990) as a feature of enclave organization.
6. The Agnellis, owners of Fiat, are Italy's richest family.
7. The standardizing influences of global market rationality and governmental controls have been fruitfully considered by various anthropologists. Seremetakis (1994), discussing their effects in Greece, links loss of food memory to the wider "mosaic" of loss affecting identity and reciprocity involved in food preparation and consumption. Roseman (2004) does the same discussing reduced production of "home raised foods" in Galicia, Spain, while Counihan (2004), referring to Tuscany, points to disproportionate effects on the social activities of women.

Dessert

–12–

Tipping

An Anthropological Meditation
David Sutton

"Wow, Bill came in on his off day and left me a fiver on a coffee and pie!"
"That's great. Somebody just sat a two-top in my station, both guys. You take them."
"Ok, I'll trade you the woman on table 3."
"No problem, oh, and Steve just sat in your station, I'll tell him to move to mine."
"Please do, that guy is a pain, and barely tips, how can you stand him?"
"Yeah, I know, but he's actually really nice once you get to know him, and we have interesting discussions when it's slow."

The preceding represents a typical exchange between servers[1] during the two years that I worked at Caffe Florian, a pizza, pasta and sandwich place in Chicago, serving the students and faculty of the University of Chicago as well as the wider neighborhood community. Tipping practices, strategies to increase tips, and discussions of actual tips form endless fodder for discussion among restaurant workers. As one's main source of income in most restaurants, tips form a kind of mini-lottery system. The excitement of counting one's money at the end of the night is part of the intrigue that makes the "tipping system" preferable to a regular salary for many of the college students and others working their first regular job at the Caffe Florian. Tipping is, of course, a source of comment and in some cases resentment among customers as well, as is suggested by the existence of organizations such as the "Anti-Tipping Society." And tipping is an interesting mode of communication between workers and customers, partaking simultaneously of the symbolic and the utilitarian, the meaningful and the functional. And yet, despite the clear centrality of tipping in the lives of servers (as well as bartenders and other restaurant workers, such as busboys and dishwashers, who may be entitled to a share of the servers' tips), there has been relatively little anthropological discussion of this practice, and none of it outside of "Western" contexts. Beyond its ubiquity, its interest for anthropology, and in particular for exchange theory, is that it so clearly blurs the boundaries that are supposed to be kept separate, in a modern capitalist economy, between economic and personal, public and private, commodity and gift. As such it reflects the recent turn of exchange theory away from its classical interest in defining the *differences* between "gift economies" and "commodity economies," or even "gift" vs. "commodity societies," towards a greater concern with the frequent ambiguities and overlappings of these terms, the ways that gifts can turn into commodities and then back again, and the fact that their very ambiguities make tipping practices fertile sites for cultural reflection and creativity.

In this chapter I explore the practice of restaurant tipping from the perspective of anthropological exchange theory. I draw on the sparse discussions of tipping in anthropology and the social sciences to suggest that this is an important, yet understudied, topic in the ethnography of restaurants. I will also draw on the published comments and memories of servers themselves, as well as my own experiences as a server. In doing so, I will argue that tipping is not simply an interesting topic in the holistic understanding of the running of restaurants, but is the kind of marginal practice that helps us to analyze some of the contradictions inherent in the culture of capitalism.

Tips: Rational, Irrational, or...

Economists and social psychologists have dominated the study of tipping, up until now. These studies are almost exclusively quantitative in nature; generating data to assess the various factors that are seen to influence tip size. Economists tend, unsurprisingly, to attempt to place tips in a rational context: they are a way of improving the service delivered. Says Orn Bodvarsson, "If we didn't have such a system, as was the case in communist countries, we'd get lousy service" (cited in Speer 1997: 51; cf. Bodvarsson and Gibson 1994). Tipping is seen as a good system in this regard because restaurant managers are not always in a position to monitor the service their staff are providing, so it puts the customers in the position of monitors (Boyes *et al.* 2004: 2624). In this view, the 15 percent standard tip is used as a benchmark against which to judge service. In tipping above or below that mark they are rewarding or penalizing the server. More importantly, according to Bodvarsson, they are investing in future good service. Some economists puzzle over why customers don't "free ride," presumably employing the rational strategy that the tips of others will ensure good service, so they may as well save their money (Boyes *et al.* 2004). Boyes *et al.* must fall back on social custom, or the desire for acceptance, to explain this apparently nonrational fact of tipping behavior. Indeed, one would think that if the tipping system were based on such concerns, someone would have figured out a long time ago that customers should tip *before* they receive service. Leaving it afterwards means, in such a view, that the customers have to trust that they will get the same server next time, and that the server will remember their previous tipping behavior. In fact, most tipping in restaurants is effectively anonymous, lost in the shuffle of the 30–40 tables that a server may service in the course of a shift. And as a result, most economists simply remain puzzled by tipping behavior. As the economist Steven Landsburg muses: "I do not know why people leave anonymous tips in restaurants, and the fact that I leave them myself in no way alleviates my sense of mystery" (cited in Seligman 1998: 138).

This economistic and "rational" approach to tipping is countered by social psychologists, who claim, for the most part, that there is extremely little relationship between perceptions of good service and the size of tips. They seem to have backed this claim with a considerable number of quantitative studies. And many servers will confirm anecdotally their own sense that there is little relation between perceived quality of service and tip – in stories of very positive interactions that ended with surprisingly small tips (Ginsberg 2001: 36), or the reverse: disastrous service experiences that led to spectacularly large tips.

Rather than service, then, social psychologists suggest a combination of factors influencing tips, from the customer's mood, to fear of breaching normative expectations, to national character differences. Thus numerous studies have suggested a strong relationship between tipping and factors such as the weather and whether the server introduces himself or herself, touches the customer or crouches down while taking the order, offers candy or draws a smiley face on the check (see Harris 1995; Hubbard *et al.* 2003; Lynn and Latane 1984; Lynn and Mynier 1993; Rind and Strohmetz 1999). Lynn suggests that tipping is related to national character traits such as individualism or collectivism, "masculine or feminine values" and "National levels of extraversion, neuroticism and psychoticism" (Lynn 2000: 396). Others suggest that tipping takes place because of fear of social disapproval, or "being known as 'cheap,'" though this concern seems greater for men than for women (Boyes *et al.* 2004). Along similar lines, and somewhat in contradiction to his other work, Lynn argues that ethnic and racial differentials in tipping within the United States may be a function of familiarity or lack of familiarity with tipping norms (Lynn 2004).

While these studies help predict the size of tips, they tell us almost nothing about the meaning of the interaction, except that, as the *New Yorker* writer James Surowiecki (2005) notes, tipping seems to be about personalizing the relationship: surely this is why strategies of touching, using first names, and so on work to raise tips. Or to invert a phrase from *The Godfather*: it's not business, it's personal. What, then, have anthropologists told us about tipping practices and the meaning of tipping? And what might anthropology offer that would help us to understand this personal aspect of restaurant interactions?

What Is a Tip, Anyway?

The origin of the word "tip" is shrouded in mystery, with some suggesting that it was one of the first acronyms, standing for "To Insure Prompt Service," a sign displayed over boxes that received customer change in London coffeehouses (Paules 1991: 42). More likely, it was derived from the Latin "stips," which means "gift." The most

Figure 12.1 Xtremebean Coffee Shop, Tempe, AZ. Photo credit: used by the kind permission of Tian Tang.

extensive ethnographic study of tipping is a chapter in Greta Foff Paules' monograph *Dishing It Out: Power and Resistance among Waitresses in a New Jersey Restaurant* (Paules 1991). Paules focused on a downscale chain diner, similar to Denny's, in her analysis of tipping practices and symbolism. Given that this is the most extended anthropological analysis of tipping, I make it a focus for this section, while also referring to other, less developed ethnographic writings on the tip.

Paules suggests that "tip" should be seen as the same as "gratuity," defined as something "freely bestowed." She argues that the tip is indeed a "gift" in this sense, but that it is not a gift "exchange": the customer freely bestows, while the server renders an economic service for which she has been contracted: "What the waitress gives, namely service, cannot be described as a gift, for a gift is by definition voluntary (ostensibly at least), while the delivery of service is a formal duty of the waitress's job. For this reason, the transfer of a tip is more accurately compared to unilateral gift giving than to gift exchange" (Paules 1991: 43). I will return to consider whether these distinctions hold up in a moment. But first it is important to note the implications drawn from this. If the tip is indeed a "unilateral gift," then it is clearly an act of dominance, as Marcel Mauss suggested long ago, one in which one party is superior because they have the power to give and the other party can only receive in subservience. Thus Paules compares the tip to the "gifts" given by women to their domestic servants: the discarded clothes or leftover food that implicitly devalue the servant forced to accept this gift. In this respect, Paules' analysis is in agreement with earlier restaurant ethnographers' discussions of tipping. Whyte (1948: 372) reports that servers see the tipping system as "a great evil" that "lowers the status of the recipient" (p. 99), and often causes the server great emotional distress and sense of personal failure: "'I failed today. After all I did for them, they didn't like me'" (p. 98). Mars and Nicod, by contrast, suggest that tipping involves an exchange – "something given – service – must typically be returned with something of equivalent value – a tip … it cannot be pressed for as an economic right" (1984: 75). However, they too see the tip as promoting the superiority of the customer.

Paules then goes on to show that, within this structure, waitresses can often "turn the tables" on the symbolism of hierarchy. Waitresses at the diner where she conducted fieldwork would find ways to humiliate the customer who had left an insulting tip. This often involved returning it as "change" to the customer, and if the customer insisted in pressing the small tip, saying to them "It's OK, you need it more than I do" (Paules 1991: 37). Thus Paules argues that the waitress can gain agency over the customer or the situation, and further notes that – *pace* Whyte – no waitress in her study ever blamed herself for an inadequate tip.[2] Indeed, much of Paules' account argues that waitresses see customers as "objects" to be "processed" as quickly as possible, while extracting the maximum amount of tip possible. Thus Paules' account dovetails with studies by social psychologists discussed above that show how servers can increase their tip by touching the customer, by writing "thank you" on the check/bill, by promoting/selling the more expensive menu items, and by other practices that are seen as strategies to be cynically manipulated. Paules also documents the fierce competition that existed *among* waitresses to get the most tables and the best customers to maximize their tips. Paules' overall assessment is that tipping is a practice that systematically exploits lower-class women who work as waitresses, and that they do their best to find ways to resist.

Without denying the accuracy of Paules' ethnographic portrayal, I would suggest that the venue of her research – a downscale chain diner where almost all the servers were poor women struggling to make ends meet – gives a certain slant to her view of tipping that does not fully represent the wider experience of these practices. Let us begin a reconsideration of tipping by returning to the symbolic dimensions of the tip. Is "hierarchy" the only or main message conveyed by the tip? Is the tip a unilateral gift, as Paules argues? Remember that according to Paules, because the service provided the customer is not freely given, but part of the server's job, it cannot be considered a "gift," and thus the tip is not a part of "gift exchange." But Paules has substituted here the American notion of the "perfect gift" for Mauss's much more complicated concept. In American folk ideology the gift should be freely given, spontaneous, and should not obligate the recipient to make a return. It should be a monad of good feelings, not extending beyond itself, and not creating social relations (Carrier 1990). James Carrier analyzes what he calls the "Ideology of the Perfect Gift" in American society, in which he traces the history of the distrust of the obligatory potential of gifts. He traces this distrust back (at least) to Ralph Waldo Emerson, who writes "'It is not the office of a man to receive gifts. How dare you bestow them? We wish to be self-sustained. We do not quite forgive a giver'" (cited in Carrier 1990: 21). As Carrier argues, this is an ideology that does not reflect the reality of gift-giving (in the US or elsewhere), and is, in fact, the opposite of what Mauss intended in his analysis of gift-giving. Carrier shows that such "perfect gifts" are, in fact, impossible, the stuff of myth – O. Henry's classic "The Gifts of the Magi" being the key text here – rather than reality. The point of Mauss's analysis was to show that the gift involved a blending of freedom and obligation, of calculation and generosity, and that gifts did, indeed, have the potential to create and sustain ongoing social relationships. The server contracts to bring the food to the customer. Whatever else is offered in this act can be considered a gift. All the more so because what is being offered to the customer is *food*, the key element of sacrifice and sacrament in many religious traditions. That a burger and fries, or a bowl of soup and bread could be compared to a religious sacrament seems perhaps fanciful. But I prefer to see it as part of the way that food can potentially, and on a regular basis, bring together the ritual and the everyday.[3] The restaurant owner of Caffe Florian, where I worked, brought this home to me in saying that he could never turn away a person who was hungry from the doors of his restaurant, whether or not that person could pay. This points, I think, not simply to the generosity of this particular restaurant owner, but to the cultural dimensions of preparing and serving food, even in the context of a capitalist business. Try and imagine the owner of a local shoe store saying that he could never turn away a barefoot person, even if they had no money to buy his shoes.

Restaurant food can have this sacramental role because, as was noted above, it blurs many boundaries that capitalist modernity tries to keep separate: most obviously the distinction between the world of work and economic transactions, and the world of home, or transactions of affection and love. That is one of the reasons, I would argue, that restaurants become substitute homes for their workers and their regular customers, as a number of chapters in this volume explore. The association of the serving and eating of food with memories of home, or at least an ideal "home," as pictured in TV sitcoms, allows such meanings to migrate into the world of the restaurant, which is presumably a business organization organized around principles of profit. Lawrence Taylor suggests that this is the origin of the "bottomless cup of coffee," a mimicking of the free flow of coffee that Americans expect between friends and neighbors in their homes (Taylor 1981).

I will have more to say about restaurants' relationship to homes in my conclusion. For the moment, note how customer–server dialogue can personalize this otherwise impersonal relationship. Joanne Mulcahy recounts this from her experience of waiting on customers, and frames this transaction specifically in terms of a gift exchange: "People come to waitresses for all the assorted stereotypes and clichés, of telling their troubles and being heard. I think that's part of the gift of what waitresses give to their clients" (cited in Owings 2002: 221).

Customers can also return the gift, by becoming listeners, or becoming involved in dialogues. One regular customer at Caffe Florian was not known as a particularly good tipper, and used to demand lots of coffee and attention, so I used to avoid waiting on him. When I did wait on him, we struck up a conversation and found that we shared common interests in politics and history. Because he used to come in to the restaurant during slow periods, it was easy to wait on him and to enjoy a conversation at the same time, and he began to request me as his waiter. The tips began to reflect our developing relationship, although in retrospect this seems incidental. He became part of the landscape of the Caffe Florian for me, part of what I considered, at the time, a second home.

In this light, the tip, especially when not calculated as a flat 15 percent fee, becomes one means of personalization of a transaction that the capitalist marketplace tries to conceptualize as the exchange of goods for services. As Shamir, drawing on George Simmel, captures it:

> Pure market exchange with its reliance on fixed prices reduces human contact to a rather mechanical affair… By giving something to the other side, above and beyond the agreed upon price, the buyer or seller may demonstrate, to himself, as well as to others, that he is not fully trapped in the non-individual, unhuman market mechanism, and that he has retained some capability for voluntary non-profitable action. (1984: 69)

As the *New Yorker* writer James Surowiecki (2005) perceptively comments:

> The free market, at least in theory, is all about impersonal exchange – as long as you have goods to sell and I have money to buy them, we can make a deal, regardless of how we feel about each other. But when it comes to tipping, who we are and how we feel matter a lot, because a tip is essentially a gift, and we give better gifts to people we like than to people we don't.

Thus in this light we can interpret the findings of the social psychologists – that touching a customer, crouching down or a myriad other small actions increase tips – as making perfect sense: they are all part of the process that can potentially transform the impersonal selling of food and services into a more personal, homelike, private experience, an exchange of care and friendship, a social relationship – in short, a gift.

Figure 12.2 The Surreptitious Tip: drawing by Samuel Rowe-Sutton.

The Symbolism of the Tip

For tipping to partake of the gift as much as or more than of the commodity, for it to be even dominated by its symbolic and social dimension, it must be something flexible, not something that partakes of the fixed prices that represent prototypical fixed capitalist retail economic relations. While some customers, no doubt, use tip calculators to calculate an exact 15 percent addition to their bill, most do not, and indeed use the tip to say something about themselves, about their server, and about the relationship between the two. Here money becomes a symbolic, and perhaps even a sensual vehicle, as many anthropologists have observed in diverse contexts (Howes 2003; Lemon 1998; Vournelis 2004; cf. L. Cohen 1997). The offering of the tip is meaningful not only in relation to the 15 percent that is considered standard, but in relation to the perception of what the customer can afford. A few examples will illustrate:

- Frances Donovan, in her autobiographical account of waitressing in the 1920s, notes her befuddlement about receiving tips from "colored boys" and indigents:

"I had tipped colored boys many times but it was indeed a new experience to have one tip me" (cited in Paules 1991: 45).

- Reka Nagy, a career waitress in high-end restaurants, recounts receiving a tip from a five-year-old girl: "'There's a surprise for you under my plate.' I said, 'Really? Can I look?' So we looked and there was a nickel. She had obviously taken her very own money. Now, when you're five years old and you have a nickel and that's all you have and you give it to somebody, that's a truly generous tip" (Owings 2002: 102).

- I grumbled the first time I had to wait on a fellow waiter from Caffe Florian. He was not my favorite co-worker, and on top of that, he ordered a milkshake, the most time-consuming drink for a waiter to produce. My grumbling turned to surprise when I found $5 left on the table, in effect a 125 percent tip.

- In her memoir *Waiting*, Debra Ginsberg reports that many servers say they would rather receive no tip than a 5 or 10 percent tip. "At least that way, they can lull themselves into believing that the diner just forgot" (Ginsberg 2001: 31).

- Classic restaurant lore has it that the ideal appreciative tip includes bills plus a penny. The bills represent the monetary aspect of the tip; the penny symbolizes the recognition of good service.

- Thomas McCarter, an opponent of tipping and a wealthy 1930s businessman, used to "run up huge bills in clubs, then leave a dime tip. McCarter didn't believe in tipping and had the nerve to act on his beliefs. Why the dime? To make sure the waiters and wine stewards realized he hadn't just forgotten" (as recounted in Seligman 1998: 138).

What all these examples share is a concern for the communicative function of the tip in addition to, or instead of, any purely "rational maximizing" function. The young girl's tip of five cents shows both how tips can be memorable independent of their economic benefit to the server, but also how generosity is gauged in relation to the ability of the giver to give, not simply in relation to the size of the gift (cf. Herzfeld 1986). The first example from Donovan, despite its overtones of race and class prejudice, leads to similar conclusions. The example of waiters overtipping their fellow servers shows how extravagant tips (even for ordinary service) can be used to communicate a deep solidarity, a vision of a waiter's cornucopia where everyone, not just fellow servers, recognized the exhausting physical, emotional and intellectual work that goes into food service. Or as Ginsberg (2001: 41) puts it, "An extremely generous tip at the end of such a meal goes beyond professional courtesy, it reflects a deep emotional bond." The fourth example, of servers preferring to be stiffed rather than receive a bad tip, re-emphasizes, in contradistinction to the economists' view discussed above, that economic maximization is not the sole motivation for server behavior. It speaks to the fact that servers often willingly forgo tips (what Gatta refers to as "tip sacrificing" (2002: 62–3) rather than engage in an exchange with a customer that they find demeaning. And the dime left by the rich businessman provides a negative example of the above, that a small amount of money can be freed from its monetary function to serve a communicative function, to humiliate, to protest, or simply to make the transaction more ... negatively memorable.

What is notable about these examples is the different kinds of emotions and social relations that can be expressed through the same medium: the lack of monetary difference between the little girl's nickel, the rich man's dime, the extra penny, and the small change Frances Donovan received from "colored boys" in contrast to the range of communications that take place through these means.

The sensory and material properties of money also play a role in the symbolism of the tip. Whether the money is handed to the server, neatly stacked, hidden away in a table nook, or spread indiscriminately across the table all have communicative potential. Small change also has a materiality that can add to these symbolic dimensions: its weightiness, in contrast to paper money, means that customers may treat it as something to get rid of, to be removed from their pockets and left for the server, who presumably will gratefully take the time to collect it. At the same time, its weightiness and the noise that it makes hitting the pavement also makes it an effective medium to hurl at a retreating customer if the server feels slighted by the tip.

"A Friendly Act of Giving": A Brief Ethnographic Interlude

In modern Greek the word used for tip is "filodorima," which could be translated as "giving to a friend" or "A friendly act of giving," a phrasing that is certainly suggestive of the category blurrings that I have argued for here. One of the prods of this chapter is to put tipping practices on the ethnographic agenda for studies cross-culturally, and to raise them out of the realm of anecdote. Since almost all the materials considered here focus on US contexts, I'd like briefly to suggest a few points about tipping in the one ethnographic area I know best, modern Greece. Though it is not a topic that I investigated in depth, I piece together a few observations to suggest its richness.[4]

In what kind of establishment do you tip in Greece? By contrast with the US, tipping in bars and coffeeshops is infrequent and minimal (as it is in taxis). You tip in places that primarily serve food, but not drink. When you do tip in bars or coffeeshops, it is because you already have a longstanding relationship with the server – a situation that is thus once again the opposite of what would be predicted by economists. Much stress in Greece is placed on the performance of generosity, a performance that some have described as "agonistic" (Herzfeld 1986). As I have argued in relation to food-based generosity more generally, one must prove one's generosity in relation to the community at large through acts that are seen as memorable (Sutton 2001: 48 ff.). When this is applied to tipping, however, two seemingly opposite things can happen: one may be quite obvious about "over-tipping," the reason being simple enough:

everybody becomes witness of the tipper's generosity, which potentially hints at the tipper's social status; or one can tip without letting one's friends know about it until it's time to go, when everybody offers to pay the bill or the tip: then the tipper can say "It's already taken care of"; thus, the tipper has anticipated the reaction of his/her company and has even taken an action to show that there was never a chance of anybody else's paying the tip. Usually people prefer to do the latter of the two, since it is a more powerful performance. This "agonistic" tipping crosses gender lines, especially for younger women who have jobs. For older women who do not work, husbands may provide them with money, because their tipping performance speaks both for themselves and for their husbands (Vournelis, personal communication with author).

In typical Greek tipping practices, consideration for the waiter (i.e. personalization of the customer–server relationship) comes into play only when one is in a context where one can let one's guard down and not worry about what people will think; otherwise consideration for the waiter seems to be quite secondary. The issue of how people tip when they are by themselves would be particularly interesting for exploration.

The sensory and material aspects of tipping are also ripe for exploration in Greece. There are a number of contexts in which the giving of money is used to highlight one's performative skills, such as the "tipping" of musicians: the trick here is to dance up to the musician in the middle of a song and stick bills in his pocket, on his forehead or elsewhere on his body. Here coins would be an ineffective and inappropriate vehicle for performance. In his study of the monetary changeover from the drachma to the euro in 2003, Vournelis (2004) noted that people experienced sensory disorientation in relation to practices such as tipping. As one informant noted: "I'm used to tipping something blue. The 500 drachma note was blue, and so is the 20 euro note. But the 20 euro note is worth 11 times more. It took me a while to realize this and stop my habit of tipping 'blue.'" Thus along with substantial differences, this brief sketch hopefully suggests that tipping in Greece, as in the US, provides a practice sensitive to the changing social and sensory aspects of identity and memory.

The Gender of the Tip

There is little doubt that restaurants are deeply gendered spaces. Ethnographic research has attested to the gendered aspects of restaurant work both in terms of the server–customer relationship and hierarchies within restaurant staffs. The ways gender plays out in terms of server uniforms, the sexualized environment, typical restaurant "scripts" and the arrangement and movement of bodies have begun to be documented through careful ethnographic research. But how does gender play out in understanding the multiple meanings and social uses of the tip? Here we must once again rely on anecdote as a prod to further research, as few ethnographic studies exist.

Certainly it is a truism among servers that customers of the opposite sex tip better than same-sex customers; hence the constant trading of tables that goes on between servers. This is particularly the case in more casual establishments, where the servers and the customers are all of basically the same age and status (e.g. students), the flirtation that is so much part of restaurant work in general (Erickson 2004; Gatta 2002) extending over into the server–customer relationship. Any time that money changes hands so directly between men and women, we might surmise, there is some hint of a sexual transaction, which is why some restaurant owners and managers, and in some cases servers themselves, may attempt to exaggerate that dimension through the use, for example, of revealing uniforms, with "Hooters" restaurants representing simply one end of a long continuum (E. Hall 1993; Erickson 2004). But in restaurants where there are clear status differentials between customer and server, other possible gender dynamics seem to come into play. Gender relations have, of course, been in a huge state of flux in the United States, at least since the 1960s, and this is certainly reflected in restaurant behavior. A study conducted in the mid-1970s discusses the refusal of restaurant servers to present women with the bill in a mixed-gender party, even if the woman has requested the check/bill or clearly indicated that she will be paying for the meal (Laner *et al.* 1979). This would, most likely, no longer be the case in most restaurants in the early years of the twenty-first century. However, gender differences and inequalities are still very much part of US society and the restaurant experience, as more recent studies have carefully pointed out (Bird and Sokolofski 2005; Erickson 2004).

The tipping of women by men for serving food crosses symbolic boundaries in intriguing ways. On the one hand, for many the traditional association of women with food serving means that the restaurant can, in this context, be seen as an extension of the "home" into the public sphere. Restaurants may play on this association, and design their décor to emphasize a home-like atmosphere. It is interesting in this context to note that it is typically in high-end restaurants, which emphasize their separateness from home – the fact that they offer things that you clearly could not make at home – that men have dominated in serving positions. In the case, then, of women waiting on men, the tip suggests a paying for something that, traditionally at least, men do not pay for, or at least do not pay for so directly. This openness can be seen as more honest and "democratic" than the more roundabout hidden exchanges that characterize the traditional family. Or they can make the exchange of money around such sacred and "natural" acts as women serving food to men seem problematic. Diana Candee, for example, working in a Denny's, sees the monetary aspect of the exchange as cheapening her professionalism: "It used to make me really mad when people thought I was working for tips. I [felt] damned if you did and damned if you didn't" (cited in Owings 2002: 246). It may be equally disturbing or problematic to the customer, as Shamir (1984: 70) argues, to have such "primary-group ... intimate services" transacted in the public sphere of market exchange. Drawing on Goffman's Interactionist approach, Shamir suggests that because the server is in essence entering the private domain – the backstage – of the customer by feeding him, the whole transaction is a potential threat to the customer's public face, so that "the tip buys the server's silence, and ... reduces the customer's anxiety" while at the same time re-establishing the public, "market" nature of the exchange. How this plays out in cases of male servers and female customers, or same-sex servers and customers, remains an open question. However, I suggest that it will pose similar fruitful issues for analysis specifically because the restaurant is a "third space" outside of the normally more clear-cut distinctions between the public and the private, and thus a space where private is always potentially bleeding into public and vice versa (see Bird and Sokolofski 2005; Warde and Martens 2000: 117ff.).

Conclusion: Tips and Third Spaces

In her ethnographic study of the "Hungry Cowboy," a Minnesota restaurant, Erickson nicely captures this "third space" aspect of restaurants with specific attention to its gender implications:

> Restaurants are carefully managed stages for the exchange of cash for food and service. But restaurants are also more than that. In the process of going out to eat, we enter a social world, taking part in a play of sociability within the confines of the marketplace. Certain customers become so comfortable in the Hungry Cowboy that they start to treat it like their own living room, walking shoeless to the bathroom or greeting servers like old friends. (Erickson 2004: 87)

Erickson suggests here the function of these third spaces to personalize the anonymous world of the public sphere and commodity exchange. As I have argued throughout, this is part of a general tension at the heart of capitalism, as ordinary "consumers" refuse the distinctions of capitalism and attempt to bring more of the world of the gift economy into that supposedly reserved for the rational exchange of money for services, as numerous authors have noted (Carrier 1990; Graeber 2001; Hart 2005; Sutton and Wogan 2003). The irony here is that they are using money itself, supposedly the most impersonal and anonymous of commodities, to accomplish this goal.

Of course, restaurants play on this tension to attract customers as well. For example, Barbas (2002) traces the attempt in the early decades of the twentieth century to make restaurants palatable to middle-class patrons by a specific appeal to what was seen as under threat through modern convenience cooking: "home cooking" (see also Whitaker 2005). Restaurant trade journals specifically encouraged restaurateurs to cultivate a homelike atmosphere by employing "mature and motherly" female servers: "Deep down in every man's heart is a desire to have food handed to him by a woman," reported a trade journal in 1928. "A woman with a 'homey smile' does more to make a man feel at home in a strange eating place than anything" (Barbas: 2002: 49).

Erickson's ethnography notes the continuing saliency of "home" at the turn of the twenty-first century, if not, perhaps, in the guise of matronly mothers:

> Restaurants work hard to make customers feel at home. What happens when customers start to treat a public space like their home? What does it mean for workers' identities and workplace culture when servers willingly trade on private personal characteristics such as their sexual appeal to make more money or have more fun at work? (Erickson 2004: 87)

Here Erickson nicely brings together the spatial and the economic with issues of gender and sexuality, and asks how people negotiate this blurring of boundaries, this mixing of public and private, gift and commodity exchange. Barbas similarly notes the "formidable contradictions" of serving up "home": "If the essence of home was its individuality and intimacy, how could it be packaged and sold" (2002: 48)?[5] Erickson and Barbas both pose these ambiguities as questions, and I would as well. I've tried to suggest some of the inadequacies of previous approaches that try to clarify these ambiguities, to purify these mixtures (Latour 1993) by insisting that tipping is purely economic or purely about enforcing social hierarchies. It is in tipping's ability to represent both of these things, and considerably more – in its multiplicity – that we find its interest.

Notes

1. A gender-neutral term for waiter or waitress. Common parlance for server at Caffe Florian was the ironic "waitron."
2. Gatta (2002: 56ff.) also notes various strategies used by servers for "emotional rebalancing" after receiving an insufficient tip.
3. As I argue in Sutton 2001, bread in the Christian tradition is a food that regularly crosses boundaries between its everyday uses as a staple and its religious uses as a symbol of Christ's body. The two types of uses are not held as distinct, but commonly blur into each other.
4. I also draw from the MA thesis of Leonidas Vournelis (2004) and discussions I have had with him over the years.
5. While indicting the "commodification" of the personal waiting tables at "Smoky Joe's," Crang notes that this did not lead him to feel alienated: "I always felt that 'I' was still there: I genuinely liked people who tipped me; I genuinely wanted to help; I genuinely had fun" (Crang 1994: 698).

Digestif

Postprandial Imaginings
Michael Herzfeld

A groaning table threatens the capacity of the most voracious of readers, and I must now serve the *digestif*. On the sympathetic principle that a slight touch of the bitters, a *liquore amaro*, might counter any reflux from such a postmodern buffet, and, given a very small glass to serve up my potion, I shall avoid the cloying dessert of indiscriminate praise; these chapters can certainly speak for themselves, and certain salient themes – class and race, the rhythms of kitchen work, the peculiar relationship between the restaurant trade and capital accumulation – have already been presented in digestible form. I propose instead to take up some under-represented critical issues that in my view would repay further mastication.

The most surprising absence in this collection is a detailed consideration of the restaurant as a physical space. We encounter the choreography of restaurant work (Erickson, Mars); but surely, if restaurants have an admittedly variable and complex relation to shifting models of "home" (Erickson, Trubek, Yano, Pardue, Beriss), the equally labile tension between the display mode of the dining area and the intimacy of the kitchen is likely to reflect ideological assumptions about national and regional culture in interesting ways. If the kitchen is a family hearth (in Thai, a family, *khrobkhrua*, is precisely "those who gather around the cooking area"), the variations on the family theme that emerge as we explore multiple understandings of what a restaurant means – including familistic idioms of personal responsibility (Hernandez) – are especially susceptible of linkage with identitarian politics, given the powerful association of kinship with nationalism. Restaurants are purveyors of stereotypes; some are counter-intuitive or clearly of recent invention (e.g. Jochnowitz), but others play to existing assumptions and resources. As Lem astutely notes, moreover, some explanations of the restaurants' survival are themselves no more than unhelpful stereotypes (e.g. the supposedly "Confucian" hard work of all Chinese) that one might find equally applicable to other migrant traditions (see, for example, Carter [1997: 85–7] on Mouride Senegalese in Italy).

Décor and spatial organization often work those stereotypes hard. How do these design features reflect cosmological assumptions? What does it mean to find shrines to family ancestors, however vaguely conceived, in Southeast Asian eateries, and does this have a differential effect on the way in which the presumably savvy "ethnic" staff members and the clumsy visitors respectively move through this space? What spatial meanings are evoked by religious art or invocation of antiquity such as one encounters in Greek or Italian restaurants? And perhaps even more to the point, what transformations of spatial understanding are transgressed when, for example, a customer manages to enter the homely kitchen that is shielded from prying eyes both by the formalism of the restaurant décor and by the forbidding weight of the servers' swing-door? In one restaurant in Patras, Greece (see Herzfeld 1987: 85) a blown-up reproduction of an old French print, firmly located over the kitchen entrance on the dining-room side and showing a family celebration with champagne, seemed to warn that entering the intimate domain of sweaty labor put the diners' fragile claims to European culture at risk.

Several authors here do indeed show how restaurants serve as arenas for repeated performances that speak to an almost Turnerian (Turner 1974) "social drama" of grand values (Jochnowitz); we see too little of the physical staging and hear too little about how the choreography utilizes the actual organization of tables, equipment, and exits. Amidst all the interesting discussion of how restaurants provide a locus for the recalibration of "authenticity," moreover, there is no discussion of table manners – another locus of inculcation, stereotypes, parody and resistance.

Attention to the mutual entailment of bodily movement and spatial arrangements allows us to calibrate what happens in a restaurant to much larger concerns. The Patras décor explicitly emphasized a spatial division, one that reflected Greeks' well-inculcated concealment of cultural associations that threatened their membership in "Europe." Two further, exemplary illustrations of such wider linkages are Malaby's (2003: 134–5) realization that learning how to carry a coffee tray in a Greek *kafenio* illustrated the dynamics of local economic risk-taking; and Chee's (2006) investigation of the comparative irrelevance of "native place" to the alliances formed among migrant workers within the spatial compression of a Beijing restaurant. The restaurant is, as the editors remind us in their introduction, a microcosm; it is important to understand both how that metonymic/synecdochic relationship is experienced and how it affects the habitus of actors while also responding dynamically to the inevitable innovations that their performances bring to bear.

Hubbert's probing of Chinese restaurants paradoxically evoking nostalgia for the Cultural Revolution is, for example, not solely about restaurants. It is about the current economic practices through which something as profoundly discordant with these as the Cultural Revolution gets retrospectively recast as a training ground for the self-discipline that made capitalism possible. (It is perhaps no coincidence that the rather folkloric and abstract older Chinese banknotes were recently succeeded by newer ones bearing the portrait of Chairman Mao.)

Habitus is compelling, as Hernandez found when he began to pare raw materials according to the norms of the Chinese restaurant where he was working. But humans can also refashion both hexis and habitus, especially through a willed awareness of the provisionality of such seemingly inflexible structures (*pace* Bourdieu 1977;

see Ardener 2006: 103–4). Restaurants, with their optical complexity and their internal analysts and critics, are an important setting for such self-crafting. Careful ethnographic analyses of individuals' bodily comportment and *tempo* (Bourdieu 1977: 7) in the changing spaces of gastronomic consumption would thus reveal how people playfully explore new conventions of both *savoir faire* and savoring fare.

Think, for example, of the Italian *barista*, who almost simultaneously prepares several cups of espresso, hauls down bottles of liquor and measures out a couple of glasses, stows used crockery in a miniature counter-top dishwasher, and banters with his customers while watching out for potential thieves and troublemakers. By contrast, in virtually any American chain coffee-house such as Starbucks a beep announces that one of the carefully measured amounts of variously complicated espresso-based hot drinks is ready for pouring into a pre-marked cup, while the employee at the cash register calls out, "One *doppio* for here," eliciting the well-trained response, "One for-here *doppio!*" A very successful *Gesellschaft* has brought Max Weber and Henry Ford together in an Italianate coffee-shop. But the original Italian model that this staging purports to imitate still effortlessly reproduces *Gemeinschaft* amid the swirl of congested traffic and incessant cyber-chatter. Both are rituals; but one embodies sociability, while the other celebrates automation.

Clearly a detailed analysis of these differences – an obvious candidate for video-based research – would be revealing of the relationship among capital accumulation, cultural values and images, the organization of labor, and the training of bodies and manners in different societies around the world. Such analysis begins to appear in this volume; for example, Mars offers a vivid image of women in an upscale Italian restaurant confined to making fresh pasta in an idiom that reproduces older and more widespread ideas about the male monopoly of meat (Herzfeld 1985: 52; see also Schweder 2003) – ideas that, in tandem with bodily exhaustion, ultimately push the modernization of tradition beyond practical tolerability. Does the collapsing body of the weary old woman, overstrained (as Mars smartly observes) by a variation on older themes of *onore*, presage the collapse of a business unable to merge the smooth pace of slow food and sharecropping with the "time–space compression" (Harvey 1989) of postmodernity?

In an undeservedly unobtrusive footnote, Trubek notes that the shift from fixed agricultural rhythms to the more serendipitous discoveries of a global market spells the end of the locally grounded gastronomic habitus. What Pardue calls "corporate intentionality" cannot stave off that kind of change; indeed, it cultivates an increasing demand for both rapidity and choice. These changes also register in bodily comportment.

Such thoughts hint at nostalgia, and nostalgia easily serves inequality. As Beriss notes, the New Orleans elite were able to tolerate satire at the expense of their well-fed self-absorption because it nostalgically invoked a past that defined their present, privileged position. We can nevertheless resist the temptation of such easy judgments by contextualizing the relevant social practices. For example, waiting and tipping, as Erickson and Sutton remark, do not entail simple exchange; writers like Carrier (1995) and Herrmann (1997) have already debunked the evolutionist Maussian nostalgia that made such a formulation imaginable. Such practices do not occur in a vacuum; they are indeed, as Sutton notes, often agonistic, charged with the residual imitation of sociability that we find in the "hospitality industry" – an industry that is no more eager to point up its own aggressions than is the "traditional hospitality" of a Greek village (Herzfeld 1987). Lest readers of this book fall into the trap of imagining restaurants devoid of larger settings (or the chapters themselves as complete ethnographies), let me urge, once again, close attention to the mutual reproduction of features internal to each enterprise and those prevalent in the larger cultural setting.

Because so many of these essays address American life, it might be all too easy to forget the lesson of *Golden Arches East* (Watson 1997): customers and workers alike enter restaurants with culturally specific dispositions as well as personal idiosyncrasies that filter and reshape their experiences, even as they accommodate to the powerful models they encounter. Restoring historical time to our analyses, as Ray suggests, also displaces nostalgia in favor of analysis. If Italian food in America no longer tastes "Italian," sensory orientations have shifted in concert with the status of the immigrant producers. We need an ethnographic and historical investigation of the *uses* of pace and rhythm, the temporal frames of cultural change, in restaurant spaces. Such an approach would induce the pleasant postprandial leaps of the imagination that a *digestif* can, and should, induce at the end of a pleasant but complex meal such as the repast offered to us in this book.

References

Allison, Anne (1997) Japanese Mothers and Obentōs; The Lunch-Box as Ideological State Apparatus. In *Food and Culture: A Reader*, ed. Carole Counihan and Penny Van Esterik, pp. 296–314. New York: Routledge.

Anderson, Brett (2002) Creole Contretemps. *The Times-Picayune* July 7, Living, p. 1.

Anderson, Brett (2003) The Art of the Meal. *The Times-Picayune* July 6, Living, p. 1.

Anderson, E. N. (1997) Chinese Traditional Medical Value of Foods. In *Food and Culture: A Reader*, ed. C. Counihan and P. Van Estrick, pp. 80–92. London: Routledge.

Appadurai, Arjun (1981) Gastro-Politics in Hindu South Asia. *American Ethnologist* 8(3): 494–511.

Appadurai, Arjun (1986) On Culinary Authenticity. *Anthropology Today* 2(4): 25.

Ardener, Edwin (2006) *Voice of Prophecy and Other Essays*, 2nd edition. Oxford: Berghahn.

Barbas, Samantha (2002) Just Like Home: "Home Cooking" and the Domestication of the American Restaurant. *Gastronomica* 2(4): 43–52.

Barndt, Deborah (2004) *Tangled Routes: Women, Work and Globalization on the Tomato Trail*. Lanham, MD: Rowman & Littlefield.

Batterberry, Michael and Ariane Batterberry (1973) *On the Town in New York*. New York: Routledge.

Baudrillard, Jean (1994) *Simulacra and Simulation*, trans. Sheila Faria Glaser. Ann Arbor, MI: University of Michigan Press.

Baum, Dan (2006) Deluged. When Katrina hit, where were the police? *The New Yorker* 81(43): 50–63.

Belasco, Warren (1989) *Appetite for Change*. New York: Pantheon Books.

Belasco, Warren and Philip Scranton (eds) (2002) *Food Nations: Selling Taste in Consumer Societies*. New York: Routledge.

Bell, David and Gill Valentine (1997) *Consuming Geographies: We Are Where We Eat*. London: Routledge.

Benton, Gregor and Frank Pieke (eds) (1998) *The Chinese in Europe*. New York: St Martin's Press.

Beriss, David (2006a) Restaurants and Culture in Post Katrina New Orleans, Part One. *Anthropology News* 47(3): 49–50.

Beriss, David (2006b) What to Eat After the Storm, Restaurants and Hope, Part Two. *Anthropology News* 47(4): 49.

Bernardo, Rosemarie (2005) Store Bids Aloha to Waialua. *Honolulu Star-Bulletin* July 21: A3.

Berry, Wendell (2002) *The Art of the Commonplace*. Washington, DC: Counterpoint.

Bestor, Theodore C. (1999) Wholesale Sushi: Culture and Commodity in Tokyo's Tsukiji Market. In *Theorizing the City: The New Urban Anthropology Reader*, ed. Setha M. Low, pp. 201–42. New Brunswick, NJ: Rutgers University Press.

Bestor, Theodore C. (2004) *Tsukiji: The Fish Market at the Center of the World*. Berkeley, CA: University of California Press.

Bird, Sharon, and Leah Sokolofski (2005) Gendered Socio-Spatial Practices in Public Eating and Drinking Establishments in the Midwest United States. *Gender, Place and Culture* 12: 213–30.

Bloomer, J. Philip (1994) Champaign's Northern Fringe Going to Town. *Champaign News Gazette*, December 18: A10.

Bodenheim, Barbara (2000) He Used to be My Relative: Exploring the Bases of Relatedness among Iñupiat of Northern Alaska. In *Cultures of Relatedness: New Approaches to the Study of Kinship*, ed. J. Carsten, pp. 128–48. Cambridge: Cambridge University Press.

Bodvarsson, Orn and William Gibson (1994) Gratuities and Customer Appraisal of Service: Evidence from Minnesota Restaurants. *Journal of Socio-Economics* 23: 287–302.

Bonacich, Edna and John Modell (1980) *The Economic Basis of Ethnic Solidarity*. Berkeley, CA and Los Angeles: University of California Press.

Bourdain, Anthony (2000) *Kitchen Confidential: Adventures in the Culinary Underbelly*. London: Bloomsbury.

Bourdieu, Pierre (1977) *Outline of a Theory of Practice*, trans. Richard Nice. Cambridge: Cambridge University Press.

Bourdieu, Pierre (1984) *Distinction: A Social Critique of the Judgment of Taste*, trans. Richard Nice. Cambridge, MA: Harvard University Press.

Boyes, William, William Mounts and Clifford Sowell (2004) Restaurant Tipping: Free Riding, Social Acceptance, and Gender Difference. *Journal of Applied Social Psychology* 34: 2616–28.

Boym, Svetlana (2001) *The Future of Nostalgia*. New York: Basic Books.

Braudel, Fernand (1981) *Civilization and Capitalism, 15th–18th Century*. Volume 1: *The Structures of Everyday Life. The Limits of the Possible*, trans. and revised by Siân Reynolds. New York: Harper & Row.

Brenner, Leslie. (1999) *American Appetite: The Coming of Age of a Cuisine*. New York: Avon Books.

Brodkin, Karen (1998) *How Jews Became White Folks*. New Brunswick, NJ: Rutgers University Press.

Brubaker, W. Rogers (1985) Rethinking Classical Theory: The Sociological Vision of Pierre Bourdieu. *Theory and Society* 14: 745–75.

Brubaker, W. Rogers (1992) *Citizenship and Nationhood in France and Germany.* Cambridge, MA: Harvard University Press.

Bruni, Frank (2005) The Contemporary Dining Scene, Est. 1985. *The New York Times*, Dining Out section (October 12), F1 & F4.

Bubinas, Kathleen (2003) The Commodification of Ethnicity in an Asian Indian Economy in Chicago. *City and Society* 15: 195–223.

Burros, Marian (1984) What Alice Taught Them: Disciples of Chez Panisse. *The New York Times* September 26, C1.

Burton, Marda and W. Kenneth Holditch (2004) *Galatoire's: Biography of a Bistro.* Athens, GA: Hill Street Press.

Burton, Nathaniel and Rudy Lombard (1978) *Creole Feast: 15 Master Chefs of New Orleans Reveal Their Secrets.* New York: Random House.

Caplan, Pat (ed.) (1997) *Food, Health, and Identity.* London: Routledge.

Carrier, James (1990) Gifts in a World of Commodities: The Ideology of the Perfect Gift in American Society. *Social Analysis* 29: 19–37.

Carrier, James (1995) *Gifts and Commodities: Exchange and Western Capitalism since 1700.* New York: Routledge.

Carsten, Janet (1995) The Substance of Kinship and the Heat of the Hearth: Feeding, Personhood and Relatedness among Malays in Pulau Langkawi. *American Ethnologist* 22: 223–41.

Carter, Donald Martin (1997) *States of Grace: Senegalese in Italy and the New European Immigration.* Minneapolis, MN: University of Minnesota Press.

Castañeda, Quetzil (1996) *In The Museum Of Maya Culture: Touring Chichén Itzá.* Minneapolis, MN: University of Minnesota Press.

Castelvetro, Giacomo (1989) *The Fruits, Herbs and Vegetables of Italy,* trans. and annotated by Gillian Riley. London and New York: Viking.

Castles, Stephen and Mark Miller (2003) *The Age of Migration: International Popular Movements in the Modern World.* London: Palgrave.

Chang, K. C. (ed.) (1977) *Food in Chinese Culture: Anthropological and Historical Perspectives.* New Haven, CT: Yale University Press.

Chee, Bernadine Wai Larn (2006) Beyond Native Place Identity in China: Valuation, Agency, and Household Registration in a Beijing Restaurant. Ph.D. dissertation, Department of Anthropology, Harvard University.

Chen, Tina Mai (2003) Proletarian White and Working Bodies in Mao's China. *Positions: East Asia Cultures Critique* 11(2): 361–93.

Cohen, Leah Hagen (1997) *Glass, Paper, Beans: Revelations on the Nature and Value of Ordinary Things.* New York: Currency Paperback.

Cohen, Marilyn (1991) Petty Commodity Producers in Tullylish, 1690–1825, *Marxist Approaches in Economic Anthropology: Monographs in Economic Anthropology,* No. 9, ed. Alice Littlefield and Hill Gates, pp. 37–64. Lanham, MD: University Press of America.

Collin, Richard H. (1970) *The New Orleans Underground Gourmet*. New York: Simon and Schuster.

Counihan, Carole (2004) *Around the Tuscan Table: Food, Family and Gender in Twentieth-Century Florence*. London: Routledge.

Counihan, Carole and Penny Van Esterik (eds) (1997) *Food and Culture: A Reader*. New York: Routledge.

Crang, Philip (1994) It's Showtime: On the Workplace Geographies of Display in a Restaurant in Southeast England. *Environment and Planning D: Society and Space* 12: 675–704.

Cummings, Richard Osborn (1970) *The American and His Food*. New York: Ayer.

David, Elizabeth (1960) *French Provincial Cookery*. New York: Penguin.

Dávila, Arlene (1997) *Sponsored Identities: Cultural Politics in Puerto Rico*. Philadelphia: Temple University Press.

Dela Cruz, Donovan and Jodi Endo Chai (2002) *The Okazu Guide; Oh, 'Cause You Hungry!'*. Honolulu: Watermark Publishing.

Denker, Joel (2003) *The World on a Plate: A Tour through the History of America's Ethnic Cuisines*. Boulder, CO: Westview Press.

DeNora, Tia (2000) *Music in Everyday Life*. Cambridge: Cambridge University Press.

Diner, Hasia R. (2001) *Hungering for America: Italian, Irish, and Jewish Foodways in the Age of Migration*. Cambridge, MA: Harvard University Press.

Dornenburg, Andrew and Karen Page (2003) *Becoming a Chef*, revised edn. Hoboken, NJ: John Wiley & Sons.

Douglas, Mary (1976) *Purity and Danger: An Analysis of Concepts of Pollution and Taboo*. London: Routledge.

Douglas, Mary (1992) *Risk and Blame: Essays in Cultural Theory*. New York: Routledge.

Douglas, Mary (1997) Deciphering a Meal. In *Food and Culture; A Reader*. ed. Carole Counihan and Penny Van Esterik, pp. 36–54. New York: Routledge.

Duffy, Richard (1909) New York at the Table. *Putnam's* 5(5): 567 (February).

Duneier, Mitchell (1992) *Slim's Table: Race, Respectability, and Masculinity*. Chicago: University of Chicago Press.

Easterling, Mickey (2002) Letter to Galatoire's. http://www.welovegilberto.com/Galatoires/12.pdf.

Elie, Lolis Eric (1997) Blackened? Try Tarred. *The Times-Picayune* May 12.

Erickson, Karla (2004) Bodies at Work: Performing Service in American Restaurants. *Space and Culture* 7: 76–89.

Esteva, Gustavo and Madhu Suri Prakash (1998) *Grassroots Postmodernism: Remaking the Soil of Cultures*. New York: Zed Books.

Fantasia, Rick (1995) Fast Food in France. *Theory and Society* 24(2): 201–43.

Farquhar, Judith (2002) *Appetites: Food and Sex in Post-Socialist China*. Durham, NC: Duke University Press.

Ferguson, Priscilla Parkhurst (2004) *Accounting for Taste: The Triumph of French Cuisine*. Chicago: University of Chicago Press.

Ferguson, Priscilla Parkhurst and Sharon Zukin (1998 The Careers of Chefs. In *Eating Culture*. ed. Ron Scapp and Brian Seitz, pp. 92–111. Albany, NY: SUNY Press.

Ferrero, Sylvia (2002) *Comida Sin Par*. Consumption of Mexican Food in Los Angeles: "Foodscapes" in a Transnational Consumer Society. In *Food Nations: Selling Taste in Consumer Societies*, ed. Warren Belasco and Philip Scranton, pp. 194–219. New York: Routledge.

Filippini, Alessandro (1889) *The Table*. New York: Charles Webster.

Fine, Gary Alan (1996) *Kitchens: The Culture of Restaurant Work*. Berkeley, CA: University of California Press.

Finkelstein, Joanne (1989) *Dining Out: A Sociology of Modern Manners*. New York: NYU Press.

Fitzmorris, Tom (1996) *The Eclectic Guide to New Orleans*. Birmingham, AL: Menasha Ridge Press.

Florida, Richard (2002) *The Rise of the Creative Class*. New York: Basic Books.

Fussell, Paul (1988) Travel, Tourism and "International Understanding". In *Thank God for the Atom Bomb*. ed. Paul Fussell, pp. 151–76. New York: Summit Books.

Gabaccia, Donna R. (1998) *We Are What We Eat. Ethnic Food and the Making of Americans*. Cambridge, MA: Harvard University Press.

Galatoire, Leon (1994) *Galatoire's Cookbook*. Gretna, LA: Pelican Publishing.

Gatta, Mary Lizabeth (2002) *Juggling Food and Feelings: Emotional Balance in the Workplace*. Lanham, MD: Lexington Books.

Ginsberg, Debra (2001) *Waiting: The True Confessions of a Waitress*. New York: HarperCollins.

Girardelli, Davide (2004) Commodified Identities: The Myth of Italian Food. *Journal of Communication Inquiry* 28: 307–24.

Gladney, Dru (1994) Representing Nationality in China: Refiguring Majority/ Minority Identities. *Journal of Asian Studies* 53(1): 92–123.

Glick Schiller, Nina (1998) Transmigrants and Nation-states: Something Old and Something New in the U.S. Immigrant Experience. In *The Handbook of International Migration: The American Experience*, ed. Charles Hirschman, Philip Kasinitz and Josh Dewind, pp. 94–119. New York: Russell Sage Foundation.

Glick Schiller, Nina, Linda Basch and Cristina Szanton Blanc (eds) (1992) *Toward a Transnational Perspective on Migration: Race, Class, Ethnicity and Nationalism Reconsidered*. New York: New York Academy of Sciences.

Globe and Mail (2004) China Rising October 23.

Gluckman, Max (1955) *Custom and Conflict in Africa*. Oxford: Blackwell.

Goffman, Erving (1959) *The Presentation of Self in Everyday Life*. New York: Anchor Books.

Goffman, Erving (1967) *Interaction Ritual*. New York: Doubleday & Company.

Goffman, Erving (1969) *Where the Action Is*. London: Allen Lane.

Goffman, Erving (1973) Role Distance. In *People in Places: The Sociology of the Familiar*, ed. Arnold Birenbaum and Edward Sagarin. New York: Praeger Publishers.

Gold, Thomas, Bough Guthrie and David Wank (eds) (2002) *Social Connections in China: Institutions and the Changing Nature of Guanxi*. London: Cambridge University Press.

Goody, Jack (1982) *Cooking, Cuisine and Class: A Study in Comparative Sociology*. Cambridge: Cambridge University Press.

Graeber, David (2001) *Toward an Anthropological Theory of Value: The False Coin of Our Own Dreams*. New York: Palgrave.

Granovetter, Mark S. (1995) The Economic Sociology of Firms and Entrepreneurs. In *Economic Sociology of Immigration*, ed. Alejandro Portes, pp. 128–65. New York: Russell Sage.

Greenhalgh, Susan (1994) De-Orientalising the Chinese Family Firm. *American Ethnologist* 21 (4): 746–75.

Habermas, Jurgen (1989) *The Structural Transformation of the Public Sphere*. Cambridge, MA: MIT Press.

Hall, Elaine (1993) Waitering/Waitressing: Engendering the Work of Table Servers. *Gender and Society* 7: 329–46.

Hall, Trish (1993) Family Tree Nurtures a New Generation of Chefs. *The New York Times* April 14, C1.

Hamilton, Gary G. (ed.) (1996) *Asian Business Networks*. Berlin/New York: Walter de Gruyter.

Hannerz, Ulf (1996) *Transnational Connections*. London: Routledge.

Harbottle, Lynn (1997) Fast Food/Spoiled Identity: Iranian Migrants in the British Catering Trade. In *Food, Health, and Identity*, ed. Pat Caplan, pp. 87–110. London/New York: Routledge.

Harris, Mary (1995) Waiters, Customers and Service: Some Tips about Tipping. *Journal of Applied Social Psychology* 25: 725–44.

Hart, Keith (2005) *The Hit Man's Dilemma: Business, Personal and Impersonal*. Chicago: Prickly Paradigm Press.

Harvey, David (1989) *The Condition of Postmodernity: An Enquiry into the Origins of Cultural Change*. Oxford: Blackwell.

Heffernan, William and Mary Hendrickson (2005) Concentration of Agricultural Markets http://www.foodcircles.missouri.edu/CRJanuary05.pdf

Herrmann, Gretchen M. (1997) Gift or Commodity: What Changes Hands in the U.S. Garage Sale? *American Ethnologist* 24: 910–30.

Herzfeld, Michael (1985) *The Poetics of Manhood: Contest and Identity in a Greek Mountain Village*. Princeton, NJ: Princeton University Press.

Herzfeld, Michael (1986) Within and Without: The Category of 'Female' in the Ethnography of Modern Greece. In *Gender and Power in Rural Greece*, ed. Jill Dubisch, pp. 215–34 Princeton, NJ: Princeton University Press.

Herzfeld, Michael (1987) "As in Your Own House": Hospitality, Ethnography, and the Stereotype of Mediterranean Society. In *Honor and Shame and the Unity of the Mediterranean*, ed. David D. Gilmore, pp. 75–89. Washington, DC: AAA Publications.

Hess, John and Karen Hess (1977) *The Taste of America*. Harmondsworth: Penguin.

Hochschild, Arlie Russell (1983) *The Managed Heart: Commercialization of Human Feeling*. Berkeley, CA: University of California Press.

Hoebel, Anderson (1954) *The Law of Primitive Man*. Cambridge, MA: Harvard University Press.

Hoffman, Lisa (2001) Guiding College Graduates to Work: Social Constructions of Labor Markets in Dalian. In *China Urban: Ethnographies of Contemporary Culture*, ed. Nancy Chen, Constance Clark, Suzanne Gottschang and Lyn Jeffery, pp. 43–66. Durham, NC: Duke University Press.

Holditch, W. Kenneth (2002) Letter to Galatoire's. http://www.welovegilberto.com/Galatoires/13.pdf.

Hong, Paul (1999) The Indian Restaurant and the (In)-Visibility of Ethnicity in London, Ontario. Master's Thesis, University of Western Ontario.

Howe, Alyssa Cymene (2001) Queer Pilgrimage: The San Francisco Homeland and Identity Tourism. *Cultural Anthropology* 16(1): 35–61.

Howes, David (2003) *Sensual Relations: Engaging the Senses in Culture and Social Theory*. Ann Arbor, MI: University of Michigan Press.

Hubbard, Amy, A. Tsuji, Christine Williams and Virgilio Seatriz, Jr. (2003) Effects of Touch on Gratuities Received in Same-Gender and Cross-Gender Dyads. *Journal of Applied Social Psychology* 33: 2427–8.

Hubbert, Jennifer (2003) Signs of the Modern: Intellectual Authority, Pain, and Pleasure in Reform China. In *Trans-Pacific Relations: America, Europe, and Asia in the Twentieth Century*, ed. Richard Jensen, Jon Davidann, and Yoneyuku Sugita, pp. 269–91. Westport, CT: Praeger Publishers.

Hubbert, Jennifer (2006) (Re)collecting Mao: Memory and Fetish in Contemporary China, *American Ethnologist* 33(2): 145–61.

Ignatiev, Noel (1995) *How The Irish Became White*. New York: Routledge.

Ikels, Charlotte (1989) Becoming a Human Being in Theory and Practice: Chinese Views of Human Development. In *Comparative Perspectives on Age Structuring in Modern Societies*, ed. David Kertzer and K. Warner Schaie, pp. 109–34. Hillsdale, NJ: Lawrence Erlbaum Associates.

Jenkins, Nancy Harmon (1994) Choice Tables: Boston Chefs: A Family Tree. *New York Times* January 9, Section 5, p. 6.

Jenner, W. J. F. (ed.) (1988) *China: A Photohistory, 1937–1987*. New York: Pantheon.

Jochnowitz, Eve (1999) Feasting on the Future: Foods of the World of Tomorrow at the New York World's Fair of 1939–40. *Performance Research* 4(1): 110–20.

Jochnowitz, Eve (2000) Send a Salami to Your Boy in the Army. In *Remembering the Lower East Side*, ed. Hasia Diner, Jeffrey Shandler and Beth Wenger, pp. 215–25. Bloomington, IN: University of Indiana Press.

Jochnowitz, Eve (2004) Flavors of memory. In L. Long (ed.), *Culinary Tourism*. Lexington, KY: University of Kentucky Press.

Johns, P. S. (1999) *Balsamico!*, Berkeley, CA: Ten Speed Press.

Kahn, Herman (1979) *World Economic Development; 1979 and Beyond*. London: Croom Helm.

Kalcik, Susan (1984) Ethnic Foodways in America: Symbol and the Performance of Identity. In *Ethnic and Regional Foodways in the United States; The Performance of Group Identity*, ed. Linda Brown and Kay Mussell, pp. 37–65. Knoxville, TN: University of Tennessee Press.

Kao, John (1993) The World Wide Web of Chinese Business. *Harvard Business Review* March–April: 24–37.

Kasinitz, Phillip, Aviva Zeltzer-Zubida, and Zoya Simakhodskaya (2001) *The Next Generation: Russian Jewish Young Adults in Contemporary New York*. Working Paper #178. New York: Russell Sage Foundation.

Kirschenbaum, Jacob (1939) *Amerike: Dos Land Fun Vunder [America: The Land of Wonder]*. Warsaw: Kh. Brzoza.

Kirshenblatt-Gimblett, Barbara (1998) *Destination Culture: Tourism, Museums, and Heritage*. Berkeley, CA: University of California Press.

Kirshenblatt-Gimblett, Barbara (2004) Foreword. In *Culinary Tourism*. ed. Lucy Long, pp. xi–xiv. Lexington, KY: University Press of Kentucky.

Kishimoto, Fukuko (2006) From Restaurant Nippon and Kaiseki Ryori to Megu and Japanese Fusion Food: A Brief History of Japanese Restaurants in New York City. Master's Thesis, Food Studies, New York University.

Koh, Tommy (1993) Ten Asian Values that Help East Asia's Economic Progress, Prosperity. *Straits Times* (Singapore) 14: 7.

Krogstad, Anne (2004) From Chop Suey to Sushi, Champagne, and VIP Lounges: Culinary Entrepreneurship through Two Generations. *Social Analysis* 48(1): 196–217.

Kugelmass, Jack (1990) Green Bagels: An Essay on Food, Nostalgia, and the Carnivalesque. *YIVO Annual* 19: 57–80.

Kuh, Patric (2001) *The Last Days of Haute Cuisine*. New York: Viking.

Kulick, Don and Anne Meneley (2005) *Fat: The Anthropology of an Obsession*. New York: Penguin.

Kurlansky, Mark (1997) *Cod: A Biography of the Fish that Changed the World*. New York: Walker and Company.

Kurlansky, Mark (2002) *Salt: A World History*. New York: Walker and Company.

Lagasse, Emeril (1996) *Louisiana Real and Rustic*. New York: William Morrow.

Landa, Janet (1981) A Theory of the Ethnically Homogenous Middleman Group: An Institutional Alternative to Contract Law. *Journal of Legal Studies* 10: 349–62.

Lane, J. F. (2000) *Pierre Bourdieu: A Critical Introduction*. London: Pluto Press.

Laner, Mary Riege, Morris Axelrod and Roy H. Laner (1979) Sex and the Single Check: The Patron/Server Relationship. *Pacific Sociological Review* 22, No. 3 (July): 382–400.

Latham, Robert and William Matthews (eds) (1970–83) *The Diary of Samuel Pepys*, 11 vols. London: Bell and Hyman.

Latour, Bruno (1993) *We Have Never Been Modern*. Cambridge, MA: Harvard University Press.

Laurier, Eric, Angus Whyte and Kathy Buckner (2001) An Ethnography of a Neighbourhood Café: Informality, Table Arrangements and Background Noise. *Journal of Mundane Behavior* 2(2). Available URL: http://mundanebehavior.org/index2.htm

Legge, James (1996) *I Ching: Book of Changes*, trans. James Legge, New York: Gramercy Books.

Leidner, Robin (1993) *Fast Food, Fast Talk: Service Work and the Routinization of Everyday Life*. Berkeley, CA: University of California Press.

Leitch, Alison (2003) Slow Food and the Politics of Pork Fat: Italian Food and European Identity. *Ethnos* 68(4): 437–62.

Lem, Winnie (1997) *Cultivating Dissent: Work, Identity and Praxis in Rural Languedoc*. Albany, NY: State University of New York Press.

Lem, Winnie (2008) Migrants, Mobilization and the Making of Neoliberal Citizens in Contemporary France. In Special Section "Migrants, Mobility and Mobilization." ed. Pauline Gardiner Barber and Winnie Lem, *Focaal – European Journal of Anthropology*, forthcoming.

Lemon, Alaina (1998) Your Eyes Are Green Like Dollars: Counterfeit Cash, National Substance and Currency Apartheid in 1990s Russia. *Cultural Anthropology* 13: 22–55.

Levenstein, Harvey (1988) *Revolution at the Table: The Transformation of the American Diet*. New York: Oxford University Press.

Levenstein, Harvey (1989) Two Hundred Years of French Food in America. *Journal of Gastronomy* 5(1): 66–89.

Levenstein, Harvey (1994) *Paradox of Plenty: A Social History of Eating in Modern America*. New York: Oxford University Press.

Levenstein, Harvey (2003a) The American Response to Italian Food, 1880–1930. In *Food in the USA*, ed. Carole M. Counihan, pp. 75–90. New York: Routledge.

Levenstein, Harvey (2003b) *Paradox of Plenty: A Social History of Eating in Modern America*, rev. edn. Berkeley, CA: University of California Press.

Lew, Roland (2004) The China Dossier. *Le monde diplomatique*, October 2004.

Li, Minghuan (1999) To Get Rich Quickly in Europe!: Reflections on Migration and Motivation in Wenzhou. In *Internal and International Migration*, ed. Frank N. Pieke and Hein Mallee. London: Curzon.

Li, Peter (1993) Chinese Investment and Business in Canada: Ethnic Entrepreneurship Reconsidered. *Pacific Affairs* 62: 219–43.

Li, Peter (2001) Immigrants' Propensity to Self-Employment: Evidence from Canada. *International Migration Review* 35(14): 1106–23.

Lieberson, Stanley (2000) *A Matter of Taste. How Names, Fashions, and Culture Change*. New Haven, CT: Yale University Press.

Liechty, Mark (2005) Carnal Economies: The Commodification of Food and Sex in Kathmandu. *Cultural Anthropology* 20(1): 1–38.

Lien, Marianne Elisabeth and Brigitte Nerlich (eds) (2004) *The Politics of Food*. Oxford: Berg.

Light, Ivan (1972) *Ethnic Enterprise in America: Business and Welfare among Chinese, Japanese, and Blacks*. Berkeley, CA: University of California Press.

Light, Ivan and S. J. Gold (2000) *Ethnic Economies*. San Diego: Academic Press.

Litzinger, Ralph (2000) *Other Chinas: The Yao and the Politics of National Belonging*. Durham, NC: Duke University Press.

Liu, Yia-Ling (1992) Reform from Below: The Private Economy and Local Politics in the Rural Industrialization of Wenzhou. *China Quarterly* 130: 293–316.

Live, Yu-Sion (1998) The Chinese Community in France. In *The Chinese in Europe*, ed. Gregor Benton and Frank Pieke, pp. 96–124. New York: St Martin's Press.

Lloyd, Timothy (1981) The Cincinnati Chili Culinary Complex. *Western Folklore* 40(1): 28–40.

Lockwood, William G. and Yvonne R. Lockwood (2000) Continuity and Adaptation in Arab American Foodways. In *Arab Detroit: From Margin to Mainstream*, ed. Nabeel Abraham and Andrew Shryock, pp. 515–54. Detroit, MI: Wayne State University Press.

Long, Lucy (1998) Culinary Tourism: A Folkloristic Perspective on Eating and Otherness. *Southern Folklore* 35(3): 181–204.

Los Angeles Times (1897) New York Greeks. May 23, p. 19.

Lovell-Troy, Lawrence (1990) *The Social Basis of an Ethnic Enterprise: Greeks in the Pizza Business*. New York: Taylor & Francis.

Lowry, Helen Bullitt (1921) The Old World in New York. *New York Times* (April 3), p. 37.

Lutz, Brobson (2002) In Closing: An Email Exchange Between Two New Orlenians. In *Letter to Galatoire's*. http://www.welovegilberto.com/Galatoires/121.pdf

Lynn, Michael (2000) National Personality and Tipping Customs. *Personality and Individual Differences* 28: 395–404.

Lynn, Michael (2004) Ethnic Differences in Tipping: A Matter of Familiarity with Tipping Norms. *Cornell Hotel and Restaurant Administration Quarterly* 45: 12–22.

Lynn, Michael and Bibi Latane (1984) The Psychology of Restaurant Tipping. *Journal of Applied Social Psychology* 14: 549–61.

Lynn, Michael and K. Mynier (1993) Effect of Server Posture on Restaurant Tipping. *Journal of Applied Social Psychology* 23: 678–85.

McCaffety, Kerri (2002) *Etouffée, Mon Amour: The Great Restaurants of New Orleans*. Gretna, LA: Pelican.

MacClancey, J. V. (Forthcoming) *Expressing Identities in the Basque Arena*. Oxford: James Currey Ltd (in press).

Malaby, Thomas M. (2003) *Gambling Life: Dealing in Contingency in a Greek City*. Urbana, IL: University of Illinois Press.

Manzo, Joseph T. (1998) From Pushcart to Modular Restaurant: The Diner on the Landscape. In *The Taste of American Place: A Reader on Regional and Ethnic Foods*, ed. Barbara G. Shortridge and James R. Shortridge. New York: Rowman & Littlefield.

Markowitz, Fran (1993) *A Community in Spite of Itself: Soviet Jewish Émigrés in New York*. Smithsonian Series in Ethnographic Inquiry. Washington, DC: Smithsonian Institution Press.

Mars, Gerald and Peter Mitchell (1976) *Room for Reform: Industrial Relations in the Hotel Industry*. Milton Keynes: The Open University Press.

Mars, Gerald and Michael Nicod (1984) *The World of Waiters*. London: George Allen & Unwin.

Mars, Gerald, Bryant, Don and Peter Mitchell (1979) *Manpower Problems in the Hotel Industry*. Farnborough: Saxon House.

Martens, Lydia and Alan Warde (1997) Urban Pleasure?: On the Meaning of Eating Out in a Northern City. In *Food, Health, and Identity*, ed. Pat Caplan, pp. 131–50. New York: Routledge.

Massey, Douglas *et al.* (1993) Theories of International Migration: A Review and Appraisal. *Population and Development Review* 19(3): 431–46.

Meigs, Anna (1984) *Food, Sex and Pollution: A New Guinea Religion*. New Brunswick, NJ: Rutgers University Press.

Mennell, Stephen (1996) *All Manners of Food: Eating and Taste in England and France from the Middle Ages to the Present*. Urbana, IL: University of Illinois Press.

Merriam Webster's Collegiate Dictionary. 10th edn, retrieved March 1, 2003 from the World Wide Web: http://onelook.com.

Miele, Mara and Jonathan Murdoch (2002) The Practical Aesthetics of Traditional Cuisines: Slow Food in Tuscany. *Sociologia Ruralis* 42(4): 312–28.

Mintz, Sidney (1985) *Sweetness and Power: The Place of Sugar in Modern History*. New York: Viking.

Mintz, Sidney (1996) *Tasting Food, Tasting Freedom*. Boston: Beacon Press.

Mintz, Sidney (2002) Food and Eating: Some Persisting Questions. In *Food Nations: Selling Taste in Consumer Societies*, ed. W. Belasco and P. Scranton, pp. 24–32. London: Routledge.

re, Mick (1997) Societies, Polities and Capitalists in Developing Countries: A literature Survey. *Journal of Development Studies* 33(3): 287–362.

Morgan, Helen (1935) Our Wide Taste in Food. *New York Times* October 13, p. SM17.

Mullener, Elizabeth (1998) The Palace Guard. *The Times-Picayune* June 6, National, p. 1.

Murphy, Rachel (2002) *How Migrant Labor is Changing Rural China*. Cambridge: Cambridge University Press.

Narayan, Uma (1995) Eating Cultures: Incorporation, Identity, and Indian Food. *Social Identities* 1: 63-86.

National Restaurant Association (1985) *Restaurant Industry Operations Report 1984*. Washington, DC: NRA.

National Restaurant Association (1992) *Restaurant Industry Operations Report 1991*. Washington, DC: NRA.

National Restaurant Association (1999) *Ethnic Food*. Washington, DC: NRA.

National Restaurant Association (2001) *Restaurant Industry Operations Report 2000*. Washington, DC: NRA.

National Restaurant Association (2003) *Restaurant Spending 2003*. National Restaurant Association report. www.restaurant.org/research/consumer/spending. cfm.

National Restaurant Association (2004) *Restaurant Industry Operations Report 2003*. Washington, DC: NRA.

Nestle, Marion (2002) *Food Politics: How the Food Industry Influences Nutrition and Health*. Berkeley, CA: University of California Press.

New York Times (1862) Delmonico's New Restaurant. April 7, 1862, p. 5.

New York Times (1873) Naples in Italy. January 4, 1873, p. 4.

New York Times (1873) German Restaurants. January 19, 1873, p. 5.

New York Times (1881) Beefsteak in Rome. December 5, 1881, p. 3

Nolan, Peter and Dong Furen (eds) (1991) *Market Forces in China: Competition and Small Business - The Wenzhou Debate*. London: Zed Books.

Ohira, Rod (1999) Okazuya Leaves Sweet Memories. *Honolulu Star-Bulletin* January 4: A4.

Ohnuki-Tierney, Emiko (1993) *Rice as Self: Japanese Identities Through Time*. Princeton, NJ: Princeton University Press.

Oi, Cynthia (1999a) A Day at Fukuya, the Food's in the Making Well Before Dawn. *Honolulu Star-Bulletin* March 3: D1, D6.

Oi, Cynthia (1999b) Much Ado About Okazu. *Honolulu Star-Bulletin* March 3: D1, D6.

O'Keefe, Kevin (2005) *The Average American: The Extraordinary Search for the Nation's Most Ordinary Citizen*. New York: Public Affairs.

Ong, Aihwa and Donald Nonini (eds) (1997) *Ungrounded Empires: The Cultural Politics of Chinese Transnationalism*. New York: Routledge.

Ongwat, Pareena (2006) Let's Have Thai Tonight: Exploring Thai Restaurants in New York City. Master's Thesis, Food Studies, New York University.

Ory, Pascal (1996) Gastronomy. In *Realms of Memory: The Construction of the French Past, II: Traditions*, ed. Pierre Nora and D. Lawrence Kritzman, pp. 443–67. New York: Columbia University Press.

Owings, Alison (2002) *Hey Waitress! The USA from the Other Side of the Tray*. Berkeley, CA: University of California Press.

Pairault, Thierry (1990) *L'intégration silencieuse: La Petite Entreprise Chinoise en France*. Paris: l'Harmattan.

Parkins, Wendy and Geoffrey Craig (2006) *Slow Living*. Oxford: Berg.

Parris, Kirsten (1993) Local Initiative and National Reform: The Wenzhou Model of Development. *China Quarterly* 134: 242–63.

Paules, Greta Foff (1991) *Dishing It Out: Power and Resistance Among Waitresses in a New Jersey Restaurant*. Princeton, NJ: Princeton University Press.

Pillsbury, Richard (1987) From Hamburger Alley to Hedgerose Heights: Toward a Model of Restaurant Location Dynamics. *The Professional Geographer* 39(3): 326–44.

Portes, Alejandro (ed.) (1995) *The Economic Sociology of Immigration. Essays on Networks, Ethnicity, and Entrepreneurship*. New York: Russell Sage Foundation.

Povinelli, Elizabeth (1993) *Labor's Lot: The Power, History, and Culture of Aboriginal Action*. Chicago: University of Chicago Press.

Pressey, Debra (1990) Other Landowners Also See Area's Potential. *Champaign News Gazette* May 6: C8.

Prewitt, Milford (2000) Not For Men Only: Fine Dining Urged To Hire Females. *Nation's Restaurant News* July 24, p. 1.

Probyn, Elspeth (2004) Eating for a Living: A Rhizo-ethology of Bodies. In *Cultural Bodies: Ethnography and Theory*, ed. H. Thomas and J. Ahmed, pp. 215–40. London: Blackwell.

Rascoll, Charles (2004) *Personal Communications*. Hyde Park, NY: CIA Chef.

Ray, Krishnendu (1998) Meals, Migration and Modernity: Domestic Cooking and Bengali Indian Ethnicity in the United States. *Amerasia* 24(1): 105–27.

Ray, Krishnendu (2004) *The Migrant's Table. Meals and Memories in Bengali-American Households*. Philadelphia: Temple University Press.

Ray, Krishnendu (2006) Feeding Modern Desires. *Seminar 566* (October): 30–4, Delhi, India.

Ray, Krishnendu (2007) Domesticating Cuisine. Food and Aesthetics on American Television. *Gastronomica*. 7(1): 50–63.

Reardon, Joan (1994) *M. F. K. Fisher, Julia Child, and Alice Waters: Celebrating the Pleasures of the Table*. New York: Harmony.

Redding, Gordon (1990) *The Spirit of Chinese Capitalism*. Berlin/New York: Walter de Gruyter.

Regis, Helen (2001) Blackness and the Politics of Memory in the New Orleans Second Line. *American Ethnologist* 28(4): 752–77.

Reiter, Ester (1997) *Making Fast Food*. Montreal: McGill-Queens University Press.

Restaurant News (2004) Refining the Family Focus. August 23: 16–18.

Rind, B. and D. Strohmetz (1999) Effects on Restaurant Tipping of a Helpful Message Written on the Back of Customers' Checks. *Journal of Applied Social Psychology* 29: 139–44.

Ritzer, George (1991) *The McDonaldization of Society*. Thousand Oaks, CA: Pine Forge Press.

Ritzer, George (2002) Credit Cards, Fast Food Restaurants, and Rationalization. In *McDonaldization: The Reader*, ed. George Ritzer, pp. 178–84. Thousand Oaks, CA: Pine Forge Press.

ROC-NY (The Restaurant Opportunities Center of New York) (2005) *Behind the Kitchen Door*. New York: The Restaurant Opportunities Center of New York.

Rodrigue, Melvin (2005) *Galatoire's Cookbook: Recipes and Family History from the Time-Honored New Orleans Restaurant*. New York: Clarkson Potter.

Root, Waverley (1992) *The Food of France*. New York: Vintage.

Root, Waverley and Richard de Rochemont (1976) *Eating in America: A History*. New York: Ecco Press.

Rosa, Craig (1997) Shmura Matsoh Baking in Crown Heights Brooklyn: A Proselytourist Production. Master's Thesis, New York University.

Rose, Chris (2002) Fine Whining. *The Times-Picayune* July 16, Living, p. 1.

Roseberry, William (1986) The Ideology of Domestic Production. Special Issue "Petty Commodity Production," ed. Gavin Smith and Jonathan Barker. *Labor Capital and Society* 19(1): 70–93.

Roseman, Sharon (2004) Bioregulation and Comida Caseira in Rural Galicia, Spain. *Identities: Global Studies in Culture and Power* 2(1): 9–37.

Ruggles, Steven *et al.* (2004) Integrated Public Use Microdata Series [IPUMS]: Version 3.0, Machine-Readable Database. Minneapolis, MN: Minnesota Population Center. Available at http://www.ipums.org

San Francisco Chronicle (1991) Chez Panisse: The Restaurant's Alumni Blaze Their Own Trails. August 21, Food, Z1.

Sassen, Saskia (1995) Immigration and Local Labor Markets. In *Economic Sociology of Immigration*, ed. Alejandro Portes, pp. 87–127. New York: Russell Sage.

Sausmikat, Nora (1999) Female Autobiographies from the Cultural Revolution: Returned Xiaxiang Educated Women in the 1990s. In *Internal and International Migration: Chinese Perspectives*, ed. Frank N. Pieke and Hein Mallee, pp. 297–314. London: Curzon Press.

Scapp, Ron and Brian Seitz (eds) (1998) *Eating Culture*. Albany, NY: State University of New York Press.

Schechner, Richard (1985) *Between Theater and Anthropology*. Philadelphia: University of Pennsylvania Press.

Schein, Louisa (2000) *Minority Rules: The Miao and the Feminine in China's Cultural Politics*. Durham, NC: Duke University Press.

Scher, Philip (2002) Copyright Heritage: Preservation, Carnival and the State in Trinidad. *Anthropological Quarterly* 75(3): 453-84.

Schweder, Richard A. (2003) *Why Do Men Barbecue? Recipes for Cultural Psychology*. Cambridge, MA: Harvard University Press.

Seligman, Dan (1998) Why do you leave tips? *Forbes* 14: 138–40.

Sennett, Richard (1976) *The Fall of Public Man*. Cambridge: Cambridge University Press.

Seremetakis, C. Nadia (1994) The Memory of the Senses, Part I: Marks of the Transitory. In *The Senses Still: Perception and Memory as Material Culture in Modernity*, ed. C. N. Seremetakis, pp. 1–18. Chicago: University of Chicago Press.

Sereni, Emilio (1997) *History of the Italian Landscape*, trans. R. Burr Litchfield. Princeton, NJ: Princeton University Press.

Shamir, Boas (1984) Between Gratitude and Gratuity: An Analysis of Tipping. *Annals of Tourism Research* 11: 59–78.

Shelton, A. (1990) A Theatre for Eating, Looking and Thinking: The Restaurant as Symbolic Space. *Sociological Spectrum* 10: 507–26.

Shriver, Jerry (2002) Delicious food fight embroils New Orleans. *USA Today. Life*: 1D.

Shternshis, Anna (2001) Kosher and Soviet: Jewish Cultural Identity in the Soviet Union, 1917–41. Ph.D. dissertation, Oxford University.

Shteyngart, Gary (2004) My Leningrad on the Hudson. *Gourmet* March: 136–41, 170.

Simon, Scott (2002) Gene Bourg discusses Galatoire's Restaurant in New Orleans and the firing of a waiter over claims of sexual harassment. July 13, Weekend Edition Saturday, National Public Radio.

Simoons, Frederick (1991) *Food in China: A Cultural and Historical Inquiry*. Boston: CRC Press.

Smart, Alan and Josephine Smart (eds) (2005) *Petty Capitalists and Globalization: Flexibility, Entrepreneurship and Economic Development*. Albany, NY: State University of New York Press.

Smart, Josephine (2003) Ethnic Entrepreneurship, Transmigration, and Social Integration: An Ethnographic Study of Chinese Restaurant Owners in Rural Western Canada. *Urban Anthropology* 32: 311–42.

Smith, Andrew (2005) The French Culinary Influence in America since World War II. Unpublished manuscript owned by Krishnendu Ray.

Soloveitchik, Haym (1994) Rupture and Reconstruction: The Transformation of Contemporary Orthodoxy. *Tradition* 28(4).

Spang, Rebecca (2000) *The Invention of the Restaurant: Paris and Modern Gastronomic Culture*. Cambridge, MA: Harvard University Press.

Speer, T. (1997) The Give and Take of Tipping. *American Demographics* 19: 51–4.

Spindel, Carol (2002) *Dancing at Halftime*. New York: NYU Press.

Spradley, James and Brenda Mann (1975) *The Cocktail Waitress: Woman's Work in a Man's World*. New York: John Wiley & Sons.

Stanley, Thomas J. and William D. Danko (1996) *The Millionaire Next Door. The Surprising Secrets of America's Wealthy*. New York: Pocket Books.

Staub, Shalom (1989) *Yemenis in New York City: The Folklore of Ethnicity*. Philadelphia: The Balch Institute Press.

Steinberg, Stephen (1989) *The Ethnic Myth. Race, Ethnicity, and Class in America*. Boston: Beacon Press.

Stephenson, Peter H. (1989) Going to McDonald's in Leiden: Reflections on the Concept of Self and Society in the Netherlands. *Ethos* 17(2): 226–47.

Sterne, Jonathan (1997) Sounds Like the Mall of America. *Ethnomusicology* 41: 22–50.

Stewart, Kathleen (1996) *A Space on the Side of the Road: Cultural Poetics in an "Other" America*. Princeton, NJ: Princeton University Press.

Su, Xiaokang and Luxiang Wang (eds) (1992) *Deathsong of the River: A Reader's Guide to the Chinese TV Series He Shang*, trans. Richard Bodman and Pin Wan, Cornell East Asia Series. Ithaca, NY: Cornell University Press.

Surowiecki, James (2005) The Financial Page: Check, Please. *The New Yorker* September 5: 58.

Sutton, David E. (2001) *Remembrance of Repasts: An Anthropology of Food and Memory*. Oxford: Berg.

Sutton, David E. (2004) Toward an Ethnography of Restaurants. *Food and Foodways* 12: 53–61.

Sutton, David, and Peter Wogan (2003) The Gun, The Pen and the Cannoli: Orality and Writing in The Godfather, Part I. *Anthropology and Humanism Quarterly* 28:155–67.

Szathmary, L. (1983) How Festive Foods of the Old World Became Commonplace In the New. In *Food in Motion*, Oxford Symposium Proceedings, ed. Alan Davidson. Leeds, England: Prospect Books Ltd.

Taylor, Lawrence (1981) Coffee: The Bottomless Cup. In *The American Dimension: Cultural Myths and Social Realities*, 2nd edn, ed. W. Arens and S. Montague, pp. 107–112. Sherman Oaks, CA: Alfred Publishing Co.

Thomas, Jerry (1862) The Bartender's Guide. How to Mix Drinks Or The Bon Vivant's Companion. New York: New Day Publishing.

Thompson, M., Ellis, R. and Wildavsky, A. (1990) *Cultural Theory*. Boulder, CO: Westview Press.

Time Magazine (1966) Everyone in the Kitchen. November 25.

Times-Picayune (2006) Restaurants, Chef, Writer are Honored. May 11: Living, p. 1.

Trillin, Calvin (1994) *The Tummy Trilogy*. New York: Farrar, Straus and Giroux.

Trubek, Amy B. (2000) *Haute Cuisine: How the French Invented the Culinary Profession*. Philadelphia: University of Pennsylvania Press.

Trubek, Amy B. (2004) Tasting Wisconsin. The Art of Eating 68. www.artofeating. com.

Turgeon, Laurier and Madeleine Pastinelli (2002) Eat the World: Postcolonial Encounters in Quebec City's Ethnic Restaurants. *Journal of American Folklore* 112: 247–68.

Turner, V. W. (1974) *Dramas, Fields, and Metaphors: Symbolic Action in Human Society*. Ithaca, NY: Cornell University Press.

Veblen, Thorsten (2001 [1899]) *The Theory of the Leisure Class*. New York: Modern Library.

"Victor" (1852) Philadelphia: Chronology – Anecdote of Baron Stackleburg – Saloons and 'Subterraneans,' *New York Times* October 27: 2.

Visser, Margaret (1986) *Much Depends on Dinner: The Extraordinary History, Mythology, Allure and Obsession, Perils and Taboos of an Ordinary Meal*. New York: Grove Press.

Vournelis, Leonidas (2004) Monies That Matter: Refashioning Identity With Old and New Money. Master's Thesis. Department of Anthropology. Southern Illinois University.

Warde, Alan and Lydia Martens (2000) *Eating Out: Social Differentiation, Consumption and Pleasure*. Cambridge: Cambridge University Press.

Wasserstrom, Jeffrey and Elizabeth Perry (1992) *Popular Protest and Political Culture in Modern China: Learning from 1989*. Boulder, CO: Westview Press.

Waters, Malcolm (2002) McDonaldization and the Global Culture of Consumption. In *McDonaldization: The Reader*, ed. George Ritzer, pp. 178–84. Thousand Oaks, CA: Pine Forge Press.

Watson, James (ed.) (1997) *Golden Arches East: McDonald's in East Asia*. Stanford, CA: Stanford University Press.

Watson, James and Melissa Caldwell (eds) (2005) *The Cultural Politics of Food and Eating*. Oxford: Blackwell.

Watts, Jonathan (2003) Mao Returns to Haunt and Comfort His People. *The Guardian*, December 27, 2003, available from http://www.guardian.co.uk/china/story/0,7369,1112844,00.html.

Weber, Max (1970 [1930]) *The Protestant Ethic and the Spirit of Capitalism*. London: Unwin University Books.

Weinreich, Beatrice (1960) The Americanization of Passover. In *Studies in Biblical and Jewish Folklore*, ed. Raphael Patai, Dov Noy and Francis Lee Utley, pp. 329–66. Bloomington, IN: Indiana University Press.

Weismantel, Mary (1995) Making Kin: Kinship Theory and Zumbagua Adoptions. *American Ethnologist* 22: 685–703.

Weiss, Allen S. (2002) *Feast and Folly: Cuisine, Intoxication, and the Poetics of the Sublime*. The SUNY Series in Postmodern Culture. Albany, NY: State University of New York Press.

Weston, Kath (1995) Forever is a Long Time: Romancing the Real in Gay Kinship Ideologies. In *Naturalizing Power: Essays in Feminist Cultural Analysis*, ed. S. Yanagisako and C. Delaney, pp. 87–110. London: Routledge.

Whitaker, Jan (2005) Domesticating the Restaurant: Marketing the Anglo-American Home. In *From Betty Crocker to Feminist Food Studies: Critical Perspectives on Women and Food*, ed. Arlene V. Avakian and Barbara Haber, pp. 89–105. Amherst, MA: University of Massachusetts Press.

Whyte, William Foote (1948) *Human Relations in the Restaurant Industry*. New York: McGraw-Hill.

Wilson, Thomas (2005) *Drinking Cultures: Alcohol and Identity*. Oxford: Berg.

Wong, Siu Lun (1988) The Applicability of Asian Family Values to Other Social Cultural Settings. In *In Search of an Asian Development Model*. ed. Peter Berger and H. H. M. Hsiao. Oxford: Transaction Books.

Wong, Siu Lun (1996) Chinese Entrepreneurs and Business Trust. In *Asian Business Networks*, ed. Gary G. Hamilton. Berlin/New York: Walter de Gruyter.

Wu, Xu (2004) Ethnic Foods and Regional Identity: The Hezha Restaurants in Enshi. *Food and Foodways* 12: 225–46.

Yang, Fan (1991) *Gongheguo de Disandai* (The Third Generation of the Republic). Chengdu: Sichuan Renmin Chubanshe.

Yang, Guobin (2003) China's Zhiqing Generation: Nostalgia, Identity and Cultural Resistance in the 1990s. *Modern China* 29(3): 267–96.

Yang, Mayfair (1994) *Gifts, Favors and Banquets: The Art of Social Relationships in China*. Ithaca, NY: Cornell University Press.

Yang, Mayfair (1999) From Gender Erasure to Gender Difference: State Feminism, Consumer Sexuality, and the Women's Public Sphere in China. In *Spaces of Their Own: Women's Public Sphere in Transnational China*, ed. Mayfair Yang, pp. 35–67. Minneapolis: University of Minnesota Press.

Yao, Souchou (2003) *Confucian Capitalism: Discourse, Practice and the Myth of Chinese Enterprise*. London: Routledge.

Yue, Gang (1999) *The Mouth that Begs: Hunger, Cannibalism and the Politics of Eating in Modern China*. Durham, NC: Duke University Press.

Yurchak, Alexei (2003) Mundane Life of Ideology. Presented at the American Anthropological Association Annual Meeting, New Orleans, LA, 2003.

Zagat (1986) *New York City Restaurant Survey*. New York: Zagat.

Zagat (1990) *New York City Restaurant Survey*. New York: Zagat.

Zagat (1992) *America's Top Restaurants*. New York: Zagat.

Zagat (2000) *America's Top Restaurants*. New York: Zagat.

Zagat (2000) *New York City Restaurants*. New York: Zagat.

Zagat (2006) *America's Top Restaurants*. New York: Zagat.

Zagat (2006) *New York City Restaurants*. New York: Zagat.

Zhang, Changlei (2003) How to Be a Good Capitalist, by Mao. *The Taipei Times* December 25: 5. Available from http://www.taipeitimes.com/News/world/archives/2003/12/25/2003084844

Zhang, Li (2001) *Strangers in the City: Reconfigurations of Space, Power and Social Networks within China's Floating Population*. Stanford, CA: Stanford University Press.

Zhang, Mei (2003) *China's Poor Regions: Rural Urban Migration, Poverty, Economic Reform and Urbanization*. London: Routledge Curzon.

Zukin, Sharon (1991) *Landscapes of Power: From Detroit to Disney World*. Berkeley, CA: University of California Press.

Zukin, Sharon (1995) *The Cultures of Cities*. Oxford: Blackwell.

Zukin, Sharon (1998) Urban Lifestyles: Diversity and Standardization in Spaces of Consumption. *Urban Studies* 35(5–6): 825–39.

Author Index

Subject Index